Laura Anne Moore
(1963)

A very interesting
book. At times I
felt the author was
stretching certain
things and elimina-
ting certain facts to
make a point (comments
on Fr. Rev.; footnote on
p. 221) — but the
last chapter was
especially good — as
much so as nearly
anything I've read.

THE ASTONISHED MUSE

The Astonished Muse

S. L. M. BARLOW

THE JOHN DAY COMPANY • NEW YORK

This book is dedicated
with love
to Florence Hallett Matthews
and to the memory
of my uncle
Brander Matthews

The astonished muse finds
thousands at her side.
                    —Emerson

But the liberal deviseth liberal things; and
by liberal things shall he stand.
                    —Isaiah XXXII,18

Social Justice is the plea of the many against the few,
of the nation against the class, of mankind against
the nation, of the future against the present.
                    —Lowes Dickenson

It is not the revelation of the absurdity of existence
but of the pangs and travail of history, not the revelation of the root baseness and contemptibleness of man
but of his distress laid bare when he falls from his pride,
and of the trials and catastrophes, through which the
abiding greatness of his destiny asserts itself.
                    —Jacques Maritain

Foreword

Too many people have presumed that politicians have bowed to artists as from a howdah and passed by, and that in general artists have returned the aloof salutation. I believe this to be a false presumption. There has always been a close connection between art and politics, between the creative mind and the created state. If this book renews forgotten connections and unearths the buried line of ancient continuities, it will have served its purpose.

Shelley would have it that all true poets are lawgivers. Less broadly, we may allow that the poet, writing memorably, has been remembered when the rhetoric of demagogues has been discarded. If we cherish liberty and justice it is because, for close on three thousand years, artists have stripped their sensibilities and fired their talents to communicate man's intense longing for the "good life."

This is not a book on art. Nowhere have I used the word "esthetics." It is not a series of biographies, though men are present as a cloud of witnesses—witnesses who have interpreted those surviving truths of the past most cordial to the benign impulses of the future. This book is the history of a longing and of those artists who, often in unpropitious circumstances, expressed that longing in terms we still cherish.

A historical sequence is necessary to set those witnesses in their own proper environment. Some of the greatest names—Swift, Goethe, Hugo—have received scant treatment where their inclusion tended to prolong a sequence into a catalogue.

It is my contention that artists have provoked those revolutions whereby civilization has made progress. The artist, sustaining the spirit in times of transition and ultimately selecting for commemoration the beneficent residues of history, cannot be far from the heart of our tradition.

Tradition must be viewed from a distance, lest current fashion and prejudice intrude. I have, therefore, carried the historical sequence up to the end of the nineteenth century, and no farther.

Contents

THE ASTONISHED MUSE

Introduction: The Artist

I.

An artist is one who has sufficient technique to communicate his vision. I have sought for many definitions. This is the shortest and most comprehensive I can devise. Inclusive as it may be—encompassing Isaiah, some Greek potter, Machiavelli, William James, the Theodore Roosevelt of the letters to his children—it is sharply exclusive: above all it embraces a vision and a power to communicate. Those who possess both are few. Those who used their gifts to make a better world are fewer. But it is these last, altruists, who have created the durable forms and concepts upon which our civilizations are based.

As to the practice of art—the stages which occupy a creator —it seems to me that in general the practice resembles the potter at his wheel. He conceives the image of the shape. Herein comes inspiration or the impulse to create. He then chooses the clothing or vehicle for his vision, deciding, rejecting, and arranging the color and design, and this personal discrimination we may call "style." He then turns his wheel and molds with his hands—he labors. Conception, style, and labor are present, like three Norns, beside any artist's endeavor. Without the first it is not a creative work; without

15

the second it is not a work of art; and without the third it is not a work at all, but a stillborn aspiration.

Art is essentially craftsmanship. The Greeks and the medieval schoolmen were well aware of this, but their tastes and their snobbery caused them to exalt some arts above craftsmanship and to debase others into mere manual labor. In the teaching of the seven liberal arts, the quadrivium expounded arithmetic, geometry, astronomy, and music; the trivium was confined to grammar, rhetoric, and logic. Below the salt sat the "servile arts," constricted by the limitations of their material: sculpture and painting. Happily, we know better today. We realize that the writer or scientist and research worker, the orator or astronomer, like the dancer and actor, are craftsmen, and that sculpture and painting are not limited by their material any more than is mathematics. Indeed, as we discuss art and artists, we find ourselves not only facing the difficulty of weighing the imponderable but also thrusting aside a mass of nonsense which has become attached to the terms in which art is usually discussed.

"The word of ambition at the present day," said Emerson, "is Culture." As culture for some is a means of social climbing, so art for many is a pleasant emotional escape. To the artist art is work. He has felt, thought, perceived something beyond the normal, obvious range. He must get it out—partly because it makes him uncomfortable to have it bottled within him; partly because, as an altruist, he feels he has a message to deliver—of delight, solace, or incitement; and partly because as a craftsman he is filled with curiosity to know what it will look like when turned out. But I have never known a good artist who worried over "self-expression." Artists worry over having something real to express and then over finding someone to pay them handsomely for expressing it.

What other personal urges has the artist? Wherefore, ex-

16

cept through an excess of egotism or equally of altruism, should he labor for little wage and often for obloquy? One of the stimuli which prompt to the creation of art is no doubt the artist's own unsuccessful attack upon life. Creation becomes a compensation for being sensitive, unworldly. Perhaps, if one could evolve a perfect existence for oneself, one would beget neither symphonies nor children. Both are efforts to hand hopefully on what one has been unable to live.

Car en enfer vont li beaux clercs, wrote Aucassin. But I think he was not consigning writers and poets to any ecclesiastical hell (for impiety or any other reason) but merely, from experience, acknowledging the particular *enfer* or torment which abides with all seekers, all artists, all men who would come by knowledge, all those who by their power of imagination can compare the world as it is with what it might be, all students who measure man's triumph over nature and man's tragic failure before his own kind, all the saints who know that, by having conceived of freedom and love, mankind has half the wings of an angel, but only half.

Yet, because—like the heels of Hermes—the artist has something more of wings, he is capable of a flight denied to others. With levitation comes power. Physical power, like Goliath's, is apt to crumble before the pebble of an idea or a faith. In the physical world victory is not always on the side of the heaviest artillery, as was proven at Marathon and Agincourt. There are Powers of Darkness (as any doctor will tell) and Powers of Light; few artists have elected the former. By some special grace, the gift of creation does not abide in the destructors. I never heard of an architect who specialized in demolition.

The subtitle of one of Henry Focillon's historical studies is *Survivances et Reveils.* Every moment of history, including

17

today, is but a sum of survivals and reawakenings. The most momentous modern discovery or invention would not escape this axiom.

In both the survival and reawakening, the artist has been the sustaining and provocative agent. Antiquity survives for us almost wholly through the efforts of creative artists. Ancient religions, political theories, and sciences are known to us, indeed influence us; but our knowledge is almost entirely due to the work of artists who made these matters intelligible to their own day and so to us. I am told that 1066 is a memorable date; but I know how the actors in that dramatic conquest looked from a piece of needlework preserved at Bayeux, and I know how the tide of battle went from the handiwork of such gifted chroniclers as William of Malmesbury. Roman law was preserved in various later codifications and commentaries; but the true spirit, in equity and in practice, was preserved for us through and because of the purity and elegance of Cicero's style. Much of what we know of Greek banking and business has been learned from the massive legal arguments of Demosthenes. And if we consider statues, temples, palaces, potteries, paintings, poems, surely there is no doubt of what survives: the work of art. It is the beneficent residue.

The two words could serve as a subtitle to this book. By "beneficent residue" I mean the quality or virtue in anything which has been found worthy of being remembered and cherished. The beneficent residue of a probably squalid trade war in Asia Minor is the *Iliad*. Each generation elects for memorializing those things which appeal to its highest aspirations; out of these is formed the tradition. The selection and presentation have been the labor of artists. It could hardly be otherwise.

As selector, it is the artist who "reawakens" the forgetful to a contemporary awareness and evaluation of what survives.

Atomic theories were propounded by the Greeks. Today we have new combinations, emphases, techniques, adapted to our needs and environments. Jefferson's classic revival in architecture was a most happy reawakening, a summing up of the past for the present use. Every year poets greet the spring, painters paint self-portraits, historians write new histories of their country, composers compose symphonies. Each is working in an effort to reinterpret the dead in terms of the living. Indeed, one might maintain that the function of the arts has ever been to fix in a current mold the valid survivals of the past and to reawaken, through the communication of present vision, the drowsy imaginations of contemporary men to understanding and motion. The process is continuous and essentially prophetic. Prophecy is not the foretelling of the future in tea leaves or crystal balls, but the act and the art of interpretation—the communication of a vision. The labor of the prophet is to wrest the meaning of the Word from God and impart it to mankind.

Everything that is subject to interpretation has been the province of the artist. And if we consider politics to be merely a strategy for maintaining society in certain forms, then the artist certainly has played a notable part—as a citizen among citizens or an exile among exiles—in interpreting the success of those forms, by his gifts adorning them, by his vitality altering them, by his wrath destroying them, or by his creative ability forging them anew.

More than he is given credit for, the artist has fashioned this culture we are pleased to call our civilization. If we look upon him as the master craftsman, we realize (with Ecclesiasticus) that he maintains the fabric of the world. Without him "no city shall be inhabited and men shall not walk up and down therein." The artist has made visible and outward the inner visions of religion; through the poets—consider Solon or Hesiod or Milton, or, one might almost add, Rouget

19

de L'Isle—he has fathered the law; his hand made the wheel; one of his kind taught the Gothic tribes to construct a mechanical reaper, to the astonishment of the Romans. Master of propaganda, he has not only led causes but also conceived them; and he has been the master of the most powerful agent in the world: the word.

It may seem as though, today, science were king.* But wherever science has riven the partnership with art, science has led our world into an insane flight. The mechanical means, the airplane, moves in one century and the pilot a thousand years behind. Man, with a mind still twin to that of a Phoenician trader, has been given an atom to play with. Science does little to educate man to this gift, for she deals with facts and means and not with values. Art, in the broadest sense of vision and craft, alone can do that. As Ruskin said, "You do not educate a man by telling him what he knew not but by making him what he was not."

We have used the broadest terms. It is time to be specific. Before we study the artist as liberator and, hence, as the architect of liberality and of the American tradition, it would be well to discuss the actual powers of an artist. If we claim powers for him we should be able to specify them. Then, with the claim established, we can point to those artists who have used their powers to form and preserve the beneficent residue. We can point to the causes of failure to use that power and to the happy flowering of art under solicitous and enlightened governments, the true marriage of politics and art.

II.

The artist is master of the word, of the name, of the myth (and hence very close to being master of religions), of the

* Note A, *Science*, page 293.

20

hero, of history, of symbols; he is a masterful moralist, and through the sum of these powers, a masterful politician.

We are assured that "in the beginning was the Word, and the Word was with God," and we may be equally assured that it did not remain long in His keeping. Together with fire, it was stolen from heaven. Debased though it often is, the word is yet the greatest invention of man, the means of his humanity as against his brutishness, the symbol for his ideas, the basis, through intelligibility, of cooperation or progress. As it was in the beginning, so also it will be in the final throe of this world. Whether lapped in a nebula of atomic lightnings or locked in a last cold night, somewhere some cry or whisper, some question or prayer, some *word* will be the last expression of our humanity.

The master of the word was and still is the artist: the poet, dramatist, philosopher, prophet—the creative writer or orator. Words are among the tools of the artist, his special endowment. With them he elucidates; names and describes; creates art with ritual, beneficent myth from anxious ignorance. And in verse and prose, in song and speech, he interprets and carries on the living formulas of tradition.

The Name

The savage, cowering at a clap of thunder, is in the most primitive state of ignorance and hence of terror. As soon as one of his wisemen has named the awful peal and called it "the god Jub-jub," a second stage is reached. Something can be done about Jub-jub because, to some extent, he is in man's image and susceptible of placation. The naming, however erroneous, is the beginning of partial control, not over the thunder, but at least over man's reaction to thunder. The third stage is reached by definition: what thunder is, as far as we can at present know. I am told that it is composed of, or caused by, precipitations of moisture, hot and cold

21

currents of air, all of which we can define exactly, and by electricity, which we can but partially define. With knowledge, some fear has been removed. Fear has not been removed by the technician but by the man of creative imagination: not by Edison but by Franklin; by the poet-priests who gave us names and by the artist-philosophers who gave us definitions.

We do not know the name of God. In no religion is it conceded, for then men might call His name and God (presumably polite) would answer. "Jehovah" and "Yahveh" mean "He who causes all things." They are appellations and not names. The alchemists and astrologers, practitioners of black magic or necromancy, the ancestors of Dr. Faustus and the doctor himself, were searching for the name of the Devil; for, once known by name, he could be summoned. If you cannot raise Ormazd, you can always try Ahriman.

But do not let us fool ourselves with the thought that such nomenclature power is primitive, the preoccupation of primitives. Today, if a man is seriously ill, and the doctors come and say, "We do not know what it is; we cannot name it," the old fear descends on the patient—and rightly. He knows that when a thing is named, its antithesis or antidote is probably named also. Diagnosis and definition, here, are the same. And the lack of them throws mankind back, in one second, to the fears and insecurities of the cave man. The nameless dread descends. Of all the controllers of fear, nothing is so salutary or so potent as the correct naming of the cause thereof. (And this would apply most cogently to our political fears. If we can drop the big, meaningless words and just say "I fear for my pocket," then fear is on its way out.)

To return to primitive man, to "God's stew-pots" as Heine called the early stirrings wherein our modern ways were adumbrated. How shall we share the intense excitement of the first man to name a "love song"? Up to that moment, at certain seasons (perhaps bearing pretty shells in one hand, a club in the other—unsure which was to be appropriate to the occasion) man, like the birds or the beasts, had sniffed around his lady, making peculiar noises and grunts. Later, he might learn to bellow something like a tune, and probably tried to exhibit a greater range than his rivals. Then, one day, word ran around the steppes that this rumpus was not a natural function, almost an automatic reflex, but an art, a love song. The touch of civility was laid upon it; man began to polish and design consciously. And then he said, "I will make a God-song," and he offered that up too. The song was *named* and so delivered into his hands, not he into its hands as before. The medicine man or shaman who called fire the Red Flower, snatched the element from God and delivered it to his fellow man as surely as Prometheus.

Even good and evil did not exist till one could call them so, till Adam and Eve ate of the Tree of Knowledge, when nakedness became more than the absence of clothes. Sin is but the custom of a country till the missionary puts a name to it. So the word, unhappily, may create fear as it may assuage it, for Scribblerius can invent false names and spread them, like Hitler and Mussolini and Franco, over the new-made instruments, over waves both long and short but irresponsible of themselves. Even so, the false priest but proves the immense potentiality for fear or serenity, for disruption or control, which pertains to the faculty of clothing the abstract in the concrete name, of lifting an inert abstraction with a soaring word. The artist began by being and continues to be the one who "puts a name to it," who delivers the unknown into our hands, into the familiarity of our understanding, delivering us thereby out of a fear-control by "it."

The Myth

As the artist names phenomena he creates myth, through

23

the magic of verbal metaphor. "It is a great sorrow to see the year die, for if it be not born again there will be no new crops nor green thing, and man must perish with the tame and the wild beasts about him. Yet the old year dies, dies like an old woman. What would her name be? Her name is Gaea, the Earth. She is dead, and it is a great sorrow." And into the mouth of Gaea, the poet might put words of comfort and explanation. He would invent a tale of Demeter, searching for a daughter snatched out of sight of men for the hard winter months, and of Demeter's return, bringing divine Persephone and the vernal seasons. With comfort for man and due regard to the gods, the poet would continue his poem, telling how and when to plant, what herbs were salubrious, what was the best food for horses and cattle, how to guess the times of the year by moon and star and do what was appropriate to the season. Your ancient poet was almanac and textbook too. Still today, in search of the date, many of us recite "Thirty days hath September."

Later poets—a Hesiod or Leviticus or Virgil—might then come along, see deeper implications in the myth and, in turn, adapt the message to their contemporaries. Refurbishing as well as reawakening is one of the prerogatives of the artist. Like Lazarus, some long-dead, once inspiring myth must be revived to comfort new generations. Material suitable to one age or one people must, to have a valid communion, be adapted to another people, another age. Parts of a story, no longer comprehensible, are sloughed off, new parts added, and the whole presented afresh to a changed world—a world altered in taste and manners, not amused by this or that as were the elders, not instructed. In short, not nourished. Our Old Testament was refined and polished in this manner until just before the Christian Era.

Perhaps the neatest example of myth adaptation is the cycle of Irish-Welsh stories, lusty and pagan, in which, together with the Fisher King and the Castle Dolorous, great mention is made of the magic creel or box (probably not unconnected with Pandora). Here, in these tales from the eighth century, picturing Mag Mell, the Happy Other World, journeys into Fairyland, matriarchal queens, lay the most exciting material for the storyteller. Yet, four centuries later, it had become very confusing, not to say sacrilegious: Arthur and Guinevere had got in somehow, and alien legends from Burgundy and the Pyrenees. Furthermore, the tales were indecent and a scandal to Christendom. A minor Homer of the twelfth century, Crétien de Troyes, who adapted, bowdlerized, synthesized, pruned, and gloriously recreated the cycles for the gentry of his own day, very adroitly turned the Celtic *criol* into the Holy Grail, connected the wound of the Fisher King with Calvary, and gave to his generation and to us, in the Arthurian legends, a new morality adapted to the highest of those conventions we now call chivalrous. This is exactly what the Hebrews did with root oriental tales —bringing in tributaries to the stream of their national tradition—putting Esther to the service of their God, as the Muslims took the same story and expounded it to the glory of Islam in the *Thousand and One Nights*.

Here we find the artist remolding, revivifying the earlier mythos into a new dispensation. Each political scientist does much the same thing, transmuting not symbols but theories, as the mathematician also gives fresh meaning to ancient symbols and ancient signs. Each may be said to deal in wonders. Here, too, we find the artist in the tabernacle, for religion enjoys a lavish use of signs and symbols. We shall see the artist as *imaginifex,* the creator of our mental images of Zeus, Buddha, Moses, Christ, even of God. And, since he is image maker, he is also refurbisher. He resuscitates, for modern comprehension, the signs and wonders which have tended to disintegrate in the dead crypts of hagiolatry. Truly, we

25

may say that Shaw and Boutet de Monvel and Falguiers, the sculptor, did more for Joan of Arc than the pope who belatedly canonized her.

Time was when myth and symbol occupied that place in the habit and mind now occupied by science, or scientific fact. But myth dwelt also in the heart, and science has no writ of dispossess. Myth dwells there still, irradiating the religions we believe today. Our daily press, our calendar, observances, political prejudices, policies, are shot through with myth and symbol and allegory. "The white man's burden" is an arrant myth, named by a poet, the cause of half a hundred years of political aberration. When we sing "Holy Night" under the mistletoe, by a Christmas tree, with Santa Claus in the offing, we are embroiled in myth as was the chorus at the bull-driving dithyramb in Athens. "Hail Columbia," "by Jove," "Uncle Sam," "The Blue and the Gray," *Deutschland über Alles,* the gold standard, a white elephant, most advertising, Hallowe'en, *L'état c'est moi,* the Yellow Peril, Washington's cherry tree, the Big Stick or the New Deal (depending on which Roosevelt you favor)—with these we are deep in personifications and allegories whose influence on the magpie mentality of man it would be rash to underestimate.

Let us add to these the word images created by artists, personifications of another sort, so deeply embedded that we do not realize we are bowing to the formulas of art: a Turner sky, the look of a Madonna, a veritable Galahad, "she is a siren," a Dostoevsky character, a Sherlock Holmes, Cinderella, an Adonis, and innumerable others.

The Hero

Myth enters the political arena most directly with the hero; he is the creation of poets; he must needs be sung. Caesar died indeed with the last breath of the last legionary who could remember him, yet he lives in books, in plays, in pictures, in sculpture, and now in the cinema. Great Caesar, the historical character, might have survived meagerly in some army account book or some list carved on a cliff, or recorded on a trophy or a coin. Caesar's existence would be known to us, but never his glory. A tarnished version, perhaps, from his detractors, or from his own gruesome memoirs.

Transcending the historical, we cherish the mythical heroes, for in them the fancy of their creators has been unhampered by such sad circumstances as that Washington was more often defeated than conquering, or that Bolivar died in despair. Here your artist has truly formed and informed his own race, increased its tradition, given its young in heart an ideal more powerful than twenty Caesars. Galahad, Paul Bunyan, Hercules, King Arthur, Roland, Siegfried, Samson; the names cluster. "The joy of worship," Swinburne has said, "the delight of admiration, is in itself so excellent, so noble a thing, that even error cannot make it unvenerable. No one need repent of reverence. It has done him good to worship though there were no godhead behind the shrine." To worship so is not to abdicate but to fulfil.

Had Shakespeare been born, lived and died on a small island off the English coast, had his works been kept alive only through minstrels and those who remembered them by heart, and then had James I commanded his finest scholars to sift and order them, put them on paper, and give them to Englishmen, the king would have performed an act parallel to that of Peisistratos in giving Homer to Athens. Suddenly, in the early sixth century B.C., the Greeks came into their inheritance. From that moment on, there was a synthesis and a liberation in Hellenic life. By showing whence the Hellenes came, Homer showed them how they could go forward more heroically. At once, the old-new tradition worked increase in the minds of men. The tedious rituals, such as the

27

dromena of Dionysius, had been festivals of dancing and slaughter which never quite proved their worth as crop bringers; there were lean years despite. But from these earlier propitiations, true drama grew to flower. Heroes now could be verily portrayed, new Homeric heroes, replacing the sham impersonations of a God whose features were doubtful and whose portrayal might be risky, possibly sacrilegious.

With the hero, the individual enters glory. No longer a fragment of tribe or class or nation, but the vivid and valiant man anyone may aspire to be. He is here and there and everywhere, a traveler, a mover who leaves nothing quite the same where he has passed (not even, like Washington or Charles I, the bed he once slept in). He is a contriver and "fixer"; an agitator; a fighter for honor, not for honors. In settled social conditions, remarks J. E. Harrison, "most of the heroes would sooner or later have found themselves in prison." Your hero is a frontiersman, par excellence.

It would be interesting to study the effect of heroes upon their following. French youth, for centuries, has aped Roland, as English youth has aped Galahad or Lancelot, or Italian youth the Conte Rosso. Alas, German youth has aped Siegfried. (Wagner began his work on the cycle well over a hundred years ago.) And here we may have touched on a profound psychological problem: how has a shoddy and contemptible national hero affected generation after generation of his worshipers? The shrine hid no godhead behind it—but a mountebank. Had Washington lied about the cherry tree, or Roland sold out to the Saracens, or Galahad resorted to subterfuge to win a lady, or Columbus been less than the unhappy visionary he was, our heroes would have toppled long since; our poets would have given us other heroes; and our tradition would be different. Siegfried remains a Wagnerian cad; and the racial psychologist may well wonder.

History

Powerfully as the poet has imagined the fictitious heroes, it is this same poet who has, more largely than his fellows, been our historian of fact. King Alfred and the Venerable Bede, a few Church chronicles, and a mass of dry state papers would not have brought early England to life for us. Herodotus alone would not have dispelled the first mists of Ionia. The plastic arts (the broken cup or shattered frieze) teach us much, but Chaucer or Homer gives us the larger picture. What we know of the Aryan invasion of India is found in the Rig Veda. I am sure to be in good company in confessing that I learned much of my French history from Dumas and my English history from Shakespeare and Henty. Among the supreme histories is the Bible. From the poets whose names we know and from anonymous epics, almost exclusively has come our knowledge of how early people felt, worshiped, behaved, what civility they owned, what trades they followed. Such are the materials out of which tradition is made—for tradition is not concerned with a date, 1066, but with the legend that a king carried a singing sword into battle; not with the fall of Jericho in such and such a year, but with the tale that its walls fell before the trumpets of Israel. Even the minor poets, Petronius or Theocritus, contribute certain small but glowing pictures which help to mitigate the stultifying scriptures of all but a few of the greatest artist-historians, like Thucydides or Gibbon.

Since the strictly reliable historian is gunning for accuracy he must avoid the luxury of prejudice or the recklessness of narrative sweep. Excitement and identification are found in the legend makers, chroniclers, troubadour-storytellers, from Europe to the Orient. It is the raconteurs who feed tradition and are often the sources which scientific historians must tap. Above all, the romanticizers create that myth-truth (the noncorporeal side of history) which keeps the story so alive that of itself it has power, political power. The business at the Alamo was, in reality, a seedy affair. But any Texan would go to war tomorrow because of the legend.

With word, brush, and chisel the artist has recorded history. The painter has perhaps been more evocative than his brother poet in recording his own day, as historian *imaginifex*. How people looked, how they dressed at court, how they plowed fields in the time of Louis XI, we know more vividly from contemporary miniatures or illuminations than, for instance, from Scott's *Quentin Durward*. *Les Trés Riches Heures* of the Duc de Berry captures the daily life of the fourteenth century as exactly as the later Breughel caught the scenes that were familiar to him, so making them familiar to us. One of the first modern historians, Philippe de Commines, chronicled the events of Louis' reign; but the record is without imagined life for us unless our mind's eye is enlivened with the images that the painters also have left us.

Not all the Boccaccios nor Machiavellis would reawaken the Renaissance for us—with our visual sense and memory so much more cultivated than our taste or smell or hearing. But, awake and alive, the Renaissance jostles us with a contemporary familiarity in many a great portrait. The Medici family, making royal progress in company with the Magi kings, hawking and hunting and talking and trotting around the walls of the Ricardi Chapel in Florence, are caught *sur le vif* by Benozzo Gozzoli and delivered intimately to us. So have I heard Cocteau, with a vivid description of how he went to market that morning in a bus, deliver provincial France into the keeping of his listeners. Great frescoes, little miniatures; the Tanagra statuettes conveying all but the words of the Greek lady as she went for a stroll under her parasol; the coin bearing the profile of Alexander; the unbelieving stare of the defeated Darius, congealed in mosaic;

the crowding figures on the stairs of Nineveh or the paintings in the tombs of Egypt—these are the very marrow of
history; of the instant and yet forever; as quick as a newsreel;
the witnesses of the eye.

The Symbol

Thus far we have seen the artist using his power over the
word to name the unknown, to turn dark forces into gods,
to create myths and to sing the hero, real or imaginary. We
have considered the artist as historian, through his power
either over the word or over the implements of the painter
and sculptor. These manifestations in general would fall under the rubric "personification," since they are efforts to
bring phenomena into man's ken by making them manlike.
Personification may take place through sculpture or paint,
even through music (as in the *Dance of the Hours* or the Bird
in *Siegfried*). In mankind, anthropomorphic desire is sharp.
I do not know if cows wish that all other animals were cows.
But it is certain that, where possible, man has rendered everything, even his god, into his own image.

Personification and depersonification are twin expressions
of the same impulse. Water becomes Neptune by personification and H_2O by depersonification; a dove personifies the
Holy Spirit; a cross may stand, by depersonification for
Christ. Into religion, philosophy, politics, art, and science—
at the very center of man's culture—symbolism is inextricably
twined. Enormous and varied as the subject is, I linger over
it only long enough to contend that the artists who created
the symbols have been as powerful and important as symbolism itself.

In politics too, we encounter a lavish use of the symbol.
The fasces or swastika, the Crescent or Cross, the Stars and
Stripes, the Lion of St. Marks, the Cross of St. George, the
lily and the rose (Lily of France or of Florence and Rose of

31

Lancaster or York), these are the symbols which, fluttering from yards of bunting, in two thousand years have led man into battle and political intrigue—in flagrant disregard of the original meaning of the sign. No one of these symbols calls for conquest or oppression, though it is greed that usually sets the emblem fluttering aggressively in the breeze.

Before man knew that the functions of sex were related to those of propagating the race, certain symbols appeared. Long after—and it is then that these symbols become of interest to us—they were adjoined to religious ritual and eventually were subverted to the priestly desires for personification. Through symbols, the wizards, priests, king-priests, were able to keep the religious, ethical, governmental, or tribal customs in fixed and remembered array. The greatest Greek statues were symbolic and ritualistic personifications, created expressly to embody the traditional truth in significance and in permanence.

The superb Elgin marbles, a frieze from the Parthenon, is such a personification, such an illustration (in the sense also of making illustrious). A rite frozen to a monument. Like the fresco in the Ricardi chapel, the frieze depicts a religious procession. Preparations for departure, the turmoil of chariots and men on horseback, musicians, then the sacrificial animals and maidens with sacred vessels; magistrates to welcome them; gods observing; and, in the center of the east wall, the crux of the ceremony: the priest receiving, for Athena, the gift of a great robe or *peplos*. This was the procession of the Panathenaia, in July, when all the gentry of Athens turned out to honor the goddess's birthday. If New York City were to combine Father Knickerbocker, Washington's Birthday, and "I am an American" day—and to add a high seriousness and elevation among actors and audience—the resulting celebration would not be very dissimilar in significance. As such, it might well be portrayed in frieze and fresco for later civilizations to admire.

Often, as I have said, symbolism takes place in a reverse order, not of personification but of depersonification: the symbol standing for the man—the Cross (or the Fish, in the early iconography) for Christ, the owl for Athena (being the wise virgin and originally a night goddess), the miter for the bishop (as in heraldry or chess), the elephant for the Republican Party. The symbol, of course, is paramount in mathematics; the word "word," too, is but four symbols to express a sound which is in itself a symbol of a meaning.

In politics the symbol has been as powerful as the slogan, perhaps more so, since the symbol is painted or carved on fairly enduring material, whereas the slogan reposes usually upon another kind of brass. If the fasces and swastikas of modern times have been restricted to a salutary brevity, the fasces of ancient Rome, together with the SPQR, are happily still visible from the Danube to the Douro; and the ancient swastika of the Mexicans and Chinese need not be effaced. The Chinese, in fact, have a far-reaching and multitudinous symbolism, wherein almost all the forces of nature or the acquired forces of man, the things of the spirit or of the emotions, are symbolized in figures which in turn are often, by depersonification, reduced to ideographs. The dragon is power, of nature or of the dynast; the tortoise is the universe; and so, too, the phoenix, the shape of the lozenge, the primary colors (five colors, five elements, five planets, five notes in the pentatonic scale), the tiger full of yin (dark female) force; pheasants, the "hearers of thunder"; the serpent, of course, in touch with the underworld—all these have symbolic significance. For the primitive watcher, bewildered by the wheeling constellations or the rotation of seasons, it was but a step from the blessed fixedness of the polestar to the conception of a fixed axle upon which the world was impaled (a not unreasonable metamorphosis of the actual truth). From there to the phallic symbol was but another step in the desire to reduce the forces of nature to the scale of man. Thence, by a last step of the imagination, it was almost inevitable to conceive of the unicorn.

This same unicorn enters Christian symbolism through a quite common mistranslation from the Greek Bible; the wild buffalo had been intended. It is the unicorn, however, who browses in the Gothic tapestries as a symbol of man's salvation from the poisonous serpent of Eden. Healing virtue was presumed to reside in the horn—an early form of homeopathy, since the poison was Original Sin and the horn was obviously phallic.

This somewhat light-minded symbolizing was a source of anxiety to the Church Fathers. They feared the corruption of political implications and the debasement of worship into idolatry. The Fathers, close to biblical times, had not forgotten the Calf of Gold; they were near enough the Greek Zeno to agree unconsciously—and for un-Hellenic reasons—that no product of the hands of common craftsmen could have great worth or be accounted holy. In fact, the early Church regarded the profession of sculptor as one which a Christian could not consistently follow. In a pseudo-Clementine Church order, painters were classed with "harlots, brothel-keepers, drunkards, actors, and athletes." The thirty-sixth canon of the Synod of Elvira, of the fourth century, stipulated that "there should be no pictures in a church lest 'the holy thing' be depicted on the walls." By A.D. 600 there was a tempered abhorrence: "It is one thing to offer homage to a picture and quite another thing to learn, by a story told in a picture, to what the homage should be offered . . . if any one desire to make images, do not forbid him; only prohibit by every means in your power the worshipping of images" (Pope Gregory I, to Bishop Serenus). Yet in spite of the protest of Charlemagne, Hadrian I, at the Council of Nicaea, in A.D. 787, admitted image worship into the canon of sound dogma.

The innocent piety which turned a Roman bath into a baptismal font, or—despite the ban—an ancient statue of Hermes and his lamb into "The Good Shepherd," was not mistaken. And the thrift which put a kirtle on the nude statue of the notorious Count Fersen and placed it in the church at Capri in the niche of the young St. John, was based on a precious instinct to keep the symbols living and to keep the heroes heroic. This, too, is the function of the arts.

When the gods progressed from stellar entities to natural forces—rain, thunder, fruitful season, day or night—and again progressed into the acquisition of some of man's characteristics, virtues, and emotions, these too must be presented to worshipers whose simplicity demanded more than a philosophic concept. We of today, sophisticated and skeptical, yet have need of such personifications as Rodin's "Thought" or "The Thinker," of St.-Gaudens' "Grief," or the innumerable Victories that perch on our war memorials. The necessity of early people was more direct. To touch a symbol of victory might mean a victorious battle; to touch the symbol of a bison might mean a full larder after the hunt. A god perhaps possessed bull-like strength (as others owl-like wisdom or sowlike fecundity). To partake of that strength, it seemed reasonable for a man to drink the blood of a dedicated bull, or to erect a statue of the bull-like characteristics of the god and then touch the statue. The god was not a bull, nor the bull a god, but the bull was the symbol of the god's strength and, in some natural affinity, presumably a proper channel for divine contact or solicitude. In many religions (as in early Christianity) it was sacrilege to portray the god himself. In one Canaanitish relief, the bull is shown and the indication that the god has alighted *on* the bull; but the god, being invisible, is not shown. In the earliest Buddhist sculpture, Gautama, having achieved Nirvana and divinity, could not be shown, not rudely snatched back from immortality. Only his footstep, once he had passed, might be displayed. The symbol for him was permitted—as, in Christianity, the dove was permitted to represent the spirit of God.

To the historian, anthropologist, and archeologist, these surviving symbols are of inestimable value. Through them, dates may be assigned, migrations charted, for people would no more leave their symbols behind them than their food or clothes. Through symbols the inner meaning of present rites or observances may be traced from today's obscurity to the reasonable light of the past. Even such practical matters as trade routes are clarified by the voyage of those who sought the Golden Fleece.

We have briefly touched on that small branch of symbolism wherein personification has taken place, for there the hand of the artist is visible beyond dispute. Even from so cursory a glance, one may realize to what extent the painter and sculptor have sustained religion and government. Through symbols, ritual and its essential meaning have been perpetuated, and philosophic concepts conveyed in a sign. For our delight, men have, in so doing, left us the greatest works of art.

Symbols and personifications, like the myths and heroes, persist and lead us on. The statue is but the signature of the godhead. Through it, the artist who has fashioned the image shows forth the truth of those things not obviously divined by man. He clothes the vision of the saint, and presents an imperishable transcription of the memorabilia of humanity to its forgetful senses. "God himself," wrote Maximus of Tyre, "the father and fashioner of all that is, greater than time and eternity, is unnamable by any lawgiver, unutterable

36

by any voice, not to be seen by any eye. But we, being unable to apprehend his essence, use the help of sounds and names and pictures, yearning for a knowledge of Him, and in our weakness naming all that is beautiful in this world after His nature, just as happens to earthly lovers. . . . Let men know what is divine, let them know: that is all. If a Greek is stirred to the remembrance of God by the art of Phidias, an Egyptian by paying worship to animals, another man by a river, another by fire—I have no anger for their divergences. Only let them know, let them love, let them remember!" *

The Moral

The minute that a man declares "thus-and-so is right" he enters the realm of morality. When the justice of his saying has been accepted by even a few people, the concept, by awakening or renewing a group urge, is on its way into politics and perhaps eventually into law. Politics is founded on the accepted canons of morality. The same is true of tradition. Frankie and Johnny, quite as much as Priscilla and John Alden, are in our tradition; prudery is not a criterion of what should or should not be memorable. To make morality synonymous with daintiness is a debasement. Morality, art, tradition, and politics are firmly bound by an inclusive link: the search for salvation.

Salvation can be sought only by the maladjusted. No one would desire to be saved from serene happiness. Mankind is not nor ever has been happily adjusted to a world in which sickness and sorrow are everyone's portion, where man's inhumanity to man is ubiquitous, and where the compensating rewards of an afterlife are so much a matter of pious faith. According to its catastrophes, every age desires a different

* Translated by Gilbert Murray.

37

salvation. I suppose that in the Ice Age, the collective desire was for central heating. Let us sum it up in one generality: the desired end of religion, art, science, and politics is the greatest good for the greatest number of mankind—namely, salvation, achieved by illumination (knowledge of truth), freedom, and order. Salvation or the "good life," must be the desired end of tradition itself, ever progressive and cumulative, since tradition is the compound of religion, art, science, and politics.

The desire for salvation was one of the earliest desires. The cave dwellers undoubtedly sat by their fires wondering how to attract the edible bison and how to repel the terrible tiger. Out of their collective need, one man arose—he of the clever whittling, handy in shaping axes and sharpening shells. With a burnt stick and some ocher he drew on the wall of the cave, miraculous to see, the bison to be allured or the tiger to be repelled. Much later, when icecaps moved or prey grew scarce or drought continued, the urge to better its condition waxed great in the tribe. Then the artist-hero would come forward, his imagination stronger than his fear—an early Moses—and he would lead them out, formulating not a new philosophy but a picture of some Happy Hunting Ground. He would teach the people to wall their habitations and to plant crops, as a *modus vivendi* and yearly habit. He caught the collective urge for stability and repose and gave the formulas to his kind. With advance of civilization, the law givers came. They, too, were catalyzers, carving on their small tablets great laws in answer to the yearning for order. "What shall we do to be saved?" And Moses, Hammurabi, or Asoka, like the later Spartacus or Gregory or Cromwell or Jefferson, found his answer, born of his day and generation, to remove fear.

These are again generalities. But the artist himself was always specific; and in matters of religion and morality we find him being particularly specific in giving concise form to contemporary aspiration. By 50,000 B.C. there are evidences of decent burial. Not long after, a few millennia, we find images and carvings in the tombs. Here is proof that man has reached the stage of some belief in afterlife and that the artist has responded to an urge for that belief. Before the conception of afterlife, a man's carcass was disposed of as one disposes of a dead horse. Later, man came to realize there were forces he was aware of but could not comprehend. The moment had arrived for the seer, the soothsayer, the priest, inventor, and artist. Through him, some answer to the questing, collective mind was crystallized. Vocabularies were small, but the eye was as perfect an instrument as it is today. By 20,000 B.C. the hand had achieved a cunning to match the eye. The first real expression of Homo sapiens' new dignity was art.

Early drawings, carvings, and clay figures were probably destined, at first, to attract the good and propitious things and repel or appease the hurtful ones. The name usually applied to such manifestations is "sympathetic magic." Berthollet calls it "dynamism": the depiction of a hunt in order to "magic" or "put a hex on" the prey. The practice comes from a very valid instinct which we have already examined: if you can depict or name something, you can control it.

Over the roofs and walls of the great Cro-Magnon caves at Les Eyzies and Lascaux, in that loveliest of French valleys, the Dordogne, are spread colored drawings of bison, deer, and tiger. For all their dexterity and charm, these drawings may yet be "dynamistic." But I am certain that the frieze of galloping horses is pure art. The exuberance of those sculptures could not spring from fear or appeasement, unless we allow that all art is a form of sympathetic magic. I confess the theory pleases me. After all, art is a form of interpretative relationship between the concrete and the transcendent. And

39

the man with vision—witch doctor, philosopher, scientist, artist—only interprets the relationship, either with a theory or an image. The theories of Plato—the known, miserable thing on earth reflecting the glorious unknowable Ideal; the symphonies of Beethoven; the paintings of any age—are these not sympathetic magic, the harnessing of forces beyond our immediacy and the interpretation of those forces to relieve the collective, human bewilderment? Are they not positive, however inconclusive, indications of the road to salvation? *

The connection between art and morality need not be elaborated. Almost every moral conception we own has been clarified or fixed for us by the word of a prophet, by a painting, a statue, a poem, or a piece of music. The high moral tone of John Adams and Jefferson has touched all of our public life. If the writers, from Amos to Emerson, have most affected our morality, the other creative artists are not far behind. Our morals, perhaps, are concentrated in ten commandments, transmitted to us by poets and scholars. But the religious aspect of our morality—let us say, our moralities— are also largely conditioned by the plastic arts and music. The cult of the Madonna would be virtually impossible without the painter; a true Christmas unthinkable without the carol.

From earliest, prehistoric emergence, art and morality show a twin origin. For the cave dweller as for us, art was the Word made flesh: not the representation but the presentation of an inner vision in apprehendable form. Art is communion, as it is communication. All this has been said often, in many ways. But a truism may yet be true; and it is

* Cro-Magnon man (our ancestor) . . . wandered into Europe . . . and carved himself out a hunting range in the teeth of the glaciers and in competition with an established race no worse equipped materially than he was himself. The only point in which he was clearly head and shoulders above his Neanderthal adversary was in artistic sensibility—and it is not impossible that it was sensibility, with the greater imagination and breadth of concept which it must have induced, that decided the issue between them." (*The Testimony of the Spade*, Geoffrey Bibby, 1956.)

40

pertinent to remember here that the word "cliché" means a "photographic negative." Even the most carefully arrayed of Brady's Civil War photographs remains documentary, in the same category as a clay tablet recording a sale in Nineveh. The eye that arranged the subjects, as the hand that pressed the clay, may have been so expert as to have approximated a work of art. Yet, for Brady as for the potter, art was accidental. Personal vision must be the origin of art, and significance its aim. A photographer may achieve it; an artist must. A painter may paint a tree; but what is transferred to canvas is not, of course, the tree but the painter's response thereto.

Another source of confusion is the word "propaganda." In a sense, all art is propaganda. A work which sustains or expresses itself through ritual, myth, morality, symbolism, must, if it is serious, be the very essence of propaganda in behalf of the values underlying such rituals, myths, morals, or symbols. The frieze of the Parthenon—as truly as a Russian ikon —was commemorative and interpretative propaganda. Fra Angelico surely could not have conceived of painting except for the "cause." (I know of no secular works by him.) The same is true of Dante. In lesser degree, all artists must perforce, in transmitting their visions, transmit the significance of those visions. Beethoven invented a new thunder, broke with past reticences, and expressed the disappointments and effulgences of a romantic and revolutionary society. He expressed the mood of a mass of people who were even then on their way to the barricades. Sustaining and exacerbating that mood, Beethoven was among the propagandists of liberty. Cézanne, without any subversive subject or statement, but by a newness of approach in his intense search for expressive form, became the agent of a propaganda which rattled every academic door. Many an artist who would disclaim any connection with politics has, by his innovations, accustomed people to new concepts in art, therefore rendering people

41

more receptive to new concepts in thought. Iconoclasm has
far-reaching consequences. Who breaks a form breaks precedent. Here is propaganda—and but one step from politics.

Moreover, this question of propaganda is closely tied to
our subject of morals, for I presume that the good moral is
the sincere one. Every expression of a sincere belief is propaganda for that belief. (Triviality also can be propaganda, as
we know from the phrase "something is vitiating the public
taste.") The harm is done, and immorality enters, when for
any reason—cupidity, fashion, or fear—the artist distorts his
vision to the uses of propaganda. To traduce his own vision
is the great sin for an artist. More than any other, the artist
has to be free. He obeys rules he believes in, he accepts many
canons; but he cannot be forced into having an orthodox
vision. A case in point is St. Francis, poet and saint.

Not long ago, Aldous Huxley was disturbed because in
the last seven hundred years the nations have spent at least
a quarter of their time at war. How, asked Huxley, have art
and letters reacted to this state of affairs? And he concluded
his short article with a partial and dolorous answer (from
his observance of modern authors): since a host of pacific
writers have not discouraged the warlike, artists should "gen-
uinely believe in transcendental values and give effective
expression to their beliefs in plastic or literary forms." He
therewith commends the artist to an ivory tower with the
words, "Seek ye first the kingdom of God and His righteousness, and all the rest shall be added."

Huxley implies, I take it, that not through propaganda
but through art shall the artist prevail. Few would deny it.
The efficacy of Callot's *Les Misères de la Guerre* or of Voltaire's *Candide* sprang from the primary ability of Callot to
draw and of Voltaire to write. An artistic conviction, for an

42

artist, must precede anything else when a work of art is in hand. Other convictions—like the piety of Fra Angelico—may enrich his imagination or purpose but not his hand. Here lies the true answer. The extra-artistic convictions of Fra Angelico were precisely the ones which contributed to the richness of his personality, the serenity of his subjects, the assurance of his attitude. Like Beethoven, like Delacroix, he transferred himself and his beliefs to paper or canvas. And the richness of personality so transferred must depend on more than a knowledge of sound craft. Otherwise the mind is paltry and febrile which creates through virtuosity alone— as the forms so created must ever remain hollow.

In short, the rich-minded artist produces great work, and the great work is one of substance and influence. The artist may be more sensitive to his canvas than to his wife; he may be subtle with rhyme and callous about Chinese orphans. But he must possess an extraordinary quantity of sensitiveness and subtlety; his awareness of form and texture, or context, must be acute, his interest in the spirit, the inwardness of things, must be large or at least schooled and intense, or he will be something other than an artist.

The artist of cramped vision performs in a cramped manner. If a man lives in an ivory tower to such an extent that he has no opinions on war, on slavery or corruption, on power or humility, on ruthlessness or justice, if he succumbs to the easy corruptions of silence, then his work will be narrow, for his vision as well as his heart is shuttered. An artist may seek refuge in Huxley's ivory tower in order to prepare his report to the world. With permanent residence, the tower becomes a coffin.

Again, the artist is man or woman, citizen of some town, native of some country, subject to law; he is a neighbor and a relative. To avoid these relationships is to cut the cord of understanding. And if there is no understanding, where is the vision? But if there is understanding and vision, there must be solicitude. A full man cannot be disaffected from humanity.

Lastly, it would seem impertinent to assume, as does Huxley, that "all the rest shall be added" by God, automatically, rather than by the local politicians. God could so add, if He would, but I doubt the continuity of His interest if a man neglects the second, great Commandment. Seeking righteousness cannot imply indifference to the neighbor who must be loved as oneself. To seek and find God, and then to hoard the discovery, is no part of the Christian doctrine. St. Augustine said that only the fool swalloweth his wisdom, "the wise man spitteth it out." It is because artists possess the gift of communication that the finding of God is but the first step; their true responsibility is to share their vision. And their vision will be ivory and tinsel unless it is conceived in the world of men and bears directly upon those problems which confront man because he is a son of God.

1. The Sources

The artist's mission of creating our tradition began with the first artists who spoke out concerning the two fundamental tenets of that tradition: liberty and justice. We find them in Greece and in Israel.

Our chronology therefore begins in the eighth century before Christ.

1.

Many years ago I attended an evening where, after a learned
lecture by Professor W., a German, our hostess thought it
would be diverting to ask some of her guests which period
of history they would prefer to have lived in. One guest described with much brilliance the life of a Sassanid princess,
amid roses and rivulets. Another guest longed to have been
Aspasia; another—the Professor—to have flourished under the
Antonines; still another, to have attended the court of the
Medici. The last, an English novelist of modest ancestry,
would like to have cast a cloak before the great Elizabeth on
one of her royal progresses.

While the speakers dilated on their choices, I could not
but remember that Aspasia saw the collapse of Athens and
the death of Pericles through plague; that the Professor, being German, would in all probability at the court of Hadrian
have been dressed in bearskins or naked as a gladiator; that
the average age at death of the first four generations of the
Medici family was well under thirty, and the cause of death
largely violence; and lastly that, given the very small number of elite allowed into the royal presence, our novelist
would have been more likely to hold the horses than to cast

47

a cloak. When my turn came, I made some of these remembrances clear. I have no desire to have been born before the invention of anesthesia (I commend to anyone an account of surgical operations as late as 1850): I choose the future, I said, and sat down.

I present the anecdote in order to introduce an unfashionable and heretical opinion: I still believe in progress. Some thinkers today take exception to the word; and, I presume, the word "advance" leaves them equally cold. But there are certain things that are generally considered conducive to the good life, to the health of the nation; certain things that lie close to the heart of mankind. These imponderables are apparently embedded in the deepest of human aspirations, as innate as a desire for a god: freedom and justice.

There are other immortal longings surely, but I choose these two because they are cordial to our tradition and because the artist has exerted his powers in their behalf. It can, I think, be shown that the concepts of freedom and social justice have grown and that there has been an advance in their spread and application. The marshals of that advance have been the artists: those who gave tongue. "Doth not wisdom cry and understanding put forth her voice?"

Above all else, the Greeks prized the liberty to live as they wished to live in their *polis:* the Hebrews had much the same longings for freedom to live as they wished in their temple city. Both nations were ultimately defeated, their armies slaughtered in defense of their liberties, and one nation wiped out.

There are two sorts of liberty much desired by mankind; the freedom within a group for a man to be himself and fulfil himself, and the freedom of the group from the oppression of other groups. In the United States we have prided our-

48

selves, until recently, upon the possession of both liberties. A man knew that his private freedoms of speech, assembly, and above all of thought were protected by a Bill of Rights. And certainly, the group, in this case the nation, has never been seriously menaced from outside.

Within the nation are smaller groups, to at least one of which most citizens belong: clubs, neighborhoods, trades, political parties. I believe there is even a fairly strict organization of hoboes. In a free country a man can move from group to group with impunity. Such movement, though we take it for granted, is one of the manmade blessings of any free society.

Up to about A.D. 1750, such movement was rarely possible in most civilized countries. Even in freedom loving Zion, a man was born into and remained in a caste—a Pharisee, a Sadducee, a Levite—or he was, if not an outcast, still pretty much a nobody. In Athens too, he might be born free, a citizen, and only slightly more lucky if born into a family of wealth as well. But if not so born, he was a slave. (This does not take into account that small part of the population, foreigners in the main, or freedmen, with partial rights granted by courtesy.*) In 400 B.C., Athens and Israel led the world in the concept of freedom. The rest of the globe sweated under absolute tyrannies; the commonalty could hope at best for a peaceful reign and fairly equitable laws, particularly in matters of land tenure, irrigation, oaths, business contracts, and inheritances. Freedom as we know it did not exist. Happy accidents (like the rise of Joseph, or the exceptional common soldier becoming general and then potentate) are so rare as to be elaborately noted.

But from two countries, Greece and Palestine, came the concepts of liberty. How do we know this? We know of the

* See footnote on p. 74.

concepts, and have inherited them so absolutely that we too will fight and die for them, because the men who formulated them were poets and set them forth in imperishable works.

The astonishing thing about the Hebrews is that they were the first (beginning in the eighth century B.C.) to lay the foundation of our modern understanding of liberty by adding two words: *for everyone.* Here, the slave-owning Greeks withheld the stylus; not so the Jews. The Jews saw truly that nothing in their conceptions of God the Father was compatible with one of His sons being in bond to another. If souls were equal in the sight of God, so, as man struggled to be Godlike, must all souls be equal in the sight of man. It was a doctrine as subversive as it was new. And it was launched and made memorable by a handful of prophets in a small, hilly country, wedged between two great slave-holding nations, Egypt and Assyria.

From those pronouncements—made in a continuous outpouring till the death of St. Paul—came the first intimation that solicitude for *all* men was the duty of everyone who thought to live according to God's will. Nowadays, we call the formulation of such ideas "social justice." People who believe in social justice are usually called "do-gooders" by the light-minded.

We must recognize that to say "one finds only the rudiments of social justice and liberty" in Israel or Greece would be absolutely incorrect. On the contrary, we find the ultimate flower of both these conceptions springing from their first adumbration. No one has written more nobly concerning them than the poets of Athens or the Prophets; and upon their words we have based all our subsequent accomplishment, aspiration, and, I would add, advance.

To these two concepts which have sustained our efforts to lead or establish the good life we may append a few more categories. Beside liberty and social justice, we may set also the practice of democracy, a wide education, and a host of civilizing laws and customs, whose roots lie embedded in the two fundamental concepts.

In the early epochs of this world, poets were revered as "legislators and prophets." Shelley, perhaps overly aware of a high calling, wrote that "all the authors of revolutions in opinion are necessarily poets, as they are inventors," since they deal in living images, in segments of elemental truth. Their word is prophetic and often, years later, becomes legislation. Rather than dispute Shelley, let us turn the sentence around and claim, at least where liberty and justice are concerned, that many poets have been revolutionaries and the cause of revolution. Indeed, there have been countless poets and prophets whose thought was so revolutionary that to this day it is considered subversive to take it seriously.

Most of what these men so eloquently advocated remained unheeded in their day; part of it was utterly forgotten for over a thousand years. With a sinking of the heart, we contemplate the untold centuries when art certainly flourished but when almost no protest was heard; almost no word spoken against slavery, war, squalor, want, ignorance, coercion; no word in behalf of liberty or social justice. While it is true that artists have been the agents of whatever liberties were possible in their own times, it is true also that for many centuries only a few—whom we shall consider later— dared express the humanitarian vision.

No one else expressed this vision; it was simply not expressed. The generals, the bankers, the men of might, the merchants, the cardinals, did not express it. In Greece the word was spoken, and in Israel up to the death of the last apostle; but from then on there was a black eclipse of liberal expression for nearly thirteen hundred years—a darkness il-

51

luminated by occasional flashes from the less orthodox saints of the Church.

II.

The first of the provocative torchbearers whom we shall note belong to the great wellspring of our tradition: the Bible. We have quoted from one or two of the Prophets, but the magnificent procession demands a fuller account. We shall find that the seven earliest and greatest, Amos, Hosea, Micah, Isaiah I, Jeremiah, Ezekiel, and Isaiah II—with one exception—were violent dissenters, experimenters, innovators; individualists for whom man's free spirit was more precious than gold, "even than the golden wedge of Ophir"; anticlerical; despisers of priests and kings, of all who might seek any power except that to do good. In an epoch of wizards, familiar spirits, and miracles, nearly two centuries before the first stirrings of science in Greece, the Prophets had no truck with magic (except for one obviously later interpolation). They entered politics to preserve for Israel the great liberty: the liberty to worship God freely and to live the good life for God's pleasure. Dissent, liberality, individualism, the rule of conscience, a desire for autonomy, these were characteristic of the prophetic mission. They remain integral to our tradition.

The Prophets were agitators; some were uncouth, some were men of the world; all were poets. As poets and interpreters of the poetic vision, they had the gift to look closely at the world about them, at neighbors, rich and poor, at houses and animals, at the suffering of mankind and (with rarely any pity for themselves) at their own sorrows. But their gift allowed them to lift the specific, temporal instance into the general and eternal—*sub specie aeternitatis*—and to draw from an observation an everlastingly valid conclusion. Shakespeare and Keats, in a sonnet, have elevated human constancy to the level of the fixed stars, as, in a lesser way, Rossetti elevated his personal grief by observing, with bowed head, that the wood-spurge had a threefold cup.

As agitators, each of the Prophets in turn was a voice crying in the wilderness, a provocative third party incessantly piercing the shams of Church, state, and society. No interest had they in circumcision or hecatombs, theology or dogma. Man should be known by his fruits. And the just man was one who made the world of God's children a decent place in which to live and to love God. By the end of the great line (Isaiah II), God was love, and His Temple was open to any who would acknowledge Him.

The years of the great Prophets run from Amos, about 750 B.C. to the end of Isaiah II, about 500 B.C., thus before the great lights of China, India, or Greece. Amos was born under the fearful shadow of the sword of Assyria, and Isaiah II died after the long exile in Babylon had come to an end.

We meet Amos, a herdsman, delivering a subversive oration to the good folk gathered at an idolatrous celebration in Bethel. He begins with a magnificent series of curses, during which he reviews the sins of the mighty and those of King Jeroboam in particular, and, from this political indiscretion, goes on to pour contumely upon the cherished conventions and fears of his listeners. As to their religious practices, Amos tells them: " 'I hate, I despise your feast days and I will not smell in your solemn assemblies,' saith the Lord." He prophesies the fall of the king and the destruction of his kingdom of Israel, not only for the idolatry and wantonness of the citizens but chiefly for their inhumanity to their own kind.

The first two chapters are one extravagant, brilliantly sustained invective. Mark what God's curse falls upon: the powerful and rich who have sold the righteous for silver and the poor for a pair of shoes, who have panted after the very dust of the earth on the head of the poor, and have turned aside the way of the meek; upon kings who broke their pledge and upon nations that cast off pity; upon those who have crushed the needy and oppressed the poor; upon all who have taken bribes or cornered the grain market and given false weight to the humble. To do such was to break the law of the Lord; to fulfil the law was to deal in justice and mercy. When Amos had finished, the local priest begged him please to go and prophesy in some other village.

The implications of this scene are manifold. No harm came to Amos, though he spoke in the face of an entrenched priesthood. Time and again, the worn figure of a Prophet appears at the palace steps or on a roadside by a festive, orthodox procession, and gives tongue to unpalatable truths. Any other peoples on the face of the globe would have arrested or stoned such a manifestant, as the Greeks rid themselves of Socrates, the archdisturber. In Israel, he was allowed to go in peace. Ingrained in the civilization of the Hebrew was a sense of wrong-doing and a perhaps superstitious awe of one who came in the Name of the Lord. We too, today, have certain respects bred in us; and we achieve, as it were, a feeling of extension in time, of spiritual enlargement, when we hark back two thousand years and encounter an intellectual ancestor whom we can understand and still admire.

In Micah we find the same horrified concern with graven images, for these were not of God but of Asshur and Omri and Baal. Again, we find the bitter condemnation of those who judge for reward, of priests who teach for hire or of prophets who divine for money—complaints that reappear in *Piers Plowman*. From what must be a wildly garbled, ill-copied script, there still sounds the fundamental demand for "equall justice." Micah's God, like Amos', continues to be irked by the offerings of thousands of rams or ten thousand rivers of oil. The gift required of men is that they should do justly, love mercy, and walk humbly with God.

Of the three contemporaries, Amos, Micah, and Hosea, Hosea is the most touching, perhaps the most extraordinary. In an age when spring was called "the season in which kings go forth to war," when a conquered city was put to the sword and the remnants of a people sold as slaves, when the most cruel revenge was considered plainest justice, when the gods, in man's image, were jealous, vindictive, and murderous, even anthropophagous, Hosea conceived of a loving Father. In the more enlightened civilizations of the earth, at that time, the idea was dawning that a man might mitigate his tremendous fear of his gods by loving them, with a respectful and propitiating love. But nowhere except in the hills of Palestine was it told that God might, that God did, love humanity. Here was truly a new conception that should have changed the heart of mankind—that large part of his heart which was concerned with religion, afterlife, myth, morals, and worship. For Hosea saw that God would not exercise omnipotence to make man requite His love, since forced love or virtue was not what God desired. And because His love was so little requited by sinful man, Hosea saw also that God must be a suffering God.

To conceive that God forewent power in order to love, and to conceive that, because of this immortal magnanimity, God made himself vulnerable to sorrow, were imaginings of an originality matched only by their splendor. "O Israel," cried Hosea's God, "thou hast destroyed thyself, but in me is thine help." The God of all the Prophets required that men should deal mercifully. Hosea knew that his God would not require what He was unprepared to mete. Here, had mankind realized it, was an end of fear—that fear which sent votaries scuttling to the wizards and soothsayers, to the priests of Baal, to Jehovah's altars with obnoxious sacrifices. If God loved man, He would love those who were lovable in His sight and who loved Him—not those who did ill and sought to buy His favor. Not for seven hundred years, not till Jesus brought the confirming revelation, was God so to reveal Himself as He did to Hosea. Only this strange, embittered man, whose wife left him and whom he took back when her lovers had forsaken her, caught sight of a God who could say, "When Israel was a child, then I loved him. . . . I taught Ephraim also to go, taking them by their arms. . . . I drew them with cords of a man, with bands of love."

Isaiah I, Jeremiah, and Ezekiel plunge us into politics. Isaiah and Jeremiah consorted with kings; Jeremiah and Ezekiel were perhaps the first of the priest caste to be called prophets. The political atmosphere of Asia Minor in the seventh century B.C. was not wholly unlike that of Europe in 1930. In the days of Shalmaneser or the days of Hitler, there was not a great difference between the lot of a small country, reputed rich, set on the main trade routes, filled with national pride, and warlike. The question for the small country, then as now, concerned what alliances she should make. The Jews were divided; the northern kingdom was Israel, the southern, with Jerusalem, was Judaea. Each sought outside alliances. (The relations between the two were like the relations today between certain Arab states; a jealousy tempered by race and common worship.) To the east lay the great incumbent power, Assyria, with Babylon threatening that ancient supremacy. To the west lay Egypt, waiting artfully in the hope that Babylon and Nineveh would destroy each other and allow her to inherit the earth. The picture is startlingly modern.

Now, Isaiah grew up in the kingdom of Judaea, which paid yearly tribute to Assyria (Nineveh). Samaria, the capital of Israel, had played one alliance off against the other and finally defied Assyria. Shalmaneser, the Assyrian king, laid

siege to Samaria, the little city. Egypt found it inconvenient to succor her ally; after three years, the city fell and
all Israel's ten tribes were carried into captivity, to be lost
to history. Disregarding this catastrophe at his very doors, the
king of Judaea grew adventurous. Tribute was a ruinous burden. If Samaria stood out for three years, could not Jerusalem stand out for longer? Could not Egypt be induced to
keep faith? It was against this mirage of false hopes that
Isaiah set himself. He saw, as we can see now, the folly of
dependence on an Egypt who would play her own hand only
to her own advantage; the folly of hoping that Assyria would
overlook an unpaid tribute or fail to destroy her debtors. In
season and out, Isaiah heckled the king. But the king was
bent on his folly. He defied Assyria, made as many neighboring alliances as he could, and prepared to stand siege.

Isaiah had warned him: "Say ye not, a confederacy . . .
associate yourselves [against Assyria], O ye people, and ye
shall be broken to pieces. . . . Because ye have said, 'we have
made a covenant with death and with hell are we at agreement; when the overflowing scourge shall pass through, It
shall not come unto us, for we have made lies our refuge' . . .
now, therefore . . . thou shalt be brought down . . . and thy
speech shall be low out of the dust . . . for the Egyptians shall
help in vain. . . . Thus saith the Lord, 'In quietness and in
confidence shall be your strength.' " To stand for pacifism
at such a time, to urge submission, and to salt this unpopular
doctrine with root-and-branch criticism, required courage.
Isaiah's advice to a people filled with turbulence and fear
was sharply to the point. "Now, the Egyptians are men and
not God; and their horses flesh and not spirit."

It was in the fourteenth year of the reign of this restive
king Hezekiah that Sennacherib sent his armies "like a
wolf on the fold." He captured forty-six cities of Judaea and
finally invested Jerusalem. When Isaiah heard of the terms

of surrender, shouted from the Assyrian camp, he sent down word to Hezekiah. Not through the obduracy of greedy royalty nor through the wickedness of the people of Judah, but through the Lord's mercy and the fact that the Assyrian king was even more obnoxious than Hezekiah, would Jerusalem be spared. "He shall not come into this city nor shoot an arrow there," said Isaiah. And he was right. A foul plague spread in the Assyrian camp. "When they arose early in the morning, behold, they were all dead corpses." Sennacherib retired to Nineveh, to be murdered while at prayer by his sons; and Hezekiah gave thanks and made his peace with the Lord.*

So much for the political side of Isaiah's activity. As the fundamentalist poet of the school of Amos, Micah, and Hosea, as agitator and reformer, through forty-odd chapters, Isaiah delivers the searing rebuke.

Ah, sinful nation, a people laden with iniquity, children that are corrupters: they have forsaken the Lord.

Wash you, make you clean; cease to do evil.

Bring no more vain oblations; incense is an abomination unto me; the new moons and sabbaths.

Learn to do well; seek judgment, relieve the oppressed, judge the fatherless, plead for the widow.

Thy princes are rebellious and companions of thieves; every one loveth gifts and followeth after rewards.

I will turn my hand upon thee (saith the Lord) and purge away thy dross and take away all thy sin.

For he (God) looked for judgment, but behold oppression; for righteousness, but behold a cry.

For ye have eaten up the vineyard; the spoil of the poor is in your houses.

---

* It is presumed that a horde of rats, attracted by greased leather thongs, bowstrings, and harness, descended on the Assyrian camp and demolished the equipment. Also, that with the rats came plague.

The day of the Lord of hosts shall be upon every one that
is proud and lofty, and upon every one that is lifted up; and
he shall be brought low.

A scant hundred years later, Babylon of the Chaldees had
annihilated Nineveh of the Assyrians. Again the little kingdom of Judaea found herself between Egypt and a voracious
eastern power. And again the great Prophet of the age, Jeremiah, counseled the Jews to conclude any pact of peace, this
time with Babylon, and again to place no hope in help from
Egypt. But where Isaiah had prophesied that the Assyrian
would not destroy Jerusalem, this time Jeremiah prophesied
that Judaea was doomed, unless she mended her ways and
submitted abjectly to the Chaldeans. His was not a popular
ministry. Yet, like Isaiah, he was right in his prophesy.

One of the most indomitable creatures who ever lived,
Jeremiah spent his life preaching nonresistance. He was
bound in chains; he was put in the stocks. He was cast into
prison, and from his dungeon he wrote violent diatribes to
his king. The king snipped the pages off with scissors and
burned them. Jeremiah sent him a fresh copy with additions.
When one of the visiting Chaldean armies retired at the
news that Egypt was on the move, and there was some justification for calling Jeremiah a false prophet, he was thrown
into a pit, in mire up to his neck. From there he was res-
cued by a eunuch. When the Chaldeans first conquered Judaea, they found the aging Prophet in prison, and they left
him with a handful of compatriots in the deserted city. Three
times this remnant of the Jews, with incredible heroism,
revolted. The last time, the Chaldeans appeared before the
breached walls to have done with the yearly nuisance caused
by a people whose desire was toward one God and who
longed for complete liberty in which to worship Him. Jeru-

salem was destroyed. The last survivors departed to Egypt, taking the prophet with them. When this pathetic band of exiles sought some rejoicing in the festivals of the Egyptian gods and in the easier life near the Nile, Jeremiah rose once again to inveigh. But his people could stand no more. They stoned him to death.

This was a lonely man, who counseled appeasement to a warlike people and submission to a proud people, who argued with his God as freely as with his king, who dinned an unparalleled threat of future horrors into his listeners' ears and who abominated the current moral practices of his day. Whatever may have seemed harsh, exigent, even repellent in that anguished figure has, with time, been softened by our vision of his overwhelming compassion. He was very human; a poet; master of the verbal image. On page after page, there come flashes of metaphor, symbolism, and comparison which have colored the use of English ever since the Bible was known to us. Jeremiah astonishes us with his close observation of nature. And always his anger is directed against those who pursue false gods, those who worship the work of their own hands, against princes, pastors, lawyers who oppress the poor, seek vain things, and are themselves corrupt. Jeremiah's God, like that of Hosea and Isaiah, is one of compassion. In spite of all the sins of Judaea, "yet will I plead with you, said the Lord." For himself, he can hardly bear his anguish any longer, or the taunts and menaces of his neighbors. "Cursed be the man who brought tidings to my father, saying, a man child is born unto thee, making him very glad. Wherefore came I forth out of the womb to see labor and sorrow, that my days should be consumed with shame?"

This man would stand in the door of the Lord's House or the gate of the King's palace and boldly describe the fate that awaited priests and kings.

They shall die of grievous deaths;
they shall not be lamented;
neither shall they be buried;
but they shall be as dung
upon the face of the earth;
and they shall be consumed
by the sword and by famine;
and their carcasses shall be meat
for the fowls of heaven.

For from the least of them
even unto the greatest of them
every one is given to covetousness,
and from the prophet even unto the priest
every one dealeth falsely.

They were as fed horses in the morning:
every one neighed after his neighbor's wife.

Saying to a stock, Thou art my father;
and to a stone, Thou hast brought me forth.
For they have turned their back
unto me and not their face—
saith the Lord—
but in the time of their trouble
they will say, "Arise, and save us!"

Yet, to Jeremiah's mind, the Lord required of His people
no more than He had always required, since the days of
Abraham or Moses; what He had made known to them
through the mouths of His true Prophets:

Execute ye judgment and righteousness and deliver
the spoiled out of the hand of the oppressor; do
no wrong; do no violence to the stranger, the
fatherless, nor the widow, neither shed innocent blood.

There is but One God, Jeremiah proclaimed, and He is Je-hovah-tsidkenu: the Lord of Righteousness. To find him, man has but to search his own conscience and go forth and deal righteously.

Here is the essence of social reform—as well, the essence of dissent, nonconformity, Lollardry, Puritanism.

Ezekiel—the shepherd of the Babylonian Exile—was of su-preme importance to the Hebrews: he accomplished for their religious organization much that Augustine and Gregory accomplished for Christianity. He endowed it with separate, endurable form. Though often speaking with poetry and with the humanitarian fire of the elder prophets, and though no more given to elaborate curses and depictions of the why and the how of the Lord's anger than the rest, still Ezekiel's interest and mission were sacerdotal rather than prophetic.

He came to prominence among the captives in Chaldea. An exile and a lonely man, he longed for the brooks and wooded slopes of his homeland. The dry bed of Chebar, near the muddy Euphrates, brought him no solace; and from the aridity of his habitation and the verdure of his memories, Ezekiel drew many of his finest comparisons. He saw about him great contrasts. On the one hand, the stupendous luxury of Babylon, on the other, the inveterate diseases of poverty and ignorance. He saw young Hebrews being sold into slav-ery to the Greeks, through the trading ports of Tyre and Sidon. And he saw his unhappy people, as Jeremiah was to see them in Egypt, dazzled by the splendor of idolatrous tem-ples, longing to dig in, be part of, take hold of this busy land; wanting to forget their troubles, even if this meant forgetting their own customs; wanting to mingle and be at rest forever.

Upon such appeasement, Ezekiel hurled his anathema. Jeremiah had written him to submit. Ezekiel agreed: he would submit to the armed might of Babylon, but no more. He must snatch and keep forever separate and alive the ancient integrity of his people, against the day when they should once more set up the Lord's house in Jerusalem. This could only be done by multiplying the causes of divergence, by destroying the desire for collaboration and the danger of contamination, by bolstering the crushed pride of the Hebrews. Above all, by keeping them faithful to their God.

With great method, with outstanding gifts as an organizer, Ezekiel set about his task. Everything that could separate the Jews from their conquerors became a matter of Church law. Until then, circumcision had little occupied the Prophets. God's work, they had felt, could be accomplished with or without appendages. Now, food, garments, washings, holy days—all these became of supreme importance. So well was Ezekiel's labor done, that when Cyrus conquered Babylon (539 B.C.) he was forced to let a completely unassimilated, obdurate group return to its own land. (So well, indeed, did Ezekiel labor that the wall of separation has lasted to this day, preserving the integrity of Israel and also accounting for many of her woes.)

It was upon this liberation, this casual gift from the victorious Mede but, to the Hebrews, this fulfilment of all God's promises, that the second Isaiah sang his paean of praise—perhaps the greatest in any language. As his words still convey illimitable majesty, so Isaiah's thoughts dwelt in realms of heavenly joy and trust and thanksgiving. In this rapt and elevated mood there was no room for the old shadows: all is the light of heaven and the love of God. Wickedness, regret, even the merits of ritual—these were but distractions from rhapsodic contemplation. The sorrow of the past had enabled man to understand suffering and to comfort the sufferer; it had made man compassionate, even as God is

63

compassionate. But now such suffering was over; a new song was to be sung and a new lesson to be learned: how to share the divine joy of God.

In this ode to freedom, though the fierce injunctions are absent, it is made clear that the joy of God is reserved for those who deal in equity, with a humble and contrite mind, for those who "undo the heavy burdens and let the oppressed go free." "Feed the hungry and bring the poor that are cast out to thy house." In the acceptable year of the Lord, man will comfort all that mourn and offer God not lip service but a loving heart.

So is it also with the many minor prophets. Each one looks about him and recoils in fear of how a just God must punish a world given over to rapacity. "That they may do evil with both hands earnestly, the prince asketh and the judge asketh for a reward [bribe]; and the great man he uttereth his mischievous desire; so they wrap it up." Superb campaign vituperation, sparing neither the liar nor robber, the warlord, the witch monger, the purse-proud nor the covetous, prophets that are "light and treacherous persons," and all who imagine evil against their fellow men. The true Prophets' concern is rarely with theology, but rather with poverty and wealth, labor and capital, in short, with politics and economics; how to make the world a more equitable place in which to serve God. All the means have been placed in man's hand to deserve God's mercy. Yet man, in his inhumanity to man, persists in alienating that mercy. The root of all abomination is the love of power. Love, not power, is the Godlike motive. To these lonely, often outcast admonishers, such a love of God was a simple actuality, a simplicity, instinct with majesty and truth, practical truth. Because these Prophets, God's hornets, were practical men and even, at times, laconic. "Love God and Keep His Commandments, for this is the

whole duty of man." These were the Prophets Christ came
not to destroy but to fulfil.

III.

It is astonishing how literally the Prophets have survived.
Such of our literature as can lay claim to moral earnestness,
from Amos to our own day, might well become a list of the
survivals and reawakenings of the prophetic spirit, often of
the prophetic word itself. The great men of the New Testament "spake by the Prophets." And Amos would joyfully
have held the pen when the nonconformist Paul wrote to the
Hebrews—a people become almost idolatrous of their state-
supported Temple—that worship was in the heart, "the true
Tabernacle, which the Lord pitched and not man."

This spirit of compassion and equity reached its height in
the ministry of Jesus, to survive in the early Church and to
reawaken in the bosom of such saints as St. Francis and the
first secular writers who dared quote from the Bible. The
cry for "equall justice" has had a long echo. Langland and
Bunyan, mighty borrowers from the prophetic books, re-
awakened it. So too Erasmus, reminding his Church that
Christ had enjoined it to feed, not despoil, His flock, and
resuming the ancient invective against those who, rather than
serve, chose to pursue lordships, dominion, swords, keys,
powers. The long echo sounds again in the Humble Remonstrance, in the Mayflower Compact, in our Declaration of
Independence—always vibrant with the prophetic protest, a
protest charged with equalitarianism, anticlericalism, and
libertarianism. Dissident it must be; for compassion, equity,
and brotherly love do not flourish commonly in this world.
Yet it is just this desire for fellowship which irradiates our
tradition; and we may hope that it lightens our institutions.
It is an ideal that we inherit from the Prophets, not from the

Greeks. From the Greeks came forms and intellectual method and delight. The spirit is from the Jews.

In Greece there was compassion and dissent; but not of the order we seek. A people that considered it proper to butcher the excess of slaves, as did the Spartans, or that classed four-fifths of humanity—legally, religiously, politically —with the lower animals, such a people was far from the ideal of fraternity and equity which was ever present to the people of Israel and Judaea. Because these Greeks, who used the word "democracy" but never knew its spiritual meaning, could not protest in the name of a common humanity, they allowed their dissent, like their compassion, to be confined, as it were, by etiquette. Their compassion was reserved for the sorrows of kings.

We do not need to enter the ancient scholastic battle concerning the merits of the two civilizations, Hellenic and Hebrew. We accept, in our bodies, the presence of intellect and emotion, mind and heart. So we must accept, with equal thankfulness, the dual font of our culture and tradition. Our concern is to choose for review those liberal and dissident characteristics which have persisted, those humanitarian values which enliven our tradition. There is no doubt that the Bible here is the primary and greater source.

We are a sportive people. Sport is in our tradition. "Good sport" and "fair play" are words of weight. Some of our traditional feelings in the matter revert to the Spartan boy with the fox at his vitals, some go back to the Pass of Thermopylae, the Marathon runners, or Horatius at the bridge. But, for adults, the lesson is better learned in II Samuel, 12, where Nathan pointed out to David that it was not quite sporting to have gotten Uriah out of the way by sending him to the front to be killed. It is a more general lesson; for few of us are called upon to hold off, single handed, the hosts of Tarquin, yet many a man may yearn for his neighbor's wife. And

66

if we learn that the Gods did condescend to interfere in the heroic strife of mortals, if Athena snatched her favorite to safety in a cloud, our inward spirit is not moved thereby nor are we greatly enriched. But when God sent the prophet Nathan to David, it was our God—not Zeus—who sent, our God who apprised David of the "ewe lamb," and who struck down the child that Uriah's wife bore to David. By that story of compassion and equity, mercy and justice, we are moved and greatly enriched.

The finest Greek minds were hard put to it to reconcile their theology and sociology with their best instincts. Implacable fate, unadmirable gods, a slave society—for men of such supreme imaginations these were irreconcilable with any high hope, knowledge, or taste. That fatal irreconcilability was unknown to the Prophets. Their God was wholly admirable; a man's fate remained in a man's hand, to do well or ill; and none were slaves, for all were equal children of God. Long after Jeremiah and Ezekiel had repudiated the barbaric conception that the sins of the father were visited upon the children; long after Hosea had discovered a God who pitied mankind "like as a father pitieth his children," the Greek poets and dramatists were struggling with the sacrifice of Iphigenia. The most brilliant elucidation of ethics or morals was, for the Greeks, invariably brought to an impasse, to a wall made of the great irreconcilables. Beyond a point they could not go, for there was no love. There could be no answer to a prayer except by condescension or favoritism. Religion remained a ritual of appeasement. Because Zeus did not love and sorrow over mankind, there was no dear fatherhood in him. Because there was no fatherhood in heaven, there was no sonship on earth; and because there was no sonship on earth there could not be the first and last great relationship, the one that lay beyond the wall which stopped the Greeks: the brotherhood of man. Yet that is the root-

67

concept of our tradition, and that is why the Bible remains the compelling force in our traditional aspirations for the good life.

With that single but all-important exception, the Greeks, in the short span of four hundred years, made the most original and far-reaching contributions to liberal thought. On intellectual liberty and freedom from tyranny, their words were the first and remain the greatest. We owe to their inquisitiveness and logic the scientific spirit, the release of the intellect from the shackles of taboo. Endless is the catalog of our debt to them. The traditions of our European world owe more numerous and diverse facets of light to the Greeks than to the Hebrews. But the one light we owe the Hebrews is, after all, the Light of the World. Any European might demur; we in America cannot. If the essential quality of our American tradition is liberality—the brotherhood of man under the fatherhood of God—then we must trace our inheritance to the lovers of compassion and equity who antedated the Greeks and whose prophetic words were ever on the lips of Christ. Our sense of social justice is not from Aristotle or Plato, but from voices that cried in the wilderness along the hills of Palestine.

Our law may well have come from Solon. From Solon to Numa; from Roman law to the Codes of Justinian; from there into canon law; from there, the English common law. Under those laws we live, we perform in our habits and customs. But the spirit of liberality is not bound by legal convention; we know that law was made for man, not man for the law. "The Law made nothing perfect, but the bringing in of a better hope did," wrote St. Paul. No Greek or Roman could so have written. Our American tradition is founded on the better hope. Not even Euripides would have written, "Remember them that are in bonds as if ye were also bound with them." Yet our tradition is founded upon freedom.

With two quotations, we shall leave this thorny problem.

Simo: "Take up sculpture? You'll never be anything but a day-laborer, without honor; you'll live obscurely, your spirit in weariness, unable to rise. You'll be only an artisan, lost in the masses. Were you even Phidias or Polycleitos, turning out admirable work, only your art would be praised, not your rabbit-like existence. So you'd live and die a vile laborer who works with his hands" (Lucian).

Ecclesiasticus: "He that cuts engravings, his diligence is to make great variety, he will set his heart to preserve likenesses in portraiture, and will be wakeful to finish his work. So the smith: his eyes are upon the pattern of his vessel. All these put their trust in their hands and each becometh wise in his own work. Without these [artist-craftsmen] shall not a city be inhabited and men shall not walk up and down therein. They will maintain the fabric of the world and in the handiwork of their craft is their prayer" (Ecc. 38).

2. The Environment

A short study of the circumstances in which artists have labored—the handicaps usually outweighing the privileges—is essential to an understanding of any craft. Such a study is doubly necessary here to account for the annihilation of dissent during the more than thousand years after St. Paul. The post-Virgilian poets, Juvenal for example, excoriated their own times. Some of their works, like Heliogabalus, have perished in the filth of their subjects. But none of the writers expressed a solicitude for liberty and justice in terms which have enriched our tradition.

I deal briefly with the dreary facts of slavery and anonymity. With patronage we come to happier material and to a circumstance which is with us still.

2.

I

Besides the barbarian invasions and the struggle of the early Church to survive, two notable causes, left over from the pagan world, were perhaps responsible for the silence which enveloped Europe for a thousand years. These causes were anonymity and servitude.

Few are charmed by the contemplation of a slave society. The back of the canvas is not dainty. Slavery is undeniably repulsive. But there may be readers who consider that anonymity has not affected the artist adversely. Many of the greatest works have not been signed; vanity and egotism are often mixed on the brush or chisel that signs. To this I would reply that without the recognition and personal involvement attendant on a signature, the artist suffers an atrophy. The nameless child, the foundling, implies a detached, uninvolved, and feckless parent.

Anonymity and slavery together compounded a circumstance and ambience in which our artist found it all but impossible to express himself. Under the Roman empire he was no longer trained to grand techniques, he was abased below the capacity to hold the vision, and to communicate might have meant death.* In contrast to the preceding chapter, where we saw the creative beacons flame above the Judaean hills, we must now peer into the void, a void wherein the future of our twin lights—liberty and justice—is at best obscure. Fortunately, God appears to abhor a vacuum; and ultimately angels rush in where the wise have feared to tread.

Before the sixth century B.C. there is no sure record of the name of an artist, except only of a few poets. From heroes, myths, statues, potteries, and symbols, we know that artists existed. From the character of those myths and heroes and symbols, as from the advanced conceptions of the poets and of the Biblical Prophets, we know that whatever liberality existed owed its existence to those same artists. But, if those ages of anonymity (which, in some trades, lasted till the Renaissance) make it difficult for us to assign and specify, we must concede how difficult it was for the unhappy objects of that enforced anonymity to live at all. The incentives to creation were warped by it; the chances of rising to eminence were few. And the dangers of kicking against the pricks were lethal.

In spite of our schoolbooks, it is well for us to realize that the liberties of Greece—so magnificently expounded and defended, so vital to our own thought and tradition—were in their day intended only for a very small élite.† The craftsmen (and hence the great majority of artists) were excluded, not only from recognition on earth but also from any hope of heaven. Plato did not allow the workingman more than half a soul. Participation in the Eleusinian Mysteries—the crucial festival in honor of Demeter, whose breath could waft everlasting life, could lend or withdraw fertility—was denied the

---

* Among others, Euripides, Ovid and Juvenal were exiled; Seneca executed.
† Around 300 B.C. the population of Athens was counted as 400,000 slaves, 10,000 strangers, about 84,000 proletaries, and only 21,000 citizens.

proletarians. Every fifth year, for nine days beginning in September, the processions of the well-born initiated passed from Athens to the temple of Megaron. The excluded freedmen and slaves could but stand by the wayside and throw stones. They were damned, and they knew it.

As he was allowed only half a soul by Plato, the craftsman was allowed less than half a name. If a workingman achieved a tombstone, it was usually the gift of his union. The little separate inscriptions, scattered here and there in Asia Minor, Greece, and Italy, are pathetic evidences of the personal struggle for recognition. Happy was he who could even temporarily borrow a seemly death. Temporary indeed, for after death Heaven was reserved for the few.

> A Lydian, yes, a Lydian I;
> But though I was a slave
> My master let his tutor lie
> In this, a freeman's grave.
> (*Dioscorides*, Furness, tr.)

A tablet is a small thing, yet it served to break the crushing silence of a lowly anonymity.

Artist, artisan, and mechanic were among the outcasts. The few who rose to consort with the optimates, the heavenborn, had their low birth continually thrown in their teeth. To counter the paradox that evidences of genius apparently cropped out in some earthborn fellows—a painting, a bas-relief, a poem, an invention, the marvels of the potters' wheel, hydraulic devices, and arts of navigation—the philosophers propounded an exclusive theory whereby the statue was everything, the sculptor nothing.

> Often, we delight in the work and yet despise the workman. Scents and genuine sea-purple dyes we rejoice in, while

we regard the dyer and the scent-maker as a vulgar and low sort of person. So it was a good answer that Antisthenes gave when he was told that Ismenias was a fine piper: "But he's a sorry sort of man. If he were not, he'd not be so fine a piper." Philip of Macedon told his son, Alexander, when he saw him at some party peacefully and skillfully plucking on a harp, "Aren't you ashamed to play the harp as well as that?" For it is enough when a king has the time to listen to others playing the harp. A king cultivates the Muses by going to concerts.

(Shades of the Hanoverians!)

Manual labor at low tasks is a sign of indifference to fine things, for it is laboring at what is unprofitable and useless. No clever young man, at the sight of a great statue feels any desire to become either a Phidias or a Polycleitos; nor an Anacreon or Philetor, for all the pleasure he may take in their verses. It does not follow, though a graceful work of art delights you, that the man who made it is worth your attention.

(*Pericles*, C. P. Curtis, Jr., tr.)

Memorable dissent is too much to expect from such outcasts. The one potent dissent available to them was the strike or armed insurrection. Even here, in our effort to catch the least echo of what we seek, we are hampered in two ways. A great part of our standard translations from classic authors was made over a hundred years ago, mostly by professors and dons who recoiled as violently from the thought of someone in trade as from a solecism. A greater embarrassment is provided by the ancients themselves who suppressed whatever records of dissent existed. We may be sure that there were liberal protests, that the historians, at least some of them, must have set down with some sympathy the account of those who struggled for a name and a hope of heaven. But it is unexpected, to say the least, to learn that such records have been systematically suppressed. Through the ministrations of their patrons the works of the conformists survive. Yet the books devoted to the craftsman, his status, and above all his revolts, have disappeared. Three books of Livy dealing with Spartacus, as well as certain books of Sallust, Nymphodorus, and Dion Cassius have not been permitted to reach us.

We know of two occasions in antiquity when it was considered inadvisable to take a census lest the slaves learn how greatly they outnumbered the free. We may, therefore, apprehend the reasons for the distaste with which the ruling classes regarded even the historical mention of so painful a subject. Plato, Cicero, and Horace would have voted for the immediate death of Jane Addams as a disturber of the peace —Horace, who had to be a snob because he was baseborn; Cicero because he was frightened for his pocket; and Plato, whose *Republic* was kept afloat on the sea of soulless slaves. The very names (the nominal terminations) of articles in common use for artisans and craftsmen—words like "adze" and "awl" and "hook," as familiar as the words "piano key" to us, yet beneath the dignity of the Latin scribe—would be unknown today were it not for the union inscriptions.

We read of the erudite slave being well treated: of Agathocles who became a tyrant and always set an earthen pot beside his gold ones in commemoration of his first trade as a potter; of Pasion, Phormion, Hermias, who rose from slave-accountants to bank presidents; of many other exceptional freedmen. But the generality of slaves were chained, fed on refuse, branded in the face, without recourse to law until the time of Hadrian. Earlier, the owner had unquestioned powers of life and death over "animals and slaves," who worked three hundred and sixty days a year, lodged in caves, lived

77

naked, and, in Rome, sometimes were armed and forced to fight each other to extermination when the owner had a fancy for a soirée.

Plutarch, indeed with a frown of disparagement, notes that the magistrates of Sparta "dispatched privately some of the ablest young men into the countryside, from time to time, armed only with daggers. . . . In the daytime, they hid themselves in out of the way places, but, in the night, issued into the highways and killed all the Helots they could light upon." Helots were not foreigners, blacks, nor barbarians; but they were excess mouths to feed. Some of the Helots who had fought in the Peloponnesian war were singled out for bravery by the Spartans, garlanded as enfranchised persons, and led to the temples in token of honor—and quietly murdered. This was not approved custom, but Thucydides mentions it as merely being strange.

To underline anonymity and, for a moment, brood upon its unhappy effects: in general, Greek statues were not signed; we know the names of the sculptors largely from contemporary men of letters or from later commentators like Pausanias who wrote, in the main, hearsay. Very few signed examples survive. Masons' marks, from Minoan days on, abound; but they are not what we are searching for. To be sure, many specimens of the potters' art were signed: for example, there is, among many others, a vase inscribed by Clitias and Ergotimus—perhaps because, having depicted the victor in the Olympic games of 564 B.C., the artists felt entitled to a shaft of reflected glory themselves. There are also signed Etruscan bronzes; but as we cannot yet read the language, the signatures confer but a cloudy immortality. The makers of Roman tableware regularly signed their works; often one finds the name of the owner coupled with that of the artist, slave or freedman. We possess the names of a few Greek painters, but I think none of their works. I doubt, if, from Greece and Rome together, there is record of a score of architects.*

Literature itself faltered into a succession of Alexandrine writers, late Latin historians, and copiers of earlier Greek masterpieces. Even the great truce of the Antonines—when our world was more quiet and commodious and traversable than ever it has been since—was more like a great silence, as animated as an obelisk. The stupendous ruins at Baalbec, now but a dozen topaz columns in an emerald oasis, incredible in their time-worn splendor, make us ask only the more anxiously what happened to the creative spirit. Did too much peace unmarrow the structure, that so benign a paternalism produced no great writer or sculptor, no invention, no prophet? What voices there were indeed were crying in the wilderness: the caves of outcast Essenes or the desert abodes of Thebaid solitaries. Everything was as anonymous as a pavement—including many a magnificent mosaic.

If we turn hopefully to the Near East, we meet the same stultifying namelessness. Some faint signatures appear on Coptic paintings, not, I believe, earlier than the ninth century A.D. But, while Christians were permitted to indulge in portraiture, the Hebrews, on principle, looked upon representations of mankind in sculpture or painting as desecration. I have seen frescoes from a third century synagogue near Doura Europos which showed not only the usual fauna and flora but also human beings, in illustration of Old Testament stories. Obviously, the synagogue belonged to a sect which felt that as God made us in His image we were not

---

* To be sure, we know the signatures of several vase painters as well as those of a few medalists and cameo cutters. But, from Lucian and Plato and others, we know without doubt what was the status of the signers. I do not feel that a stray name alters the picture.

unworthy of depiction. But this is the exception. The Muslims also severely enforced their ban on representation. Floral and geometric designs were permitted, and acres of holy writ which, in the ancient script on tile or in gesso, became one of the most lovely motifs of decoration. Again, I know one set of palace stuccoes where man is depicted. But the early Omeyyeds may have been less doctrinaire than their successors. Certainly the Byzantines of that period saw nothing damnable in displaying the human figure, and I believe there is no warrant in the Koran for any such deletion. But the fact remains that the Jews and subsequent Muslims were not allowed that latitude in the plastic arts. If there are no signatures, it is because there was less to sign than one might hope for.

Should we move further toward the East, we would fare little better. On the way, we might pause with one mosaic, in a private house of the fourth century in Delos, which is the only signed mosaic I know of: the artist was Asklapiades of Arados. From Antioch came signed silks of the sixth century, A.D., but the signatures almost certainly are not those of the designer but of the shop master or owner-weaver. In short, we find practically no signatures till after the year 1000; names of painters, architects, musicians, weavers we know only through literary reference. The first signed Persian rug dates from 1521: the signature is incorporated in a boastful panegyric on the artist.

We shall stumble over anonymity again—but enough has here been said, I hope, to establish its demeaning existence in the year A.D. 1. Today the very word "anonymous" is one of reproach for the writer: anonymity is something that is perpetrated. We cannot imagine a society where the painting, the piece of music, the sculpture, the pamphlet or article, the bibelot, even, is by someone unknown—like that *Ignoto Fiorentino* who was my favorite painter when I was very

young. No critic will pounce upon my failings without signing his name. Nor would I fail to sign my book. Something
is probably of pride, something of integrity. The early artist
or craftsman was denied both. Is it a wonder he created with
diminished enthusiasm? In the ancient world anonymity lay
like a caul over the birth of any work of art.

The drama, the poem—these are firmly attached to their
maker. Great statues were no longer made; frescoes and mo-
saics, no matter how glorious, were, from the altitude of
the donor or employer, considered routine, unionized, craftsman's jobs. So too with utensils, of gold, silver, or clay. Easel
painting was unknown. And, most cruel of the causes of decline: buch of the work was performed by slaves. A slave has
no name. He has little incentive to rise and even less per-
mission to assert a personality.

Aristotle, at least, had the grace to hope that slavery would
one day pass from existence; as things were, he considered
"the slave a tool with life in it." In one place Euripides conceded that, except in name, a slave "if he be good, is no
worse than a freedman." Socrates alone, perhaps because he
was a laborer born, a stone cutter, and perhaps lived and
died a union member, had compassion for all men, irre-
spective of caste. It is noteworthy that Socrates' phrase, "We
are all brothers and members of the same union, under the
God of Love," comes to us through Xenophon and not
through Plato.

There is not much one needs to add to the picture of
slavery in Rome, in its filth and abjection. Children were
brought up by slaves; their tutors (often Greeks and frequently the best educated persons in the household) were
usually slaves. The yeomen had sold themselves into slavery
when the estates, the *latifundia*, had swallowed their small

81

holdings and the state had usurped the public lands (*ager publicus*). After the battle of Pydna, Aemilius Paulus is said to have thrown 160,000 slaves into the market at a single clip, thus perhaps solving the servant problem but hardly founding the Welfare State. On one hand there were the *optimates*, on the other a horde of slaves, freedmen, proletaries, from whom there came no protest (other than half a hundred slave rebellions); the free, creative mind had been stifled. No hanger-on, no client, no one who had a patron (as all the writers had) would cry the truth. No one would forego his dinner for a diatribe.

We may leave pagan slavery to its squalor and consider the Christian world. Slavery bears most heavily on the creative artist, and his liberation is an integral part of our tale. If Rome was a great power for six hundred years, we may say that slavery flourished for six hundred years under Rome, and three times that long under Christianity. It is not a cheerful thought.

Charlemagne (*ca.* A.D. 800) instigated laws curtailing the sale of Christian slaves. Yet in the twelfth century, the kings of France were still differentiating in their beds of justice between men who were free and men who were bond. Even so, under the humanizing warmth of the Gothic Church, as serf rose from villein to villager, as a relative poverty engulfed Europe, slowly the burnings and brandings of antiquity subsided.

The great horde of slaves—the captives of Rome—had vanished. The day of servitude was apparently over, at least as a profitable venture or cornerstone of national economy. And then, in 1442, a stout Portuguese ship with white sails, bearing within her a number of Christian gentlemen and letters-patent from their king, sailed along the coast of Africa in search of yellow gold and found black gold. For the next four hundred years, at the behest of their Most Catholic

Majesties and for the comfort of their colonies, the vilest traffic in the world was reinstated in its full horror. Perhaps ten million black souls were torn from their native soil, chained below decks, and shipped to the four quarters of the globe. About half of them perished before they could labor in their new servitude. Nearly three million reached the Americas. The Roman slave had been crucified if he rebelled. The Negro slave was thrown overboard if he took sick.

II.

We turn here to a happier subject—a condition which is with us still and which can be fruitful and pleasing: patronage. It has always dominated the circumstances in which an artist works, and it also—usually by revulsion—is his closest connection with politics. The greater, the more eccentric, the artist, the more has he to rely on a patron. The expert potter sold his wares in the open market; but Phidias worked at the behest of the state and was to such an extent subject to its caprice that he spent part of his life in prison.

A patron implied and still does imply the object of his patronage: namely, a client. The word "client" comes from the Latin word implying "at the beck and call of." When the client is disobedient he is not further employed, his works are banned by the censor, or he is beaten up, like Voltaire, by my lord's lackeys. Or there is a price on his head, as there was on that of Thomas Mann.

Simo, the parasite in Lucian's brilliant dialogue, justifies his profession by calling attention to the nobility of the footsteps in which he follows. He points out that Euripides retired to the court of Archelaus, that Anarchus was sustained by Macedonia, and he names several who lived off Dionysius of Syracuse, among them Plato who made such a mess of dining out that he had to be excused from table. To Simo's list we must add Aristotle and Senaca, tutors to the royal family. They were near enough the throne, indeed, to be well fed; near enough also to be controlled by the royal whim or burned by the royal incandescence.

The decrees of patronage are as valid today as ever they were. And the condition will so continue as long as there remain the patron and the patronized, the distributor and the creator, the agent and the artist. The word "client" is falling into disuse, but the root of that word is still the root of the matter: conform or starve.

The monuments of antiquity which have been preserved to us were essentially state projects. The palace at Nineveh, the Parthenon, the Pyramids, like Versailles, were national undertakings. So, too, the Whitestone Bridge (WPA), the Delphic charioteer (possibly paid for out of the treasury of the tyrant of Syracuse), and Brahms' *Academic Overture*. Each in its way was a public monument; for, though all except the bridge were designed to exalt a king, a caste, or an event, we must remember that the works were paid for in national funds, directly or through a subsidized agency. Funds were not less national for being royal. *L'état c'est moi.* In fact, for many centuries, coinage itself remained a royal prerogative. Trade was largely a matter of barter, payment a matter of perquisite. In spite of the banking in ancient Babylonia or that in Athens and Rome, wealth was in general the privilege of office; the higher the office the greater the wealth; and, as both the source and repository of affluence, the golden vein was reached in the king's treasury.

In Greece and Rome, it was in no wise considered unbecoming to accept a grant therefrom, whereas to accept wages was beneath the dignity of the meanest scholar. Wages implied that the acceptor belonged to the servile classes. Plato, Isocrates, and the other renowned teachers would not take payment from their pupils. But they would cheerfully accept, and often pursue and acrimoniously insist upon, lavish gifts from royal parents.

Two reasons, among many, help to make clear this peculiar attitude. On the one hand, the Greek philosopher—teachers were nearer by two thousand years than we are to the sources of prerogative and taboo. The hero-king, part immortal and part founder of the race, was as close in time and far closer in thought to Plato than George Washington is to us. To accept a gift from the descendant of a demigod, such as Theseus, was both felicitous and proper. A niggardly king was a sad spectacle, showing only how large was the admixture of clay in his otherwise Olympian nature. On the other hand, only serfs took wages.

The Greeks were a frugal people. Artists and intellectuals clung to their austerities. Not until the time of Alexander and the later dominion of Caesar was it customary to find in Athens the Persian pomps which took such quick root in Alexandria or Rome. Many, perhaps most, of the wants of a Greek citizen, of that very small élite who were citizens, were cared for by the state. A few of the Greeks whose names still glow with splendor were of noble stock; the majority appear to have been yeomen, usually the owners of substantial farms. Mere wealth—unless it attained the astonishing proportions attributed to Croesus—was considered if not vulgar, at least unworthy of protracted notice. Wealth was noted only if it led the particular plutocrat to pay for a battleship or the production of a play, or if the rich man, like Nicias (who made a fortune as the lessor of slaves) was otherwise notable.

We do not know, for example, the sources of the money which enabled Herodotus to travel widely and steadily for close on seventeen years. We do know that, fairly late in life, when he left or was ejected from his native Halicarnassus, he received, by decree of the appreciative people of Athens the great sum of ten talents. Translated to our day, this municipal gift would be in value not far from one hundred thousand dollars. The generosity appears to have been unique. Admiral Dewey was given a town house by a grateful nation, and the Canadian government was recently signally liberal toward the discoverers of insulin. But even in the spacious days of Pericles, the gift to Herodotus was an exception. It would not have been wise for any artist to depend on the variable sentiments of any Greek city for his livelihood. More reasonably, the accepted method for keeping alive was for the artist to attach himself to a patron, usually a despot. This holds true from China to Peru. In time, of course, the Greek prejudice against taking money from pupils broke down. A noted writer might fare well at the schools of Alexandria or Athens, as later at the great universities of Paris or Padua.

The playwrights fared even more precariously. They were at the mercy of a *choregus*. A *choregus* was a rich man who desired the favor of the mob or a man to whom the authorities made it plain that if he hoped to display his wealth, to keep it at all perhaps, he had best (as a sort of supertax) put on at least one set of plays during the theatrical season.* It was for him to defray the expenses of engaging a chorusmaster for the *choreutae,* of purchasing or renting costumes, of paying the salaries of the chorus, and for him also to receive any prize which his productions might win. The actors proper were, in a sense, wards of the state, paid by the state and assigned by the state.

Presumably, Aeschylus and Sophocles were paid rather as

* Today, many *rentiers* put money into theatrical productions hoping to lose it, and so write it off their income tax. I prefer the Greek largess.

performers than as poets. However, after the play, the author was allowed to appear before the public with a collection box in his hand, soliciting applause and obols. In general practice, the state leased the theater to persons who attended to the upkeep in return for charging admission. Then the state gave each citizen six cents wherewith to buy his ticket. Furthermore, the state furnished the protagonists, a small and special group of male actors whose persons were regarded as sacred. Other expenses were born by the *choregus*. In a system which is to us still obscure and which apparently was never very sound financially, the playwright would seem to have fared scantily; and research tells us less of his rewards than of any other among the transactions of the theater. We may assume, I think, that the *choregus* was the temporary patron of the author. He doubtless bought the play that pleased his fancy and further employed the author in some capacity on the stage.

In Rome, with but a half dozen exceptions, all who touched the theater professionally were considered defiled. Actors were drawn exclusively from the ranks of slaves or freedmen (and what a contrast with the Greek way where these purveyors of the immortal word were ranked rather with priests!). The stage, therefore, depended entirely on patronage. The troupes were well paid, and actors might augment their earnings by tutoring in elocution or the dance. But they remained the chattels of those who hired them, of the wealthy, of princes and magistrates avid of notoriety.

The great showmaster of antiquity was the state, either directly or through the medium of enforced ostentation such as that thrust upon the *choregus*. But there were also men who loved learning and who, from their private means, could afford quietly to indulge their tastes. The Egyptian gentleman lived in luxury, with henna, ivory, linen, and spice for his family, with elaborate yachts and hunting parties for his own pleasure. If he were wealthy enough, his portrait, in sculpture or painting, adorned his tomb. And concerted music was, at all times, one of his delights. A scribe was attached to his household. But, invariably, this cultivated personage and patron was a government official. The source of his income was the state, and the condition of it was royal favor. The same is true in Rome, where the great wealth of a few families came from or was vastly augmented by a proconsular office or some other golden opportunity to dip into public monies. The Augustan age has given us the archtype of private patron in the gracious figure of Maecenas, the friend of Virgil and Horace. Bordering the Via Appia, there are many handsome private tombs (probably belonging to some of the two thousand taxable families mentioned by Strabo); and there exist several small, sculptured trophies, like the olive-circled one at St. Remy, extolling a particular general. But the military monuments were primarily for the glory of Roman arms; and private undertakings are few compared to the far-flung, might works of the royal or state builders.

The slow conversion of the ancient world to Christianity altered nothing in the relation between the artist and his patron. Where pagan emperors might have built monumental baths, Justinian built the great church to Hagia Sancta Sophia. (The only artistic complaint at this change came from members of the image-makers' guild who found themselves suddenly without employment, for the early Church looked askance at ikons and images. Opposition from the silversmiths, which St. Paul encountered on his third journey, eventually won the day at the Council of Nicaea, in A.D. 787, when the Church finally admitted the propriety of statues.) Later, when the Church became master of its own theocratic domain, as in Rome, the taste and fancy may have been those of a Pope Julius, but the funds that paid Michelangelo were the funds of the soveregin Papal States.

Throughout the Middle Ages there were but two patrons: the Church or the noble. Frequently the two patronages combined. Charlemagne called the renowned cleric, Alcuin, to be the tutor of his children, much as a princely vizier drew Hafiz from his religious seclusion to the management of a school expressly founded for the poet. Another appreciative vizier relieved Omar Khayyam of the necessity of making tents by appointing him royal astronomer. And in that incredibly modern court in Sicily where Frederic II kept open house, royalty combined not only with the Church but also with all faiths, pagan or Muslim as well. Possibly no gathering, under one patron, has so influenced the course of European thought as that galaxy of scholars who fed on the bounty of a skeptical and excommunicate emperor.

At the height of the mid-Renaissance, the pattern of patronage became more complex. There was as yet no "buying public," but the rich burgher had entered the field. The Church had lost much by the Reformation; her patronage of the arts was on the wane. In many lands, the nobles—by marriage, by the ownership of trading fleets, by banking, and by manufacture—were acquiring riches far greater than had been at an emperor's disposal two centuries earlier. These princelings, dukes or counts, must rank as royal patrons, since, on the Continent, till the end of the eighteenth century, most of them owned salves, many had the power of life and death, and all commanded the treasury of their county, barony, or dukedom.

With few exceptions, the religious paintings and sculptures of the Italian Renaissance were commissioned by the state or by corporate bodies. The Tintorettos in San Rocco were ordered by the hospital authorities, a public service corporation; those in the doge's palace were paid for out of city funds. If Isabella D'Este desired a painting by Mantegna, that price too came from the Mantuan state coffers. The works, like crown jewels, became permanent assets of the state or Church or corporation.

As we approach modern times, we find, with some fluctuations and variants, that there has been really but little diminution in civic or national patronage. Louis XIV, Frederick the Great, Anne of Austria were indefatigable builders. The czars of Russia were much given to constructing entire new cities, an example followed by the Soviets. The British crown founded a complete New Delhi. And the city of Washington has little of General Grant left about it. Perhaps, during the last fifty years—as against the long survey of history—it has seemed that the private patron would replace the state. But revolution, war, and taxes have altered that trend, if not forever, at least for a time. Today, housing projects before the parliaments and congresses of a devastated world alone require the resources of a national treasury (or an insurance company) to rise from the ground.

Before we examine with more care the most valuable, fruitful manifestation of patronage, the great state project, we should consider the rise of the private patron and also observe the fortunes of the artist amid the shifts of power since the Renaissance.

The architect, the sculptor, and the painter of large frescoes have in the logic of their requirements worked most closely with the royal builders. But secular easel painting appeared in due time, partly because the cult of madonnas had begun to pall, partly because the philosophic trends had prompted man to look about him rather than behind or above, and largely because a new purchasing class had arisen among rich burghers who, unable to lodge a huge mural painting and willing to leave Crucifixions and Annunciations to more pious walls, desired a picture to hang by the bed. ("Not figures of Madonnas or Saints, but some fine and beautiful invention"—as the Marquis of Mantua desired of Sebastianello Veneziano.) The cities of the Hanseatic League, the autonomous cities, the cities largely controlled by the guilds—cities of Holland, Flanders, or Germany—cities like Genoa—these gave birth to a comfortable bourgeoisie which has its equivalent today the world over. Its influence on sculpture and music and letters was slight at first; its influence on the crafts was enormous (textiles, jewelry, shipbuilding, plumbing); and its influence on painting was immediate.

A glance at a catalog of Rembrandt's work shows, by contrast with a catalog of Raphael's, for example, the small number of paintings commissioned by any state or any corporate group (such as the Doctors or the Corps of Watchman) as against the preponderance of landscapes and portraits executed for the casual buyer or the well-to-do neighbor.

In England, the China trade and the expansion of empire, the plantations of Jamaica or the traffic in slaves, brought untold wealth to merchant adventurers who, if successful, either married into the illusion of permanence or bought a title. Long before, in the time of Henry VIII, some of the most spendid houses of England had been built by commoners, and some, like Hampton Court, had been returned to an ungrateful monarch. (But, after all, Wolsey was merely restoring in kind what he had earlier filched from the royal treasury.)

Yet, amid all this affluence, there was still no such thing

as the "buying public." Your artist had as hard a scramble as ever to find a patron. Court and Church were still the nurseries of talent. It is well known what Michelangelo suffered at the hands of the pope, less known, I believe, that Piero di Medici set the great sculptor to make a statue out of snow—to put his art "into the service of annihilation." * The Church ministered to the wants of Palestrina and Bach; but the prince bishop of Salzburg has his name on another record than the one to which he aspired. He is remembered because he did *not* minister to Mozart but allowed him to perish in a neglect almost as dire as Shubert's. Royalty was more munificent. The Princes Esterhazy befriended Haydn as Leopold of Anhalt-Cothen had befriended Bach. In both cases, the private palace orchestra was an elysium of experience and delight. Even Beethoven tolerated several protectors.

As Versailles o'er-topped every other princely residence—built usually to emulate the French splendor—so Louis XIV outdid all others in his patronage. Every form of art (employing the talents of Lully, Molière, Le Nôtre, the painters and architects and gardeners) was gathered into one extravaganza under *Le Roi Soleil*. Beneath the warm rays of his solicitude, the Academy reached a level of excellence which it has maintained to this day.

The French Revolution changed little: it had its own

---

* "The Pope sent a second bull and a third, and the Gonfaloniere of Florence, trembling for the safety of the Republic, summoned the sculptor (Michelangelo) and said, 'You have braved the Pope as the King of France would not have done . . . We do not wish to go to war with him on your account and risk the State, so prepare yourself to return.'

"It is pleasant to record this incident if only as a reminder that there was a time when states were prepared to fight for the services of an artist. Today conditions are a little different: the Pope has no use for artists; nor has any state, nor any city, nor any individual unless it be the brigand called the dealer and the snobbish collector."

(Thomas Craven, *Men of Art*.)

favorite painters and poets, and considered some of them so potent that it executed them. Napoleon was as lavish a patron as Louis XIV. The first luxury which monarchs permitted themselves upon ascending the throne seems to have been a burst of building, if possible in a new style; and the last and best thing for which those monarchs are remembered is their munificence toward the arts.

As late as 1860, one of the greatest composers of our time was hawking his operas with little success in his native land, after utter fiasco in Paris. Only the surprising and sudden munificence of Ludwig II of Bavaria, first manifested in 1864, enabled Wagner to proceed with those grandiose and hitherto unwarranted plans for a stage where his Ring could be adequately produced. In the main, perhaps, artists tend to bite the hand that feeds them—loathing condescension more than they love food. Not so Wagner, the most egotistical of artists, in the spiritual liaison (for it can be called little else) with Ludwig. "We sometimes sit for hours," he wrote, "lost in contemplation of each other's features and expression." Rarely have the relations between patron and client been so felicitous—perhaps because, having once established Wagner in security, the unhappy Ludwig became insane. To this day, no composer—except the few who have achieved popularity with their operas or ballets—supports himself uniquely by his compositions. Today, almost all composers add to their slender incomes by teaching. And if, as is usual, your composer teaches in a foundation, then his patron is as exigent as was a Prince Bishop. His patron is the probated will of the founder and a living board.

The scribe has had a somewhat different fate. At first he was the darling of the Church. But, once he was turned loose

93

to fend for himself, the hounds of Grub Street were in full cry. He sought a secular patron and found, like as not, only capriciousness. From the time of the establishment of printing in Europe, a writer might live scantily by his wits and his works. His wits earned more than his works, in all probability, since it was the wits that located and placated the patron. Every artist or intellectual we have noted so far had one or several protectors. Galileo was in and out of favor with the Medici. The court of Weimar shielded Goethe and Schiller, helped produce their plays, and gave Goethe the leisure to pursue his studies in morphology. Addison, beginning his career with an astute *Address to King William,* extracted a pension from the object of his flattery. Another essay in glorification—this time of Marlborough—brought Addison a handsome fee and government office. Dr. Johnson's definition of a patron is the record of his failure to find one. "Is not a patron, my Lord, one who looks with unconcern on a man struggling for life in the water and, when he has reached ground, encumbers him with help? The notice which you have been pleased to take of my labors, had it been early, had been kind; but it has been delayed till I am indifferent and cannot enjoy it, till I am solitary and cannot impart it, till I am known and do not want it." Yet to secure an understanding protector, Johnson had been as patient as he knew how. And, of course, his dictionary, like the encyclopedia of d'Alembert, could be brought out only with a multiplicity of subscribers.

Particularly in the theater but to some extent also in the securing of a publisher, a patron's power could work in reverse, as it were. If that august personage did not like your prose, your case was sorry till an equally powerful defender was found. The role of genteel impresario has fascinated many a dilettante; the state-subventioned theaters and operas were apt to be controlled by a princeling. If you wanted your play produced at all, it was well to be on good terms with his lordship.

As the Greek dramatist had labored under a mixed and dubious economy, the Elizabethan dramatist also was caught in a scheme which exhibited some of the worst elements of that inconvenience or ignominy prevalent in Athens and Rome. But there was added one saving grace: for want of better, I must call it the temper of the times. The laws, redolent of Rome, still adjudged all, "common players as vagabonds and rogues." Shakespeare might have received as much as twenty pounds for a play (the average was about seven pounds). Out of this he had to bribe the Master of the Court Revels (the Censor). And, further, to avoid the charge of vagabondage or roguery, the playwright was forced to join the licensed company of some noble, and move and have his theatrical being forever "under the hand and seale of such baron or important personage."

Though this precarious existence shows little advance over antiquity and far less dignity than was allowed the Periclean actor, England enjoyed a widespred diffusion of knowledge, appreciation, and wealth which blew fresh airs through the dusty hedgerows of prudery and prerogative. The Queen, herself accomplished in many ways, had a decent if wayward respect for the genius which flourished so copiously about her. She adored a pageant or a Progress. Theatricality was *à la mode*. Poets and playwrights were seen at court, and all the town went to the play. Furthermore, there was a knowledgeable and well-to-do middle class. The Burbage brothers built the Globe Theater and had an interest in the Blackfriars, definitely controlling some "important personage's" company in the one and sometimes in the other. To what seem to us incredibly small author's rights, Shakespeare could add more substantially his good pay as an actor. And, by 1599, become a partner, he shared in the profits of the Globe. For the last years of his life Shakespeare was able to retire to Stratford with a sound income. Yet, throughout his working life in London, he had been constricted by arbitrary laws, ever at the mercy of the Master of Revels, ever in search of or in praise of some patron whose generosity alone made possible the publication of his poems. The Act of Uniformity and the Test Act, the charge of high treason waiting for those "reconciled to the See of Rome," these restrictions, if they bore heavily on the closet, how much more were they terrifying to the open and much frequented performances on a stage! Nowhere does Shakespeare greet that flowering Puritanism which was exalted in the *Fairie Queen,* nowhere does he confess to religious preoccupations. Because of the law, perhaps because his family was recusant, the "obstinate questionings" are not found in the Bard. Surely he must have thought searchingly, felt deeply, but there were depths he dared not reveal before his patrons. Conform or starve. It was thus written even in the statute books of Merrie England.

So runs the record to our own times. Today, copyright for the author, a vast number of rentable playhouses, wealthy collectors in abundance, these would seem to make the path of the creative artist straight. Yet, in this comparative comfort, the larger forms find no haven. The quartet, the orchestra, the opera still need subvention. The fresco is rarely within reach of the private purse. The collector who buys pictures to avoid paying taxes is not an edifying spectacle.

Down the length of history we may mark how the arts flourish when they have been supported by state, Church, or corporate patronage. This is most true of the great periods of art, where the prestige of a state has floated high or low on the sumptuous or meager tide of its culture. In Persia, Egypt, Greece, Rome, Byzantium, and the Caliphates, state patronage was the rule. In the Gothic period, help and direction came either from the crown, from the Church, or from the city and its corporations. (Only a few private chapels, such as that at Bourg en Bresse, were built by private funds for private use.) And, in the founding of the arts and crafts, the original impetus and the first orders were apt also to come from the state.

After the Renaissance, there appeared the rich private donor. Slowly, we have achieved an open market, impersonal and fairly ruthless. Nowadays, it would seem that writers and philosophers and teachers have slipped out from under the need of patronage. Yet we incline to forget that almost all the schools and colleges where those writers and philosophers, poets and historians teach and so earn their bread, are the recipients of government (state or federal) subsidy or are under the compulsions of private endowment!

To share in the responsibility for that condition of culture to which it has pleased God to lead us is surely as vital an interest to a community as sharing in the responsibility for the laws which purport to govern us. Today, the sentiment runs for stark individuality. But the facts are against it. The arts have never flourished when they were divorced from the general enhancement of the life of the group. And though it is fashionable now to pretend that government "interference" is the end of enterprise, it is quite easy to demonstrate that enterprises are the more noble and the more successful when undertaken in behalf of the general welfare than when undertaken in behalf of the specific pocket. Whether we like it or not, our major institutions are and must be subsidized. This also applies to the Metropolitan Opera, Harvard University, cancer research, or crop control.

97

The fetish of private patronage has been set up beside the *lares* of the wealthy. To patronize is part of the prerogative of riches. It is largely presumed that the rich man maintains art and sport. Rather, it is art and sport which now justify and relieve from boredom the very existence of Dives. He is, in art as in business, the broker. He manipulates; he does not create. And to protect his privilege, his outcry against civic collaboration takes shape: "How would you like to have your opera supervised by a board of aldermen?" Sir, even aldermen could do little to match the sordidness that has marked some of our operatic regimes, or the ignorance and provinciality that have distinguished many an orchestral board.

On the positive side, the active collaboration and interest of City Hall would open innumerable avenues of popularity. It would lend the company or the orchestra a meaning and a permanence, woven into our civic pride, not easily procured otherwise. And it is doubtful if the artistic incompetents, who too often push to the veneered surface of our boards, could remain were the mass of the people to share in the ownership. The voice of popular protest is an urgent and salutary sound in a democracy. At present, any criticism of the various philharmonics is merely a rudeness to several well-intentioned ladies. Such criticism should be a civic duty, not a breach of manners.

The alternative to private interest is public interest. The control—since there must always be a control—must therefore be either church or state. For better and for worse, the church has been removed from the scene. The state remains. Let us observe the state as patron.

Here the records are full; there is but the embarrassment of choice.

Let us begin with the record of one public project: the building of Solomon's Temple. We know the quantity of the materials used; we know the name of the contractor, Hiram, who labored "from the month Zif to the month Bul." (There are two Hirams mentioned in the Book of Kings; one the great worker in metals, who used the clay of the Jordan valley to do his casting, and who came from Tyre; and another called, perhaps due to a copyist's error, King of Tyre. From the terms of the labor contract between this second Hiram and Solomon, it would seem that this second Hiram was a great power rather than a king—a contractor whom Solomon paid regularly. The two Hirams may be identical.) At all events, in this noble public work we find an early and clear record of how such matters were handled at their best.

We read also in the Bible that Nebuchadnezzar ordered the selection of "children in whom was no blemish but well favored and skilful in all wisdom, cunning in knowledge and understanding science, and such as had ability in them to stand in the king's palace, and to whom they might teach the learning and tongue of the Chaldeans. And the king appointed them a daily provision of the king's meat and of the wine which he drank; so nourishing them three years. . . ." And we are privileged to know of the king's largess, of this gesture precursive of Rhodes scholarships or Guggenheim fellowships or State Department subsidies, because one of the brightest scholars was named Daniel.

Another and more brilliant document comes from the threshold of the Renaissance. I quote it at length for the sake of those who consider the Tennessee Valley Authority a dangerous experiment in paternalism, rather than the expert harnessing of a country's resources to the free devices of mankind. It is part of a letter, written about A.D. 800 (at the time when Charlemagne, emperor of the Franks and ruler of a large part of Europe, was unable to read) from Rashid Ud Din to his son.

We think it is of the greatest service to the people that we should encourage science, learning, and scholarship. Therefore, we have sent with utmost speed letters by couriers to all the great scholars at the time, inviting them here and promising to arrange that they shall pursue their studies in peace of mind, without the dust of poverty on their foreheads, nor in the lap of their virtue. Crowds of scholars and scientists continue to arrive, and we do our best to keep them free of cares. We have built 24 caravanserais, 1,500 shops, 30,000 fascinating houses, salubrious baths, pleasant gardens, stores, mills, factories for cloth weaving and paper making; a dye, mill, and a mint, have also been constructed. We have given 400 houses to special scholars like theologians and jurists and their street is named the Street of the Scholars. They receive daily payments, pensions, yearly clothing allowances, soap money and money for sweetmeats.

We have established a thousand other students and assigned to their maintenance the tribute from Constantinople and India, so that they may be comfortable and peacefully occupied in acquiring knowledge and profiting the people by it.

We have prescribed which and how many students should study with which professor and teacher, and have ascertained each student's aptness of mind and capacity for learning a particular branch of science; we have assigned him to learn that subject for which he is fitted.

The specific purpose of writing this letter is that you should send us quickly fifty camlet weavers from Antioch and Tarsus, not by force and compulsion, but by kindness and persuasion, so that they may come with carefree minds and voluntarily. You must ask King Theophilus to send twenty more camlet weavers. Do not delay for we are waiting.

This is a wise and astonishing document, and Lorenzo the Magnificent himself never surpassed it in magnanimity. There breathes throughout not the desire for glorification, but the desire to spread wisdom among the people.

Such moments of high civility have been rare. Usually, as we have seen, the royal coffers poured out gold for temples or churches, the Mosque of Cairo, the theater at Taormina, the great roads or the aqueduct over the Gard, for the tomb or the palace, the Invalides or the Trianon. Above all, for the paraphernalia of conquest: fortified mountains and harbor, fleets, weapons, and legions. The armies have gone, but the star-shaped Vauban fortress remains, crowning a hill or rebuffing the sea. The crusades of St. Louis have foundered. But the black battlements of Aigues Mortes, whence he sailed, still rise from the sedges like a gauntlet with fingers upraised. It is before the ruins of these walls and battlements that the tourist gapes. By these ruins we judge the power of the hands that made them. But splendid as the palaces were, magnificently as Carcassonne dominates the valley, intricate and awful as was the Iron Maiden of Nuremberg, what truly lifts our imaginations and guides us to the ancient well-springs of civilization are the documents of altruism and solicitude, the serene painting, the poems and philosophies—in other words, the work of artists. All that remains of Ozymandias is a piece of sculpture.*

* Note B, *Patronage*, page 294.

3. Survival

Patronage carried us somewhat beyond our time scheme. Here we return to our chronology.

The Church Fathers and the early Charters lead us to the lovely flowering of the fourteenth century when all the arts were devoted to the glory of God, and some of the artists to the liberation of man.

3.

I

On Ascension Sunday, in the late spring of 325, the Emperor Constantine entered the great hall at Nicaea where his first ecumenical council awaited him. From his red, embroidered buskins to his imperial diadem he blazed with jewels. Beard trimmed short, hair flowing, he was tall and immensely powerful in his look, his stature, and his spirit. Awaiting the royal entrance were more than three hundred prelates, assembled at the command to establish once for all an irrevocable creed—an answer to Christ's own question, "Who say ye that I am?"

The emperor sat on a throne between Pope Alexander of Alexandria and Bishop Hosius of Cordova; Bishop Eusebius of Caesarea delivered the opening address. Constantine replied in Latin, as befitting the last wide-ruling Roman emperor. Listening intently, waiting to fly at each other's throats, the delegates presented a spectacle of extraordinary diversity. Theophilus the Goth, a blond Scythian; John, bishop of Persia and metropolitan of India; the bishop of Nisibis in his camelskin coat; Paphnutius, one eye gouged out and leg mutilated in the dungeons of Diocletian; two presbyters representing the dying bishop of Rome.

An amazing conclave, which lasted into the summer and out of which, in the victory of Athanasius over Arian, came the Nicene Creed. We are not here concerned with dogma. But the council is of vast interest to us. It was the organized embodiment of a temper which controlled a thousand years of European history. This first official meeting of the Christian Church with the emperor tipped the balance: slowly and inevitably the Church was to replace the empire. There was less change than we generally assume; temporal power was quietly usurped by patriarch or pope without being greatly altered. Far from the Church becoming responsible for the collapse of Rome, the Church took over as the imperial powers and personalities declined. We shall see a different taking-over in the decline of feudalism.

Constantine, a Christian, had not made Christianity the only recognized religion. Pagans still outnumbered Christians. Christianity was torn by a dozen sects whose doctrinal wrangles all but wrecked the Church. The pagan sects offered a bold opposition: they enjoined the tonsuring of priests, baptism, communion, doctrines of salvation and redemption, preachings, and hours of pious contemplation and prayer. A later emperor, Julian, would even reinstate paganism for a few years as the state religion.

With the Roman empire as its model, the Church had one pressing need: unification. First, the unification of doctrine, that all might preach the same Christ and interpret the word alike. This was the preoccupation of the thousand years when heresy was the archenemy. Second, in order to impose spiritual power, wordly power was needed; and that power was assumed as it fell from the hands of the Caesars. In neither of these struggles was dissent tolerable. Rather than break with old forms, the effort was continuous to maintain them. Even the most outspoken of the Fathers clung to the established orthodoxies of life and the established forms of government. When one of the Fathers could no longer endure the incongruities of his position, he retired to a monastery.

Many other preoccupations the Father had. He read the scriptures to exhaustion. I cannot but imagine that he was immensely troubled by the violence of the Prophets in their attack on principalities and dominions as well as in their revulsion from the hollowness of ritual and ceremony. Here an accommodation was imperative. The Prophets had lived before the New Dispensation: they knew not Christ. But with the Gospels in hand and the Second Coming announced, there was no longer a need to overturn the social order or (except in a few matters) to institute an uncomfortable and disrupting reform. (The bishops, for example, had brought their slaves to Nicaea; and if the slaves were ever manumitted, it was from kindness of heart and not from principle.)

This world was but a purgatory from which the godly would be released and elevated to glory. "A future reward, not present; in heaven, not on earth; as He promised, so shall it be given," said Ambrose. Augustine went so far as to suggest that God had instigated the persecutions in order that martyrs and saints should be thus begotten. Whatever happiness a man had in this life might be docked from his joys in paradise. Such Fathers could not be expected to mitigate the injustices of a world which was in any case worthless and transitory. Rather, sanctify the immaterial soul, struggle hourly for that, but not for the hollow shell of the corporal and the mundane.

If this world was but dust and ashes, still, the ancient precepts held, along with the problem of free will and wretchedness. Obviously, man's sinfulness was responsible for most of the trouble; but he had been given free will by God's grace, and the sin and misery man chose were as arbitrary as they were nonexistent—that is, a non-sense, a negation of the reality of God, a turgid vacuum. But the problem of

107

poverty prostrated itself under the noses of the Fathers and had to be dealt with. Here they did not mince words. Themselves living poorly, ascetic, divested of all creature comforts, dedicated and assiduous, the Fathers clung to that part of Prophetic literature which excoriated the rich. Power could not be dislodged, for the Church wished, disinterestedly, to be itself accoutered with the necessary temporal power. But ostentation and luxury were emanations of hell.

To end poverty, some went so far as to suggest (for the poor) the communal ownership of land, thus harking back to the early Christians, who owned all things in common. When the Goths ravaged, Ambrose sold the gold utensils of the Church, and to the carpers made it plain that this was not sacrilege. "Behold the gold that is approved!" The gold of Christ which saved the motley company of refugees was "more glorious than the splendor of cups." Ambrose, like many another of the Fathers, had given his personal fortune to the poor. "The earth was created for all," he preached, "for rich and poor in common. Nature knows no rich; she creates all alike; and alike she encloses us in the sepulcher." Charity was but the interest due on God's gifts to them that have. (We shall find Wyclif elaborating this point.)

Whatever effect the Fathers had on economics can be largely discounted. The same is true of their unification of doctrine which ended abruptly in a split between the Eastern Orthodox Church and Rome and produced a hundred sects that flourish today. The most fruitful preoccupation of scholars was to reconcile the philosophers of Greece with Holy Writ. The effort took a myriad engaging turns which delight us still. When all else failed, the Greek stories were baptised into the true faith with the waters of allegory. This refurbishing for contemporary assimilation and convenience we have seen as one of the most precious powers of the creative mind.

108

The Prophets and Moses were difficult enough; the Stoics could be treated as cousins because of their moral elevation; the Gnostics were fairly heretical, teaching that all matter was evil. Other sects had set the fashion for anchorites. But, recognized as supreme intellects, Plato and Aristotle had somehow to be admitted into the company of the elect. In spite of much misgiving, this was ultimately arranged— centuries after Nicaea—and Aquinas was the beadle of the admission.

We do wrong to think of the Church Fathers in terms more suitable to the humble apostles. The Fathers were an extraordinary and extravagant lot, leaders in any society. And they belong in the company of artists not only because most of them were gifted, but because all were articulate and some were remarkable poets. Many of our finest hymns were written by the Fathers. They alone cherished and communicated the ideas, poems, and Prophetic works which underlie our traditions. And they incubated—perhaps unaware of the social implications involved—the concepts of liberty and social justice, which otherwise would have perished.

It was the Fathers, too, who preserved the free word. Through them we know how Aristotle linked friendship and justice, calling friendship good will in practice and justice good will in theory, and pointing out that neither could exist under tyranny, for good will is meaningless unless there is free will. The free-will offering was part, too, of Hosea's vision: that forced love was not desirable to God. In a world of barbarism, murder, serfdom, and coercion, it was this creed of the liberal heart which, in spite of all the backslidings, remained the core of the Church's doctrine. What scant social justice there was reposed in the precepts and practice of the clergy; all else was rapacity. Behind the monastic wall there was leisure to grow; without there was but time to grab. It was a Father, Tertullian, who called the

109

world a vast "republic" wherein was "a great family of God's children"; and St. John Chrysostom who wrote, "I call noble and lord the slave who is covered with chains if it accords with his life; I call him low and ignoble who in the midst of dignities retains an enslaved soul." These men were indeed of the prophetic line; and the world knew their power.

Ambrose is typical: he was the Roman governor of Liguria, which we know today as the Italian Riviera. He was of noble birth and senatorial rank, like Gregory. So troublous were the times and so admired was Ambrose as an administrator and humanitarian that, upon the bishop's death, the people of Milan elected Ambrose to the episcopal see before he was even baptised a Christian. He had been a classical scholar and could not break with his first loves. He brought with him Virgil and Homer, Cicero (above all, for there he had learned his dialectic) and Plato; also the spirit of the Stoics, housing the Stoa near the altar, but not too near. Study of the classics appeared to Ambrose almost as a dissipation; it was necessary constantly to remind himself that though one relishes the honey of Plato, how much more the hive of Moses!

Some of the Fathers studied in the great schools at Athens: grammar, rhetoric, dialectic, arithmetic, geometry, astronomy, and music. Men like Lactantius were the first humanists, planting diligently what the later Petrarch and the early Renaissance were to crop. To them it never seemed incongruous to suppose that the wine used at the marriage of Cana was Falernian. Horace would have loved the Fathers as they loved and quoted him.

The last of the great Roman writers, Boethius, consul in A.D. 510, was philosopher and statesman at the court of Theodoric the Ostrogoth. Toward the end of life Boethius was caught in the struggle for the preservation of the ancient senatorial liberties and was charged with treason. After having held every office with honor, he was cast into prison and probably strangled there. In that prison he wrote his last and greatest work, the *Consolations of Philosophy*. This book, the comfort of pious minds over the next thousand years, glowed with Boethius' disdain for the caprices of the flesh, for royal courts, and earthly ties. Even his own final catastrophe was the benignant act of Divine Providence, to be accepted joyfully in a world where the Good is God, far above chance, evil, or fortune. Before the *Consolations,* Boethius had written books on a variety of subjects: arithmetic, geometry, music. Performers, he felt, were not musicians but slaves. The composer remained at the beck and call of wayward inspiration. But the critic—ah, there you have the real musician! The critic came armed with a deep knowledge, using neither the agility of fingers nor the fluctuations of inspiration, but pure reason. Like earlier Fathers, Boethius fortified himself with Cicero's dictum: the essence of right living is the strength and nobility of the soul in contempt of things human.

Such aloofness, such transcendence is not sympathetic to us, perhaps. We remember, with more appreciation, the Prophetic injunction that this world is our proper preoccupation, to make it a better place for all of God's children. To us, the proper study of mankind is man. But, though the Fathers turned in revulsion from the priapic carnalities of Rome to an empire of the spirit, still, the Fathers were men of real and endearing humanity. Clement of Alexandria cried "When thou seest thy brother, thou seest God." And Gregory Palamas said "man is higher than the angels." Here is essential poetry upon which the future can build.

II.

Eight hundred and ninety years after the Council of Nicaea, another gathering met, not in the dry fastnesses of Asia Minor but among green and probably damp fields by the river

Thames in England. The circumstances of this conclave are the reverse of those attendant upon the earlier assembly. Not that the dignitaries of the Church are absent. But here there is no word of dogma; only of vaster temporal powers to be confirmed. Here is little splendor, though the nobility are out in force, and the monarch has come unwillingly—a virtual captive of his lordlings.

Even though there was no leader of the people present at the field of Runnymede where King John met his barons, the prelates as well as the nobility and the crown knew that the ultimate enforcement of any article lay with the men-at-arms who stood by each tent and lined the hedgerows. The nobles were aware that if the king could meddle with the serfs he could meddle with the owners. Whereas the exemptions of the master, in matters of arbitrary taxation, visitations, and drafts, were strengthened if those exemptions were extended to the villeins. The clergy, professing a concern for the body of the common man as the temple of his soul, disliked to see that body alienated to the jurisdiction of a king who confiscated the goods of widows and orphans, seized the Church lands, and tampered with ecclesiastic appointments. Thus Magna Carta, which appeared on Monday, June 15, 1215, was born as the Articles of the Barons. The Archbishop of Canterbury and Pandulf, the papal legate, labored during the following weekend to see that the Church received its due. The Charter took final shape by Tuesday the twenty third, and was sealed by the king. Men felt that this charter was but the reaffirming of old rights, rights assigned in the time of Henry I or Edward the Confessor. Actually, here was new drama, never before experienced: the king beaten to his knees, the prelates sweeping from tent to tent, insistent upon a profitable reconciliation, and the barons holding out for those individual autonomies which by osmosis would affect every shire in England and ultimately every householder.

112

Tradition has gathered the Charter of Runnymede to its own. It has sloughed off the fact that Pope Innocent III and King John immediately repudiated the document. The fortieth "chapter" or article is the shortest. Without that provision, we cannot conceive of a good society, and we rightly tremble whenever we see it imperiled: *To no man will we sell or deny or delay right or justice.*

In the centuries between Nicaea and Runnymede, the cycles of civility had swung so low that on the upswing the world presented a new face. More than in any place else, unguessed and largely unappreciated, it was in England that the fair hopes of our civilization were taking shape. In our enthusiasm for the evidences of self-government and local councils, of folk-moot and the rights of common deliberation (accompanied by the rattling of shields and loud "yeas" and "nays"), we are apt to forget that before the Saxon and the Dane, England had enjoyed the indispensable centuries of being a colony and having Roman law and Greek philosophy conferred upon her. While Spain was to congeal into an absolute monarchy implemented with an Inquisition, and the great, free Italian communes were to be crushed between two millstones, papacy and empire, Guelf and Ghibelline, Germany became a chaos of princes. In France, an astute, often wise, frequently brilliant policy of concentricity was to produce logically, lamentably, a Louis XIV. By some special grace England was to build in material not made with hands but compounded of the search for and the spirit of freedom and justice.

Plantagenet charters confirmed the generality of people in England in the rights of "equal justice by one's equals"; of local self-government; of the payment of money in lieu of arbitrary and compulsory conscription; of open courts held regularly, at stated intervals and fixed places; of exemption from all capricious taxes, over and above the recognized feudal dues, except when voted by the general council of the realm. Provision was made for the summoning of this great council, ancestor of Parliament. Specifically, the yeoman was never to be deprived of the means of his livelihood, his tenement, his wares, or his wain.* In all matters, the humblest freeman was to be dealt with, not directly by force, but "by legal judgment of his peers or by the law of the land."

The various charters are at the very root of our tradition, the origin of our twentieth century law and practice. From Runnymede we learn how ancient is the group desire, the collective urge for those rights we still prize. The political formula was cast, as yet, in old molds; there was no interpretative voice, no artist-hero in England. But the time was ripe for a champion. And from now on, the array of prophets emerges. One poetic and exquisite voice was raised at the very moment King John faced his barons. In 1215, the year of the Great Charter, Francis of Assisi was preaching that in poverty was no disgrace, but rather, the swiftest means of grace. "Carry neither gold nor silver; for the workman is worthy of his hire." To a world in which serfs and outcasts, brigands and lepers predominated under the stigma of servitude or outlawry, more compassionate stigmata were offered by the equalitarian ministry of the friars. The blessing poured upon their wretched condition did much to encourage people to get out of it.

Little by little, from the mists of a thousand years, we see emerge our twin lights of liberty and social justice, strangely fortified by their long sleep. In Europe, the slavery of whites is almost a thing of the past. Anonymity too is on the wane; the Church can claim that her pope is the greatest potentate in Christendom. The villein is on his way to becoming a burgher. Groping, ever more vocal and specific as increas-

---

* Does not blacklisting, so widely if tacitly practiced today, violate this provision by depriving a man of the means of livelihood?

ingly affective prophets raise their voices—coming to a head under grievous conditions, then checked brutally or scattered but to reassemble—through the heyday of feudalism, the cause of the people pushed forward. An insect will sometimes inhabit and lay eggs in the body of a larger insect. When an observer looks he sees no change though the host is dead, and a stronger, living guest is now the tenant of a husk, waiting to take wing. So feudalism was replaced (as the Roman empire had been)—sloughed off almost unnoticeably by the vigorous society which had sprung up in its belly.

III.

In the fourteenth century the young sprigs of our tradition flowered, as there appeared those who could quicken them, as England herself flowered in the works of craftsman, architect, sculptor, and poet. Grammar schools began to dot the land, giving a certain national cast, a uniform awareness, to the young. Abbeys and cathedrals, Westminster and Salisbury, thrust new spires into an arch of sky that covered all alike, in a great communal upsurge in which all the commonalty joined, to which every worker laid his hand. The people had become English, not Norman and Saxon, Jute and Dane; and the language followed the new affirmations. As caen-stone is soft in the ground and easy to cut, yet hardens in the air once hewn and dressed, so the malleable language wanted but the skilled hand to shape it in the light. And now the language, instrument of communion and prophecy, of explanation and questioning, was given a definition to which ready artists in their turn were to lend splendor.

By a curious coincidence, four writers were born in the first third of the fourteenth century: Langland, Gower, Chaucer, and Wyclif. One of them, Wyclif, became the father of English prose: another, Chaucer, the father of Eng-

lish poetry. The century was one of ferment, of boom and
bust, of a second revolution to dethrone an English monarch,
of calamity—"the first murrain," the Black Death of 1349.
Merchant galleys from Flanders and France, Italy and Spain,
the Levant and the Hanseatic towns, touched at English
ports, bringing an interchange of trade and ideas. As Thomas
Aquinas, a hundred years before, had reconciled Moham-
medan science with the catholic appetite of the Christian
cosmos, these traders were to reconcile the spices of the Orient with English mutton. In this century of ferment, we can
see the wielders of the new weapon of words at work, han-
dling the current ideas, giving them back in usable form to
the people, asking the questions and hurling the indictments
from which political action springs. Of the four men, Wyclif was the most effective. His influence lasted through
Cromwell. Whereas the men of politics who seemed so effective in their day left little mark of progress or enlightenment
or liberation, unless Shakespeare later called them, like
Lazarus, to come forth into immortality.

> What must the King do now? Must he submit?
> The King shall do it; must he be deposed?
>
> I wasted time, and now doth time waste me.
> *King Richard II*

Master John Wyclif wasted little time; and in that royal deposition, which Shakespeare touched with such tenderness,
Wyclif played a major role.

We can picture this master of Balliol College, Oxford—
cleric, teacher, writer, pamphleteer, translator—in the long
gown we associate with the Canterbury Pilgrims. By all
accounts gentle, virtuous, and courageous, the greatest theologian in England. Honored by the pope, rector of Lutter-

worth, envoy of the crown, versed in the sum of all that knowledge upon which our tradition is based: the Bible, the philosophers, the Church Fathers, English law and custom, and whatever science was available. But perhaps more potent than his own vast knowledge was the splendid burgeoning about him: the age that Wyclif adorned.

It was a fecund time for the concurrence of the elements for which we are searching. As the thwarted desire of the people for opportunity and growth drove them to association and common understanding the group urge became manifest. At last appeared the artist, Wyclif, with the new technique of language at his command, to carry in his heart and head the logic of these urges toward freedom. All of Wyclif's critical faculties were called upon, all his powers of acceptance and rejection, to judge the most momentous question of his day. It was a question which had disrupted ecclesiastical studies before. But now the spiritual future of the Church was at stake: whether to creep with the scholiasts in theological controversy, to wink at the "French pope," to condone the sale of what Chaucer called "Pardons hot from Rome," to ride with the prelates with face averted from the poor, or to run with St. Francis, pursuing the humbleness of holy scripture into the arms of an inevitable Reformation. Our tradition is what it is because Wyclif refused the complacent answer. Instead, he gave his people the Bible in their own tongue.

The times were indeed out of joint. The century had opened with the fall of Edward II, his deposition and most uncomfortable murder (accelerated by the application of toads, in Berkeley Castle). It closed with the fall of Richard II. After the victories of Crécy and Poitiers, English arms and prestige suffered the crash of defeat. In midcentury, the Black Death lay in devastation over the land, reducing the population by nearly half. In its wake followed a labor short-

age and consequent laws to strip the freemen of their free-
holds, institute forced labor, tie men again to the soil of the
nobility, and to confirm the law with brandings. The popes
were, for the moment, as insecurely seated as the kings.

There were two popes, one in Avignon, one in Rome, each
ardently supported by prelates and saints in good standing.
St. Catherine of Siena on one side, St. Vincent Ferrer on the
other; and between them the captain of the papal bodyguard,
referring to His Holiness not as *Urbanus* but *Turbanus,* the
rowdy. The Great Schism having put an end to reticence,
all men asked, "Where then is salvation?" The ravages of
plague, the destruction of crop and trade attendant upon
civil strife and the fluctuations of the Hundred Years' War,
these created the situation, the circumstances, in which the
people were to find for themselves a common impulse, a common refusal to persevere in these incompatible ways of coercion, serfdom, and superstition. The feudal corselet was
ripping at the seams; men were asking anxious questions
about fealty. A few exercised dominion at the expense, it
seemed, of the many. Where was justice and righteousness?
The answer lay with Wyclif.

He began his teaching quietly enough, quoting from Chrysostom and Tertullian and the other Fathers, as well as the
Prophets. Aquinas also was quotable, having written long
and deeply on politics. "It pertains to the office of a king so
to procure the good life of the many as is congruous with
their attaining eternal beatitude." Obviously, Aquinas had
not recommended squalor and ignorance as adjuncts of the
good life. Gently, then, Wyclif taught that dominion is of
grace. Since God gives all, even life, to His creatures, any
earthly power is in the nature of a stewardship and all we
own is but a hostage unto heaven. We possess in fief; the
right relapses to God when that right is abused. Gently, then,
and so far in accord with the Church Fathers. But time and

118

circumstance took a hand and forced the issue. The Church of Rome controlled a third of the land of England. And yet land was scarce; the revenues of the Church were twice those of the crown, and yet a new poll tax was being exacted from a destitute people. Was this Christian stewardship? Further: the land was England's—under the temporal care of the king who held from God, as, in spiritual matters, the pope held from God. For their earthly possessions, the prelates could be but sublessees.

What might have remained a theological hobbyhorse for the cleric at Oxford became almost at once a battlecharger for the rulers of the realm. The House of Lancaster was in need of funds—for the ultimate seizure of the crown by Henry IV. Here was a ready justification. So sharply did the king's uncle, John of Gaunt, threaten, that the prelates, fearful of losing their all, poured conscience-money into his lap. Parliament passed two statutes in which it was forbidden to review elsewhere the judgments of the king's court; the pope was forbidden to dispose of English benefices. Parliament officially noted that with the superfluous revenues of the Church, the crown could maintain an army as well as a hundred hospitals for the poor.

These matters are packed into a short scene by Shakespeare with an excoriating clarity he rarely permitted himself in dealing with ecclesiastical politics. At the opening of *Henry IV* we see the Archbishop of Canterbury and the Bishop of Ely, on a balcony, wondering if they can divert the king's mind from seizing the swollen benefices of the Church, by suggesting to him an equally profitable yet safely remote war on France. Rarely has the undertaking of war as a distraction from troubles at home been more devastatingly shown. (The trouble at home, in this case, was caused by the Lollards and the people's distress. But Shakespeare, with an eye cocked at the Tudor police, mentions neither Lollards nor Wyclif.)

119

Canterbury:

> My lord, I'll tell you; that self (same) bill is urg'd
> Which in the eleventh year of the last king's reign
> Was like, and had indeed against us passed,
> But that the scrambling and unquiet time
> Did push it out of further question. . . .
>   If it pass against us
> We lose the better half of our possession;
> For all the temporal lands which men devout
> By testament have given to the church
> Would they strip from us; being valued thus:
> As much as would maintain to the king's honor
> Full fifteen earls and fifteen hundred knights,
> Six-thousand and two hundred good esquires;
> And, to relief of lazars and weak age,
> Of indigent faint souls past corporal toil,
> A hundred almshouses right well supplied;
> And to the coffers of the king besides
> A thousand pounds by the year. Thus runs the
>   bill. . . .

Ely:

> But, my good Lord,
> How now, for mitigation of this bill
> Urged by the commons?

Canterbury:

> . . . I have made an offer to his majesty. . . .
> Which I have opened to his grace at large,
> As touching France, to give a greater sum
> Than ever at one time the clergy yet
> Did to his predecessors part withal. . . .
> Through his true title to some certain dukedoms
> And generally to the crown and seat of France,
> Derived from Edward, his great-grandfather. . . .

(LATER)

> (To the King)   Gracious Lord,
> Stand for your own; unwind your bloody flag. . . .

120

With blood and sword and fire to win your right;
In aid whereof we of the spirituality
Will raise your highness such a mighty sum
As never did the clergy at one time
Bring in to any of your ancestors.

While those "of the spirituality" plotted, and Parliament formulated statutes of "provisors" and "praemunire" to uphold a precious autonomy, the bitter cause of the poor grew in strength and noisomeness. A cause flourishes as it raises questions, as it thrusts to the fore those who have the eloquence to question. There were few sleeping dogs left lying as Wyclif aroused his fellows, raised questions, and frequently answered them.

Many creative minds have invented systems, the literal application of which would fill their authors with misgiving. I presume Plato would have been as astonished at having to live in his own *Republic* as Marx would be today in Russia. Wyclif found that in pursuing the logic of his own conscience he had become the embarrassed spokesman for a people whose subversions in society troubled him profoundly. In 1362 there was a great strike of journeymen weavers. They did not strike out of hand, but because they had an ideal of betterment and presumably a hope of success in a world they trusted was prepared to accord them that betterment. Led by John Ball, a preacher who felt that Wyclif's moral philosophy should be given immediate practical application, the people rose in the Peasants' Revolt. From north and south, from Devon and Norfolk, the people converged upon London; a hundred thousand men of Kent followed Wat Tyler. "Lollards," they were called in derision, these yeomen who came for redress of grievance: men lately returned from the wars, faced with new taxes, quickened to conviction by the very charters that had once been granted them. They sang as all

121

marchers must: * verses by Gower, snatches of Langland's *Piers Plowman*. They knew

> When Adam delved and Eve span
> Who was then the gentleman?

or

> For thief is reave, the land is penniless;
> For pride hath sleeve, the land is almsless;
> For might is right, the land is lawless.

They carried handbills signed "Jack the Miller" or "Jack Trewman." Above all, the Lollards were sustained by the thunderous dialectic of Wyclif.

Under the protection of John of Gaunt and of the university, Wyclif withstood the excommunications, the summons to trial, the charges of heresy leveled against him. Before he was done—he died, safely, of old age, after hearing mass in his own parish church—this man became truly heretical, the first Protestant. Relying upon the doubts of Ambrose, Jerome, and Augustine, Wyclif attacked the newly adopted dogma of complete Transsubstantiation. He denied that the priest had the power to create a miracle merely because he was a priest. In matters of faith, Wyclif commended the sole authority of the Bible, and to that end he left the people their first Bible in English. He did not know that what he had written would travel to Bohemia in the train of the widowed Queen of Richard II, and there fire John Huss to continue the Reformation already kindled at Oxford.

Wyclif's work in England suffered temporary eclipse, and for the same reasons that blighted the first fruits of the French Revolution or the American Revolution: exaggeration and fear. When the Lollards marched on London, they

---

* "When men first began to know themselves free to find God, apart from priestly and political interference, they began to sing." Foreword, Hymnal Notes, *Christian Science Hymnal*.

were not in a playful mood. "Free us," they cried, "that we may be never more held for serfs." Wantonly they broke down whatever palace doors were barred. The young king met them in a great field; hot words were exchanged; Tyler was murdered. But when the king promised redress, the mass of people returned to their hearths, hugging empty promise and worthless charter. Exaggeration and wantonness possessed the lords in their turn, together with the usual fear of the rich to lose their superfluities, a more ignoble fear than that of the poor to lose their necessities. The princely armies set upon the crowd; seven thousand of the people died on the gallows or were trampled under foot. (Froissart considered the massacre most exemplary.) In a spasm of vindictiveness, Parliament passed the Statutes of Heresy and the Statute of Laborers, putting the clock back a century and merely adding to the troubles they would mend. Such convulsive movements of coercion, under the impulses of fear, almost always lead to the centralization of power. In this case they led to the autocracy of the Tudors.

In a final burst of rancor, the Church Council of Constance ordered that the remains of the dead Wyclif be disinterred and scattered, with great repugnance and marked ceremony, on nearby waters. "Thus," says Fuller in his *Church History,* "this brook had conveyed his ashes into Avon, Avon into Severn, Severn in the narrow seas, then into the main ocean. And thus the ashes of Wyclif are the emblem of his doctrine, which now is dispersed all the world over."

By the year 1400, our tradition had been confirmed in its liberal course, under the guidance of Wyclif. The expansions of a later day were to be but logical conclusions, compatible conclusions, to matters stoutly begun.

Our study of England commenced with a barbarous country, backward in the arts, newly conquered, in which the generality were undoubtedly hardy but ignorant and virtually serfs. It is astonishing to find so little civility, yet so much conscience. Very slowly, the group urges took on definition, as communications were broadened and eased so that men in one village or shire had knowledge of their neighbors in another. Equally slowly, the group urges achieved that cohesive force from which movements spring to life. Then it was that Chaucer * and Gower, above all Langland and Wyclif, appeared, to give voice to what hitherto had been dumb. The sudden stabilizing of the language, in forms recognizable to all, was the great step in communication, the indispensable medium for the writer and orator.

Tradition does not carry in its bosom the dead statutes of those days, and, were it not for Marlowe and Shakespeare, the circumstances of Edward II or Richard II would gather dust with the circumstances of the last Roman emperors. These kings, like the Widow of Bath, live in the rich shadows of our tradition because later dramatists quickened them. But tradition has accepted into its full body, often into our present habit and custom, those affairs which occupied Wyclif.

Much of the glory of England shone from works of art, from the cathedrals especially; and Wyclif was an artist. The grammar schools that were to branch out so splendidly, grew in a sacred grove around him, where he was grammarian and teacher. The civil liberties and charter rights of the people increased, and the demand for them grew even into a formidable movement of which he was the liberal leader. The Bible was for the first time opened to the eyes of all the people; and Wyclif was the translator.

* Note C, *Chaucer,* page 301.

From that day, the artist-prophet no longer lags behind the urge; more and more he becomes the one who announces, rather than the one who sums up. Armed now with the word, above all with the vernacular Word of God, the artist commands a power which had but flickered since the high days of Greece and Israel.

4. Reawakening

In this chapter we continue upon ever more rewarding ground. The strands of our weaving have become hawsers. The artist enters into his own, as prophet and elucidator. The patterns of our tradition are set; and by the time of the Mayflower Compact we can see a tradition fully established—a tradition to which later accretions will be made only to confirm the ancient liberalities or to adapt them to modern times. More and more, the artist announces, leads, sums up.

When Richard III died on Bosworth Field, the crown passed to Henry VII, the first of the Tudors, in 1485. The last Tudor, Elizabeth, died in 1603—thus the Tudor century lasted 118 years. From the death of Wyclif in 1383 to the accession of Henry VII, English history is largely the tale of dynastic struggles: the Wars of the Roses. With Richard III, the Middle Ages may be said to have died at Bosworth.

4.

I

From the death of Wyclif to the defeat of the Armada was almost exactly two hundred years. Less than twenty years after the death of Elizabeth, the Pilgrims landed in America.

We must pause here for a few lines of history and a few pages of consideration: considering first what happened to our concepts of liberty and social justice and, second, what manner of men were those creative artists who irradiated the often sinister incumbency of the Tudor monarchs.

In the flurry of reaction against Lollards, the knights, prelates, and burgesses were content to let the royal artillery (today we might say "the brass hats") maintain the status quo. Through divers poll taxes, through the abolition of the rudiments of a direct primary and the substitution of election by "selectmen," Parliament became a clique. In its degradation, Parliament was not even worth summoning. So rich was the king, so gorged with confiscated baronies, that he had no need of it to levy funds. Spies and arbitrary imprisonment were encouraged in lieu of legislation.* For a hundred years Parliament fell to the desultory level of the Estates General in France or of the Cortes in Spain—an occasional gathering of the king's men at the king's pleasure.

From time to time Lollards marched again on London, as from time to time some Lollards were burned at the stake. Imprisoned in the golden amber of the new capitalism, caught in new specializations and exploitations, watching retail handicraft become wholesale, the people saw all commerce tied to the new middleman and broker. Bewildered by the activity of society as by the invention of double-entry accounting, deprived of the land by enclosure (the cheap and profitable sheep pasturage), the common people declined into pauperism, except for the few of them who rose on the kites of the new plutocracy. Quite naturally those who sank took their memories with them—memories of a tradition in which the state was essentially the frame for corporate, cooperative well-being. They remembered the days, in the Frankish and Teutonic traditional past, when kings were elected and when, as the Seneschal of Burgundy said, "the power of governing was lent to the king by the people, themselves the true givers of power." They remembered that their fathers believed that to the producers belong the products.

Rarely has suppression, as practiced by the Tudors, been accompanied by such brilliant compensations. The mitigations were so staggering that, without digging below the surface, the use of the word, the mere thought of, "reaction" seems a complete misnomer.

Yet, if we take such a mundane matter as high explosive, used first in the Wars of the Roses, a philosopher might hesitate to employ the word "progress" in connection with

---

* Indeed, the Elizabethan FBI drew up a formidable dossier on Christopher Marlowe, with all the customary insinuations.

its importation. The Chinese invented gunpowder and used it only to delight grownups and children with the delicate display of fireworks; pinwheels bursting above carp pond or pagoda. The House of Lancaster provided other uses. Gunpowder in Christian hands changed not merely the art of killing people, it also changed the balance of power. Only the royal treasury could afford a train of artillery. Before the mouths of the king's cannon, baron and castle crumbled. A whiff of grapeshot accompanied the entrance of absolute monarchy into England.

The merchant guilds and later, the craft guilds had far less use for civil liberty than for corporate privilege. The masters sought protection and control, both of which were put to the service of manipulating cheap labor and acquiring high markets. Once the Church relinquished her solicitude for the "just price" and for the lot of the poor, the laborer was at the mercy of a small class through whose hands passed the new wealth from America, whose monopolies controlled the king's cannon, and whose purses alone could afford the books which now came from Caxton's press.

For this long century brought printing (also a Chinese invention) and the use of linen paper to replace parchment. But, for decades, this great gift to civilization was a gift to the few. Later, it would bring the world of thought under every man's roof: news of the day, news of a thousand miles away, true or false, news of what had been said two thousand years back, subversive or orthodox. Later, it would set the charters where they could be read by all: the referable documents in which the tradition smouldered—known by word of mouth before; now, with the Bible, to be held in a man's hand. But truly popular diffusion of printed books did not take place till at least a century after Caxton's death in 1491.

To the spirit of discovery, the use of the blunderbuss, the power of the guilds, the influxes of wealth, and the blessings of print—all of which, in divers aspects, have affected our tradition or still live healthily in it—we must add the rise of capitalism. We have seen examples of the group urge when men combine to thrust through or out from bonds—from impossible conditions. The slave rebellions under the Roman empire, the Peasants' Revolt in England, the coming Rebellion, and our own Revolution were all cousins under the skin. There can be observed also another urge which I must call by the uncouth name of "inner urge," to avoid even more obnoxious terms like "push" or the Greek *physis*. This takes place in arts and sciences, in medicine and law, every so often. It is wont to appear at the end of cycles: the art or science must expand or die. Such an urge came upon commerce. Medieval economy was done, new worlds were opening. The new capitalism could not brook an economy founded on monastic or manorial control. The necessary freedom to trade demanded a divorce from ecclesiastical restraint; and, since the Church herself desired wealth, she was forced into compromises which filled her coffers but rifled her prestige. Worn with the struggle, she relinquished the market men to their markets, and control over them to the state. Morality and business parted company. The ideal of the "whole man" as of a "whole dominion" slipped from the papal fingers. Individualism had won a round, for both good and evil.

As the aristocracy of arms was brought to heel, a new, moneyed class of burghers came into the clear. While the *noblesse* forgot to oblige, the plutocracy busily cultivated its privileges at the expense of its obligations. Both huddled around the throne. The Church, dropping like a cumbersome umbrella her wonted solicitude for the common people, for business morality and for the increase of knowledge, hived also near the crown in fear of those same common people who, through Wyclif, had voiced such untoward ideas.

132

In fear too of Parliament which twice had demanded the expropriation of Church lands—twice, before Henry VIII.

These then, so briefly, are some of the circumstances which attended the hundred and more years of Tudor autocracy. The picture contains one notable paradox: that while liberty and social justice were incarcerated, one might say, and the only visible group urges occurred when the people rose in loyalty to and in defense of the crown itself, the number of golden voices proclaiming the need for liberty and social justice had never been so prodigious. The response to those voices did not come, in action, in political action, till half a century after the eloquent mouths were stopped with dust and the hands that wrote were withered in the grave.

With the death of Henry VIII, the laws of absolutism remained on the books. They sustained his son and his two daughters. With infinite tact, Elizabeth used them without quite mentioning them. But at her death, they appeared for what they were: the corruption of all that the best Englishmen had ever stood for. When the great loyalty that hedged the queen who had saved England from Spain, confirmed her subjects in the middle way of Anglicanism in religion, given them peace and the Bible, when this loyalty was released from obligation by her death, then the scales fell from English eyes. Parliament revived and, with its first breath, blew upon the imposed and imposing structure of autocracy, and did not relent till a whirlwind had blown it away in the Great Rebellion.

II.

We have left to the last the most powerful, most brilliant and the most beneficent part of those many components which characterized the Tudor century. Inextricably mixed with the struggle for dominion, mixed with the animating zeal of the reformers, above all with the moral and political thinking of its own day as of all the future, was the New Learning. It is properly linked in our memories to three men —artists, prophets, scholars—who were born in the fifteenth century and died in the sixteenth. Under Henry VIII each was touched by the passing finger of glory. By the end of the reign of Elizabeth their work, the inspired transmittal of this New Learning, had so freshly and pungently penetrated English thought that the American tradition—soon to embark on its own—may be said to have sprung directly from their labors.

Colet, Erasmus, and More may be counted among the most civilized men who ever lived, not just because of their gentleness, wit, and learning, but also because their civility was exalted by a simple piety and noble spirit. Deeply religious, tenaciously Catholic, still their thoughts were not cumbered with the suet of dogma, but rather bone-clean in their sharply reasoned faith.

Colet spent his life translating the Gospels from the original Greek and, as Dean of St. Paul's, preaching what he'd found therein. Erasmus carried on Colet's work, traveled everywhere, wrote constantly—commentaries, translations, popular essays, satires, political works—refused a Cardinal's hat, and said, as he died quietly, "I desire only to go home and find favor with Christ." Thomas More, artist and philosopher to his fingertips, anticipated not only the civil liberties which purport to flourish today but also most of our social welfare. He rose to be chancellor, and died on the scaffold because he would not subscribe to something he could not believe. These three friends spanned the century from Richard III to the close of the reign of Henry VIII. They felt the whole luminosity of the Renaissance and labored to diffuse its light. Above all, they strove to reform the Church, to reduce dogma to some minimum to which all could freely subscribe. "Never," said Erasmus, "was Christian

faith purer than when the world was content with the shortest creed." They strove to reconcile the sects among Catholics as well as among Protestants, and to cleanse the Church
of simony and greed. They condemned that meddling with
temporal affairs which invariably resulted in the Church
standing for reaction, to protect her holdings, rather than
for the social justice which shone from every page of the New
Testament before Colet's eyes as he pored over his manu-
scripts, over the "moving and ravishing texts."

Truly, the Reformation lay in many Roman Catholic
hearts as deeply as in Protestant hearts. Both have desired
such a redemption from the corruptions of power as was
sought by St. Francis and the purer spirits. As far as England
was concerned, the splitting rock was not dogma but prestige,
not faith but power, not charity but money. Time and again,
to assert her temporal power or to preserve it, the Roman
church appeared to be, indeed was, on the side of tyranny.
To Englishmen, to Colet and More, it was intolerable that
their ecclesiastical head, the pope, should insist that it was
the sacred duty of Englishmen to betray their king, to side
with their country's ancient enemy, and finally depose their
queen. The Inquisition of Spain and the massacres of Alva
in Holland were sustained by Rome as exemplary pro-
cedures. Such ineptitude drove men, logically, to confound
the Pope with all that was unpatriotic and illiberal. The
break up of the monastic lands had been but the culmina-
tion of a slow process. As to the divorce, Queen Catherine
was the aunt of his Catholic Majesty, the Emperor Charles V,
and that same Charles (after sacking Rome) held Pope Clement in semicaptivity. Clement urged Henry to procure his
own divorce in England, and say no more about it. There
was little cause for schism here. But the Vatican and the
emperor could not brook the example of the autonomy which
Henry cherished. The king then set up his own primate and

his own Anglican Church, both subservient to the crown. For to the Tudors, the desire of Calvin to make the state subservient to the Church, or the zeal of Luther in elaborating a whole patchwork of new dogmas, was as repugnant as it was to Colet, Erasmus, or More. Even so, Erasmus could say —and how few cardinals today would say—"In Luther's enemies I perceive more of the spirit of this world than of the Spirit of God."

These Catholic reformers attacked not a faith but a system. Unfortunately, to cleanse the system—the indulgences, mendicants, persecutions, interferences, pardons, and policies—the papal pretentions had to be shorn. In the shearing, with the ticks went the wool. From long corruption the wind was ill-tempered. Essentially, civil liberty won the day; that is, even a precarious freedom in which to worship was found to be nearer the desire of man than the cozy comforts of orthodoxy. This medieval, scholastic "system" was, at bottom, what Voltaire was to attack later: the vestigal aversions to wide secular education, independent thought, civil liberty, and personal responsibility. Erasmus cut clean through the sophistic niceties of the churchmen: "While people thus trifle away their misspent hours in trash and babble, they think that they support the Catholic Church," he cried. He regretted Luther and deplored the brutalities on either side, but he strove for freedom of conscience and liberality within a church of Christ, dependent on and animated by the word of Christ, with a success he could not live to see. Even now, we have not achieved such benevolence. "Though the old ignorance is still defended tooth and nail," he wrote, "yet is the world working out of a long deep sleep." His shadow lengthened, as far as across the sea, and touched Roger Williams.

In the martial excursions which occupied so much of the time of princes, so much of the funds of the state and blood of the citizenry, Erasmus could see nothing worthy. Even more shocking to him was the activity of popes in similar dynastic and predatory wars. "Do we not see," he lamented, "that noble cities are erected by the people, yet they are destroyed by princes? . . . The men of might are called *serene* though they turn the world upside down; *illustrious* though they grovel in ignorance of all that is noble; *catholic* though they follow anything rather than Christ. . . ." Sir Thomas More went further; beneath or beyond the might of princes he sought the might of truth, the right source of power itself, as Wyclif had done. With prophetic finger he pointed to the labor class as the true basis of any commonwealth. He recommended nine hours work per day and a decent leisure which could be devoted to the larger services of the mind. He built *Utopia* not just by tearing down the pitiful barriers of his day but by building up a compensating virtue for every vice. Where, but for Colet's grammar schools, he saw general ignorance about him, into *Utopia* he built public education; for paupery and disease, he charted a public health service. For antiquated prisons he substituted crime prevention and correction; and in his realm there was to be absolute religious tolerance. Rhode Island was to achieve that tolerance, first, in 1636; but More's great plan for social justice is only now, and only here and there, being gingerly lifted from the pages of a book and piece by piece written anew into our practice and our law.

The radiance of the New Learning outreached the acute battleground of Church reform. It brought new light to all the knowledge of antiquity. Hebrew, Aramic, Greek, all had been known hitherto through crude, often incorrect, Latin versions; now they were translated direct. Doctrine founded on error was open to a new scorn. Ovid, Homer, Plato, Euripides; the documents preserved by Byzantium or by Islandic scholars; mathematics, geography, astronomy; the

writings of the men and women of the Renaissance in Italy
and France, as well as the contentious writings out of Germany—all these were in the province of the New Learning.
All these passed through the hands of Colet and More and
Erasmus, through the hands of commentators and expound-
ers, till they seeped down, distilled, into the current knowledge of the day. How the Hebrews built a temple or the
Greeks founded a colony; how the antique world established
marine insurance or made love; how Islam made a squinch
or dealt with calculus; how the ancients considered *demos*
or the *res publica*—these were matters that depassed the struggle for ecclesiastical dominion.

This New Learning is with us still. But the moment of
its first impact—what is called the "Time of the New Learning"—lasted only to the death of Lord Bacon, in the reign
of James I. There were many agents of its diffusion, not
alone Colet and More and Erasmus. One other concerns us
especially, since his word profoundly affected the thought of
our first colonials.

In the reigns of Henry, of his son and of his two daughters,
the tracts of Wyclif were revived, printed now, and passed
from hand to hand. Henry suppressed one Bible and authorized a new one. *Piers Plowman* was read again. Alter-
nately, as the extremes of patriot-separatists, on one side, or
of Roman priests, on the other side, grew eloquent or con-
spicuous—depending on the leanings of the monarch or the
primate—the witch burnings and persecutions flared. But
even the middle way found well-nigh perfect expression,
though the way of compromise is rarely one for the prophets.
The finest prose writer of his day in England was Hooker, a
clergyman in that Anglican Church which, under Elizabeth,
had come to stay. He was a Protestant, but no fanatic; and
he was veritably a modern man. He still speaks with authority as well as sonority.

Hooker was learned and he was just, the highest type of Renaissance scholar. In his off-parsonage hours he tended sheep with the odes of Horace in his hand. His importance to us lies in the liberal philosophy, experimental and tolerant, which he developed to expound the virtues of the new Church, but which were applied, and still apply, to the state as well, since he conceived of both Church and commonwealth as fundamental aspects of the same government. Ecclesiastical government, he held, like the civil, should be reasonable and accustomed, for what the generality of reasoned men consent to must be in conformity with natural law and so with God's law. Certatin premises of his thinking were to assume a permanent importance in the minds of men, more for political than churchly reasons, since the temperate core of his argument was that "public approbation" or consent was the only foundation worthy of governments, civil or religious. As such, there was much in Hooker which foreshadowed Locke and even Rousseau, and much which was peculiarly sympathetic to Jefferson. Much, too, which we might cherish in times of political and religious prejudice and coercion. In words that touch us nearly, he said, "We covet a kind of society and fellowship even with all mankind." Hooker can not have been popular with the Puritan Separatists; but when the separatists were no longer harried, the desire for some tolerant accommodation even with an Anglican rector crept in to their defensive intransigence. Certainly in Hooker the Protestant Episcopal Church may count its intellectual founder.

The Reformation did not become a battle of the sword till long after it had been a battle of the books. The same is true of the Great Rebellion, that vicarious throe which accompanied the birth of the United States. The politicians themselves have rarely been present at the inception of an idea. They flock to table, as it were, when others—usually the

philosophers and poets and prophets, and occasionally the
hand-forcing generals—have prepared the banquet. The creative minds have always been the stewards of the feast. The
Rebellion like the Reformation was instigated and sustained
by the eloquent men, not by the mute; by the prophets, not
by the adjusters; by the "creative minds," not by the stand-
patters; and by the agitators, those greatly discomforting
people who usually, since Socrates or John the Baptist, have
been killed off only to have statues raised to them when they
were safely dead.

Eloquent, learned, illuminating as were Erasmus, More,
Colet, and Hooker, still they were men no longer medieval
but of the Renaissance, that is of a *rebirth*. Even the greatest
of the Renaissance scholars were but transmitters, like Colet
and Erasmus, or stabilizers, like Hooker, rarely prophets, like
More. In the main, the New Learning was old learning writ
new. And of all the ancient learning, the Bible contained
the greatest reward. Aristotle and Plato had been digested by
Aquinas; Horace, Ovid, even Virgil were authors of delight
rather than instruction. Daily life was little touched by them.
The laborious study of the Old Testament and the New Testament, however, was destined to alter the very conceptions
of man's relation to man, let alone his relation to God.

The rediscovery of the Bible, and its publication and
general distribution, though often the pursuit of purely pious
men, in effect was a political event of the first significance.
Slaves and peasants had periodically risen since time was, but
they were driven to rising only when their despair overcame
their fear, and in so doing they had to invent their charters
or their bills of grievance and of mutual aid as they went
along. Now, suddenly, in the Bible was discovered the Great
Charter of liberality, one above all which those in anointed
power could not tear up or disown since they too admitted
its authority. Within its covers was the very school of democ-

140

racy, not only the precepts of compassion but the models of protest, of inspired invective. "Thus saith the Lord," cried Isaiah, "Bring me no more vain oblations . . . but wash you, make you clean . . . learn to do well; seek judgment, relieve the oppressed, judge the fatherless and plead for the widow." During a reign in which the king had bought the judiciary and in which judgment was the sport of the Star Chamber, a God who desired to "restore the judges as at first and the counsellors as at the beginning" was truly a "rebellious God" and a subversive one. The works of Erasmus and Hooker, as later those of Milton and Bunyan, or the chivalric, loyal, and protestant poems of Spenser—these were memorable, effective. But the first poets and prophets who shook the world of our forefathers were those who prophesied and sang, lamented and exhorted among the hills of Palestine two thousand years ago and more.

It may seem ungracious and arbitrary not to accept into our beneficent residue all the illustrious works and figures which adorned the age of the Tudors. Some of the greatest artists—Marlow, for instance—must be rigidly excluded from this study because I can find no enhancement of the cause of social justice or liberality in him, as I must exclude also Lord Coke, through whose interest and protection Roger Williams had obtained scholarships at Charterhouse and Pembroke College. Though Coke's *Institutes* and *Reports* underwrote the coming Rebellion and sustained all the liberal common law of the colonies, I see no possibility of calling him an artist, in spite of his courageous and fertile mind. But more than enough remains, after anxious winnowing, for us to apprehend what the Pilgrims were to carry away for permanent safe-keeping out of the two centuries of creative, autocratic, gloriously contradictory turbulence.

141

To insist that gunpowder is in our tradition would be as frivolous as to insist that the common cold must be because it affects so many people. It is quite possible that such off-shoots as Daniel Boone's powderhorn pertain to our tradition. It is also more probable that Nobel, the high-explosive manufacturer, should be in it than Hiram Maxim, for obvious reasons. The journeyman guilds, as the ancestors of our unions, might well hold a higher place in our tradition than they do. The merchant and craft guilds are enshrined not so much in the practices of modern commerce as in the enormous number of works of art associated with them. Part of the inscrutable ritual of being a director was and is still to have his portrait painted. Further, it has always seemed fitting that a certain proportion of excess profits should be given to embellish a church. As to printing, it is of itself a convenience only; the measure of the author whose works are printed is the measure of the civilizing value of print.

Even discovery must not be accepted joyfully as an automatic good. The Conquistadors brought back plague as well as emeralds. But, a greater boon than the gold mines of Peru, their adventures kindled the imagination of mankind. For, truly, the great discoveries are not made when Balboa's men —gazing at each other in a wild surmise, silent upon a peak in Darien—see an ocean which is new to them, but when a poet, from the little eminence of his own integrity, gazes within himself and discovers some truth for the human heart. Of such discoveries is the Kingdom of Heaven.

To be sure the pilgrims came here rather than elsewhere because this New World had been discovered. But they brought precious little with them except qualities and conditions of mind and heart. They cherished the noblest thoughts of the New Learning which they owed entirely to such masters of art as those we have singled out. They undoubtedly brought a knowledge of corporations and guilds, but they were to practice cooperation, founding communes and reserving such lands as Boston Common to the common use.

They rejected, and our tradition has rejected, absolutism and the divine right of kings; enclosure, and the entailment of estate; foreign interference such as that of Rome; and any coercive measures which would force them to worship against their conscience. They rejected the manifestations of coercive government in secret police and Star Chambers.

Actually, they were somewhat more medieval minded than the generality of people left behind in England. It is customary to conclude that the Middle Ages closed in the time roughly of Henry VII; that is, when, in the name of a new nationalism, kings made their rule absolute, and when the Gothic idea of a world unity under Christ gave place to a web of independent sovereignties. Now, the God-conscious Puritans, dissenters, presbyters, these still clung to the central medieval tenet: that man's business on earth was only to prepare for his exit therefrom. They clung to the idea of a unity under God, all men united in a Christian discipline. If they narrowed that discipline to fit their own custom, they were but following in orthodox if unfortunate steps.

From the corpus of medieval doctrine many admirable things survived. The Church had laid particular stress on natural law, separating it carefully from conventional or coercive law. Natural law being preempted by association with Divine Law—both being "reasonable," as Aquinas said —only conventional, manmade law was left to the king, for the regulation of mundanities. The religious aspect of this concept was not alien to the Puritans, and the secular aspect was one which we shall see fully accepted by Jefferson.

As the Church could not tolerate an absolute monarchy, it repudiated the assumptions underlying divine right. In the same manner, it could not tolerate the Reasons of State, in whose name absolute monarchs bore heavily either on the Church or on the dissenters.

Lastly, medieval scholarship made much of *contract,* contracts with God or with men. Feudalism had been a mass of contracts. Kings, said the Church, were placed on the throne by contract: a contract with God to be worthy of the anointing, a contract with their subjects to deal justly. A broken contract meant a broken crown. This tenet, briefly buried under the Tudors, was not long in reappearing. Rousseau called it the *Social Contract,* and our early documents are full of it. In short, we cannot say farewell to the medieval mind; we can but say *au revoir.*

In the stress of the fifteenth and sixteenth centuries, liberalism wore many disguises. The forms were pushed out of line though the vital urges remained intact. Suppression of the Lollards had brought only a greater diffusion for their ideas. What had been a flash of lightning under Wyclif's pen became a continuous rumble of thunder among the people. In the new stratifications of society, the hidden springs remained fresh, and ideas, like earth creatures out of sight, continually turned the soil. The times were robust, enough so to carry the reaction to real glory. Reaction in one field was balanced by violent action in another. The tradition of social justice was put aside for power and magnificence, but —any vintner knows you do not bottle a fermenting liquor, in fear, hastily in a rush to paste on a gold label—the tradition was to take its revenge.

Tradition has swallowed whole the men who made the sixteenth century sound like a trumpet after the subdued viols of the Dark Ages. Drake, the pirate; Raleigh, the poet; countless poets and dramatists and historical personages; the heedless and headless: Anne Boleyn, Lady Jane Gray. Curiously enough, there were many conspiracies but few group urges. Actually, the chain, the whole chain of our tradition received a cleaning, a gold bath, an electroplating of new-old learning. It received but one new link, that of the Reformation: the acceptance of religious dissent, which would lead ultimately to that tolerance we cherish. (This link was really forged by Wyclif. But its full acceptance into our tradition must be set down to the Tudors and their Reasons of State.) It sounds ungrateful to these glorious centuries, but it must be said that during them the tradition was not so much enlarged as stuffed.

The inner urges, however, those pushes within matters rather than men, were strikingly evident. Like commercial practice, both religious and political thinking rushed from tight, orthodox cores to new expansions, in logical outbursts guided by the exigency of new conditions, new knowledges, new techniques. Thus, also, absolute monarchy pushed to its logical if catastrophic end. Furthermore, rarely has there been a time when the artist-elucidator was more in evidence. It was the work of a few men of creative talent in the sixteenth century which announced and guided the liberating revolutions of the next century. What is amazing is the time lag: the hundred years of waiting between More and Oliver Cromwell, the hundred years it took the people to catch up with their prophets.

If liberalism for a long while went by the board before the surges of the new monarchy and the new capitalism, it still floated, cumulative and urgent, below the surface, to receive fresh charters and to be brought out into the light by the third and greatest wave: that of the New Learning and the Reformation. It was upon this resurgence that it was brought to America.

III.

The first North American document was the Mayflower Compact, signed by a few members of the Pilgrim band which bobbed off the coast of New England a little before Christmas, 1620. They had come, these refugees, to escape or avoid certain things and to find or achieve certain other things. They came to live, not to conquer and return home; to sow, not just to reap.

Let us examine the brief Compact—its limitations and affirmations—in order to understand of what mind these signers were; and then we can ask how their minds came to be so garnished and appointed—in other words, what was their "mental furniture" and why?

Briefly: "In ye name of God, Amen"; this company of men loyal to King James, "having undertaken for ye glorie of God and advancement of ye Christian faith" to "plant ye first colonie" in northern Virginia (as it was then called), do mutually "covenant and combine our selves together into a civill body politick for our better ordering and preservation" and therefore do "frame such just and equall lawes . . . as shall be thought most meete for ye generall good of ye Colonie" under which we promise . . . "all due submission."

Now, short and unpretentious as the Compact appears, it is intensely special. No such spirit moved the tobacco-planting colonists of Raleigh's day, sent out to recoup *his* fortunes. No such spirit moved the conquistadors of Mexico or Peru who came to conquer by the sharp of the sword rather than by the sweat of the brow, who brought the hemophilia of primogeniture and caste, who thought somewhat of bringing infidels to God but made no voyages to facilitate their own submission to His will. For them, Eldorado; for the Pilgrims, the City of God.

To colonize rather than conquer, then, and very much "in ye name of God." Further, these dissenters did *mutually* covenant and combine, on an equal footing, as their fathers in town-moot had done. Then, again, they ordained a civil body-politic, not a rival monarchy, nor a hierarchy, nor yet a leader with his bodyguard. They quoted straight from Magna Carta when they set up "equall" laws, equal justice to all alike. And lastly they bound themselves to abide by the laws to which themselves had consented. That is all; but it is colossal by its omissions.

The Pilgrims who were but a handful, a boatful, among the thousands of Puritan emigrés, had left a Europe in which the Thirty Years' War had begun. Some had come from Holland bringing their memories of the Duke of Alva and his fire and sword and Inquisition. These refugees had shared in the Dutch refusal to endure the lash of bigotry and foreign rule and dictatorship. They had been in the resistance, the underground. Others had come from England, where the autocracy of James was daily being questioned in Parliament. In shire and town the Bible had taught people soberness of life. Of late, oppressive laws had turned the spirit of men inward or turned their minds toward the charters wherein lay the record of liberties cordial to their tradition. Charters by which to be guided amid the evils of the surrounding day in an England whence the pagan glamor had fled with the death of the red-haired queen seventeen years before.

They sought tolerance (for themselves) and jobs and farms —a place to grow, away from the cramped enclosures and espionage and violence of Europe. And if they were vague one day or didactic the next as to what was wanted, all knew what was *not* wanted: coercion of the kind they had experienced.

These men and women were educated, Protestant, Parliament-minded, Puritan. Their leaders were university bred. Bradford carried in his pocket a critique of Plato's *Republic*. All of them knew by heart the Bible, and all were acquainted with the popular serious literature of the past hundred years. The world was round, not flat, they knew. Kepler and Galileo, as well as Columbus, had recently overturned a

147

thousand years of ecclesiastial cosmography. Some of the company knew their logarithms, or had heard that the blood circulated, according to Harvey. Not ignorant people, the Pilgrims, but keenly aware of their times, and well documented, too. Nearer to the great lights of the New Learning than we are to Jefferson and to our own greatest charters, and, looking ahead, actually nearer by a hundred years to Jefferson's birth than we are today.

In no group ever was the group urge more epitomized than in the Pilgrims, forerunners of a whole Puritan people who were shortly to burst into a Great Rebellion and decapitate Charles I. Children of the Reformation as well. No expansion of thought—no urge within an intellectual category—ever, except perhaps in one century in Greece, was so revolutionary, so shattering as was the Reformation. And this Rebellion and this Reformation were largely conceived, announced, and guided by artists.

If the ears of the Pilgrims were not attuned to the euphuisms of Lyly, they had absorbed the deploring accents of Foxe's *Martyrs*. They had harkened to the wisdom of Erasmus, the subversive splendors of More's *Utopia,* the translations of Colet, and, more lately, the balanced tones of Hooker and Lord Bacon. It was with the works of such creative minds that the minds of the Pilgrims themselves were furnished. The lamp of the New Learning, its procreative radiance now softening to an afterglow, was part, a large part, of their mental baggage.

The Pilgrims, then, left an England where, even at the moment of their sailing, the Commons were resolving "that the liberties, franchises, privileges, and jurisdictions of Parliament are the ancient birthright of the subjects of England"; where the cumulative anger against the vacillations toward Spain, as against monopoly and corrupt elections, was reaching a climax. They left an England where the desire for freedom of speech was grown as urgent as a cry for food. They brought with them a fear of popery (though, as was said, a hundred thousand men might be willing to march against this popery, but they "did not know whether it was a man or a horse"). They brought a detestation of martial law. Along with Greek philosophy and the commentaries of Erasmus, they carried the popular, radical tracts of the day. These tracts had been run off on underground presses. Censorship was active in England. Even the Bible had been occasionally snatched away as the archstuff of sedition or of Lutheranism. Above all they brought this precious Gospel, and this "Gospel Truth we will maintain," said John Eliot, "not with words but with actions." They brought prejudice and conviction and habit. And out of the three, they forged the first American link in the chain of the American tradition.

Their departure was not without incident. When the Pilgrims first attempted to seek refuge in Holland, the secret police seized their children. In the end they were deported. So it is that, in the main, the further back you pursue an "old American family" the nearer you come to a deportee or refugee.

Thus they came: few bags, much mental baggage. They came armed, armed with the three R's: Renaissance, Reformation, Rebellion. Over twenty thousand Englishmen, Puritans mostly, in less than twenty years. Then the first million, almost all dissenters, from England or Scotland, Huguenots from France, Protestants from Germany, diverse yet fired alike with Reformation and revolt in the vast majority, seeking a liberty in which there would be no necessity for secret meetings, underground presses, commercial pacts at the expense of moral principle, unequal justice or caste prejudice. They came to find a life where a man could count that his charters held an ever fresh validity, to be relied on and lived by.

For the first hundred years, our colonists were somewhat more occupied with the extravagances of climate and soil than with those of empire; with experiments in crops rather than in theories of government; with naked and painted braves than with ruffled Cavaliers. Though the Puritans were themselves educated and godly, their problems were problems of primary necessity. The battle which allowed the Puritans to fulfil their remote labors was fought in the mother country, in England. There, great matters were afoot. As the contest in England went one way or the other, the tide of migration to America rose or fell. At one time, during the Protectorate of Oliver Cromwell, many colonists returned to enjoy a brief security in England, as earlier and later under the oppressions of Charles I or James II the tide turned violently back to the New World. The cause of these tides we must examine first—leaving for the while the colonists to their Indians, their plantings, and their God.

IV.

When Charles I came to the throne in 1625, he sought, with obstinate myopia, to prolong or introduce everything most abhorrent to a tradition which was by then well established. Since Wyclif and the Lollards, England had been dissident and individualistic in matters of faith. It was felt that, in the matter of credenda, the truth lay with St. John (7:17), "If any man will do His will, he shall know the doctrine." Charles, on the other hand, leaned strongly toward Roman Catholicism and even brought up his children as Catholics. The hearts of Englishmen went out to the heroic Netherlands; Charles preferred to ally himself with those who oppressed the Netherlands and who made war on the Protestant princes. Parliament was looked upon as the true voice of England, the inheritor of the "yeas and nays" of the first Grand Council, the bulwark of the people, to be summoned yearly; yet Charles summoned it only to raise money, prorogued it early, and sought by any other means to raise funds.* Monopoly and special taxes were bitterly resented, not only because they were circumventions of Parliament and irksome in themselves, but also because the funds so raised were for the king's private purse, not spent for the good of the people, but rather for favorites or foreign wars or the maintainance of a standing army whose civic virtues the people had good right to suspect. Charles, however, imposed every monopoly and tax which had a semblance of precedent and even invented new ones. He extended to the counties of the interior the Ship Money levies, as well as raising the tax in the very ports which had so gallantly resisted the Armada and which were the cause of England's prosperity. It was not, then, in general, that Englishmen were grieved for their pockets, but for their principles: they grieved that Parliament was bypassed in special taxes, and that the money so raised was spent in unpopular ways. Where Scotland had been promised its religious liberty as the price of its union with England, Charles set about to destroy the Kirk and impose Anglicanism, as a step toward reconciliation with Rome and as a surety for his own divine right which the High Church prelates were willing to accord. "No bishop, no king," James had said. Last and certainly not least, "equall justice" was found wanting. The courts of the Star Chamber and of the High Commission were manned by king's men, and dis-

---

*   *Moneys? We'll raise supplies what ways we please,*
    And force you to suscribe to blanks in which
    We'll mulct you as we shall think fit.
                                    Massinger (1583-1640)
Charles himself deleted these lines as "too insulent."

pensed not equity but that perversion of justice which consists in controlling men's thoughts. If you did not support the government actively, then you must be rebellious, unfit for government employ, probably ripe for treason, and half way on the road to the gallows.

The obstinacy of the king was matched by the steadfastness of the people. Before the Long Parliament or the Rump or the Barebones Parliaments had finished their labors, every pretention of the king had been met by a counterassertion in behalf of liberality. When there is no tolerant accomodation everyone is incommoded; when matters are not tacitly understood, everyone speaks out. Before that extraordinary triple parliamentary period came to a close, the statute books were filled with laws, projects of laws, and assertions of principle, report of which flew to America on every favorable wind. And upon these laws and projects the colonists shaped their own destinies, remote from the counterrevolutions of Europe. The colonials cherished those liberties which they found compatible with the causes of their own exodus, and resolved to apply them. The true inheritors of Oliver Cromwell were the colonies. Much of what the Parliamentarians won under the Lord Protector was, in England, given back, or "restored" to Charles II. Not so in America. The colonies were too insignificant to be asked their opinion. They had been given nothing which they could be asked to return, not even their consent. As later, in the eighteenth century, the English language was to be, if not corrupted, at least overlarded with Johnsonese and Oxfordese, though the older uses continued in Ireland, Scotland, or in New England, so the political ideas which surrounded the establishment of the colonies lingered, true and increasing, not "accommodated," in the minds and practice of the colonists.

In Grand Remonstrance, Petition of Right, or Humble Representation, Parliament set about the abolition of the

Star Chamber, the court of High Commission, and of the un-
authorized taxes. The immunities and exemptions, as well
as the wealth, of the Church courts were docked. With the
old insistence upon the observance of the law and the security
of justice, came the new doctrine of ministerial responsibility
—responsibility to the Commons. While still dealing with the
king, Oliver Cromwell besought complete religious tolerance,
triennial Parliaments, electoral reforms (the doing away
with rotten boroughs), tax reform, the end of monopoly and
special privilege, and a general amnesty. To none of this
would the king incline, except in show, to gain time while
he tried to set one faction against another, or cry up war on
Scotland, or seek foreign aid. After the death of the king,
the Barebones Parliament considered certain matters which,
accepted calmly enough by us today, must have come as a
shock to many in the year 1653: the validity of civil marriages,
the support of churches solely by voluntary contributions,
and the redistribution of land. Great land holdings were a
minor problem to the colonists, but England is still dealing
with her entailed estates. For the rest, the prophetic matters
before the Barebones Parliament found acceptance in the
thirteen colonies before they found it in any other part of
the world.

The active agents of this Rebellion were the people and
their Parliaments, Oliver Cromwell and his New Model
Army, and certain men of letters. In their day, Cromwell
appeared the most effective; but he is dead. He belongs to
history. More important to us are the members of Parliament
—disputatious, pig-headed though they were, so stuck to their
seats (like vacuum cups, which indeed they became) that
Cromwell had to lock them out—for in their meetings were
propounded those ideas and theories which were to animate

the later constitutions of our separate states and our federal Constitution itself. But most important to us today, because most lasting and still referable, were the works of a few artists.

Carved in stone on the Arc de Triomphe in Paris is the march of the French revolutionary soldiers, while above them floats the spirit of victory. So, above the battles of the Great Rebellion, extended the marmoreal spirit of Milton. "Through struggle, triumph, and catastrophe he shared in the public life of his day with passion: what he had to express, in poems as well as pamphlets, was the collective thinking of his generation, though he lifted it, alone among his contemporaries, to the level of genius" (H. N. Brailsford). Faults he had: he was not a simple democrat, not concerned with universal suffrage nor social justice, as were the Levellers (the Lollards of their day); rather one desiring an intellectual élite and, in politics, tending to favor a hand-picked oligarchy. But in matters of the intellect or of the spirit, there he thought as nobly, as freely, as man ever has—unhampered by Puritan narrowness or by his middle-class financial conservatism. Toleration and free will have never had a more resolute or eloquent champion. He said of himself that God had instilled an intense love of moral beauty into his mind —and moral beauty, though visible chiefly in the elect, did not comport with bigotry and unreason.

When Milton as a youngster went on the Grand Tour, (when he was deciding whether to become a priest), he paid a visit near Florence to the aged Galileo, lingering on in retirement as a "prisoner of the Inquisition." Galileo was totally blind, as Milton himself was to be ere long. The old man of seventy-four had been, like Milton, an accomplished music lover, a student of medicine and painting, a gifted writer. Milton, too, was to end his days theoretically in ostracism, precariously, a victim of the Church rather than of the temporal powers. Would that some prophetic being had whispered to the old man and the young man, as they sat talking in the soft Tuscean sunlight! "Youth and age," the being might have said, "with blind darkness before you and around you, your blindness is as nothing to that of those who will not see. Yet, fear nothing. In how short a time the light within you will shine bright and acceptable to all the world! A little patience. For you there is no time, only immortality. There are men alive today, Galileo, who will interpret your word; Newton shall be born before you are cold in the grave. Your eyes 'dismounted the highest stars,' the rings of Saturn were your prize, yet because of you, man will provide himself with further, mightier worlds, and in a tiny atom challenge God. And you, John Milton, may you know as you descend sightless to the grave, that twelve years thereafter the fourth Stuart will try to force (how the pendulum swings!) religious tolerance upon your England, and that, though this measure cost him his throne, yet, riding upon his downfall, shall come your triumph. You put aside your mighty Muse to travail, as you said, 'on a sea of noises and hoarse disputes.' But you pleaded for the freedom of printing, for Parliament, for the large religious view. And all this shall be England's and the world's."

Of that meeting, Milton himself wrote, "I have sat among the learned men and been counted happy to be born in such a place of philosophic freedom as they supposed England was, while themselves did nothing but bemoan the servile condition into which learning amongst them was brought. . . . There it was I found and visited the famous Galileo, grown old, a prisoner of the Inquisition, for thinking in astronomy otherwise than the [religious] licensers thought."

In that sea of noises, where from Milton's pen came pamphlet after pamphlet, whence came in truth the mightiest defense of Cromwell and of his cause, a flood of letters and

155

documents of state, there came also the quiet evidences of his compassion, the anguished cry also of the man, not the statesman but the poet, wounded by the inhumanity of those who wielded power. His sonnet *On the late Massacre in Piedmont* (when Emanuele of Savoy exterminated the Waldenses) is the first of a noble line.

If the Barebones Parliament desired the complete disestablishment of the Church (as we have it in the United States today), the words and the prompting were Milton's. In five great pamphlets he struggled for freedom of worship, as in the *Areopagitica,* he struggled for and won freedom of the press. These are freedoms dear to us; as much as to any man we owe them to Milton. In his pamphlets on the *Tenure of Kings* he justified the fate which had overtaken the sly tyranny of Charles I. Upon the execution of that monarch, a shaking-palsy seized the courts of Europe. (English ambassadors were run out of various countries, including Russia; envoys were insulted, under a hasty moral quarantine, much as the Russian diplomats were ostracised in 1918.) Indeed, England's stock sank upon the continent until, as was said at the time, "Milton's books and Cromwell's battles" restored her reputation. As secretary to the council of state of the new commonwealth, Milton wrote late and soon to preserve the republic, wrote, in fact, till his eyes gave out. After that he dictated to Andrew Marvell. All this was known to the colonists, especially to those who came back to England to share in the triumph of Parliament, who perhaps knew Milton or watched him pass on Marvell's arm. Later, those colonists who returned to America again and those who followed, like William Penn, to escape the last oppressions of the Stuarts, took the pamphlets and the books with them, and remembered the story of the blind poet, of the republican who was the incitement and the inditement (the spur and the saddle, as it were) of their collective desire.

Milton was not an isolated phenomenon: this was the century of Halley, Hobbes, Newton, and Boyle, of Descartes and Locke. Milton we shall meet again; Locke and Bunyan must detain us a moment; and, above all we must revere the philosophic and scientific temper of the age which dominated the English-speaking world. The works of the great writers of that day were read or rejected (and the authors exiled or cautiously honored) in the main by a few contemporaries, even approved perhaps and tentatively assimilated. But their accepted application came later, often a century later. Their printed works lay far enough behind our Founding Fathers to be—by 1750, say—no longer the objects of acrimonious dispute. Their broad latitude of disposition was by then part of the accepted intellectual mode. The eighteenth century was nursed upon the rationalism of the seventeenth. What shreds of the narrow scholastic garment remained were disposed of by the scientists, many of them members of the new Royal Society founded under Charles II. The theory and practice of scientific investigation accustomed people to novel truths, to novelty in those sacred spheres where only ignorance and ancestor worship had theretofore been dominant. Newton (b. 1642) and Boyle (b. 1626), in presenting new physical laws, in tearing the veil away from natural truth, presented the veil, one might say, to obsolete dogma for a winding sheet.

That this small globe of the earth was discovered to be far from the center of the universe, not even the center of its own solar system, may have dealt a blow at theological egoism, but it also conferred a greater honor in that such a minor planet as ours should have been visited with the splendor of the human spirit. We have learned since—from experiments in hypnotism—how intense faith and purest dedication can bring out on the physical body actual markings or signs of that ecstasy. Surely, it is a greater miracle that, through

157

association and faith, St. Francis could have brought out the precious marks of the Cross upon his own flesh than that an omnipotent God should have leaned from heaven and imposed those marks. Nothing is miraculous to omnipotence. The miracle lay in the power of love in the heart of the saint. Religion, then, was only strengthened by the discoveries in natural law. For the Protestants, the new truth added scientific charters to the legal and moral ones they had already acquired.

As some part of the seventeenth-century mind pushed forward in certain realms, elsewhere it turned back, with simple directness, to earlier truths, truths encumbered with centuries of dialectic. A poet, in prison for his nonconformity, searched deep within himself for sure knowledge of those things to which he could faithfully conform, and, as St. Francis had done, found them in the apostolic and communal teachings of early Christianity. In prose and poetry, John Bunyan transcribed his vision of a world where the last were indeed first, where Mr. Legality and Mr. Worldly Wiseman and Lord Luxurious sat below the fisherman of Galilee. In *Pilgrim's Progress,* Great-Heart says compassionately to Feeble-Mind, "I have it in commission to comfort the feeble-minded and to support the weak. You must needs go along with us; we will wait for you; we will lend you our help; we will deny ourselves of some things, both opinionative and practical, for your sake; we will not enter into doubtful disputations before you; we will be made all things to you, rather than you shall be left behind." In those few lines there are four direct and thoroughly assimilated quotations from the New Testament; and the emotional sense of the passage lies, as St. Francis also would have known well, in our Lord's solicitude for lepers, for the outcasts and the mute, and for little children. Nothing could better prove the absolute permeation of the Bible into every man's daily living and writing than the chapters of the most read secular work of its time. In *Pilgrim's Progress,* the collective morality of Protestantism found its artist, its prophet, and, to a large extent, its grace. As folk songs, when they travel to ruder climes and harsher circumstances—from Normandy to Canada, for example—lost their gaiety and ease, so also some of the gentleness of Bunyan, some of the compassion bred in him by the long years in prison away from his beloved family, was obscured by the harsh circumstances of winters in New England. Opinion narrowed. Apostolic and communal Christianity, within the Puritan stockade, set up its own intolerances and witch burnings. But the excess of the zealot was a transitory phase, whereas the true and burning zeal of John Bunyan remains with us even till today, among the dozen Holy Books we possess.

One last and great figure, before we rejoin the colonists. That figure is John Locke (1632–1704). Today, we know him through his disciples, through the eighteenth-century English philosophers, through Montesquieu and Voltaire, above all through Jefferson. His *Thoughts on Education* or his *Essay Concerning Human Understanding* are now for the special student. Even so, we must acknowledge that he fathered many a doctrine or practice accepted today, that he foreshadowed psychoanalysis, that he formulated much that is part of our tradition, and above all that he opened doors through which Franklin and Jefferson and Adams were to pass.

In an age of rebellions and extremes, the philosopher, particularly a skeptical one like Locke, is looked at askance by both sides. Neither Puritan nor papist rejoiced in a writer who disparaged those people who "peremptorily required demonstration and demanded certainty where probability only was to be had." He, therefore, passed much time in exile, returning to England—and to great acclaim—finally in the

159

accommodating wake of William of Orange and his wife Mary (in 1689). By then, England had settled down to a free press, to tolerance in matters of faith, to the law, written and unwritten, that the crown is subservient to Parliament and that the power in Parliament must reside in the Commons. In short, Locke returned to an England on the threshold of modern times, an England whose social and religious polity was the result of the labors of the artists and prophets, agitators and poets we have so briefly noted.

Locke was diverse in accomplishment. He was a theologian, a medical doctor, an experimental chemist, a political writer, and one-time secretary to the chancellor. To all these employments he brought a philosophic mind to which the only validity was the evidence of personal observation. He loved attainable truth for its own sake and for the good a knowledge of it could bring to mankind. He, more than most, loved liberty, but he had seen too many dictators, too many secret police, too many witch hunts, too much political chicanery, to credit the mouthings of all the self-styled guardians of liberty. Too often he had seen these guardians become the jailers of liberty. Political power, like religious power, was relative, conditional, not absolute; power, like wealth, he wrote, was a trusteeship. (So had Wyclif written.) He felt that no sect held a corner on truth which was beyond the searchings of free criticism. In his work we find the final, unhampered summation of all that had been thought before. Its originality and its daring escape us now, we are so used to philosophic freedom. Yet, as the sum of English thought, he became the rock from which leaped the speculations of the next century, speculations which were to become actions in the American and the French revolutions.

Had the rulers * of the eighteenth century understood the

* "Lord, ope the King of England's eyes," cried Tyndale, just before his execution.

implications and expressions of Milton and Bunyan and Locke, of the visions and voices of the seventeenth century; had the rulers conformed to the new truths and given rights and opportunities to the people rather than settle more obstinately than ever into prerogative, privilege, and infallibility; then the people would not have had to snatch those rights and opportunities, tear the world with two revolutions, and destroy, as revolutions will destroy, much that must be rebuilt anew. "The tyrant," it was written, "is first concerned to see that his *subjects neither wish nor dare to rise against his rule;* next, *that they do not trust one another;* third, *that they cannot attempt a revolution.*" Words of Erasmus; prophetic of the eighteenth century; and who shall say they are prophetic of only that century?

The English seventeenth century, which began with the Thirty Years' War, which saw the forced subjugation of Ireland, three wars with Holland, war with Spain, and war with the France of Louis XIV; that encompassed the execution of Charles I, the republican Protectorate under Cromwell, and the expulsion of James II; that see-sawed between the extremes of religious belief; that witnessed the early-Christian, leveling political doctrines of the Barebones Parliament as well as the pretentions of two Stuarts to divine right —such a century of contending opposites gave birth to the American colonies. It is to be noted that whatever was "left of center" remained steadfastly in the colonies. Though Charles I, Charles II, or James II leaned toward Spain, toward Catholicism, toward divine right, the colonies clung to their austere liberties, to belief in the reliable guidance of Scripture, and to a firm faith in the free spirit of man and his capacity for self-government.

Much was crowded into that century for England—much

which the colonies were slow to absorb. Occupied with primal necessity, suffering also from the refugee complex—one we are tragically aware of today—cut off from the graciousness of the arts, confined to the straits of a defensive position, the colonists were likely to be impressed by the manifestations of enmity rather than by those of benevolence. They heard directly the distressing facts about political cabals, but were too close in time to feel the happy germination of the two-party system, of the Whigs and the Tories. They learned that on the dread anniversary of an earlier disgrace, St. Bartholomew's Day (this time, 1662), the Puritan clergy would be expelled from every pulpit in England, whereby the Anglican Church was exalted to a position of lonely and upholstered malnutrition. But the colonists were unaware that England's loss was to be their gain, that many of the finest brains in England, because of that expulsion (as from the Revocation of the Edict of Nantes), would seek refuge across the Atlantic. The colonists knew of the troubles with Scotland, but not that the concept of federalism would be born of the union with Scotland. They knew that three Parliaments had stubbornly refused to disband, though long since unrepresentative of the people, and that from such irresponsible obstinacy had come tyranny, if only that circumspect and benevolent tyranny of the Protectorate. Yet that knowledge drew them into an even stricter observance of the obligations of their own town councils, under an increasing fear of arbitrary government. With horror, they learned of James II's *Declaration of Indulgence,* that spurious gesture of tolerance (which cost James his throne) whereby, in order to bring Catholicism back, all faiths were to be temporarily allowed freedom of worship. The colonists appreciated the ruse, but, despite the example of Rhode Island among them, they were not yet ready for true tolerance themselves and professed as much fear of the genuine latitudinarianism of Locke as of the fraudulent

162

measures of James. The colonies took things slower than the mother country and harder, but by the same token they held to them with more singleness.

In many ways England handed us the brick with which we were to build a wall against her or which we were to throw through her windows. Often in the next two hundred and fifty years—even as now—England would be ahead of us in social legislation, labor laws, penal laws, and in many of the far-reaching experiments of the mind. Yet, increasingly, England was caught in the compromises of empire and always forced to drag the club foot of caste, state-Church and large army. The colonists had not that limp, but could march toward their expanding West encumbered only by their finest qualities of independence and courage, by a few fundamental and liberal concepts, and by a rather primitive but infinitely sustaining faith.

Looking across the sea, back to England, the Americans could well be grateful for the gifts of the seventeenth century, for habeas corpus, for the acknowledgment of Parliament's authority over the crown and over the army, for freedom of the press, above all for the liberal generalizations (call it the temper of the times) or the philosophic and scientific assertions that were to bear such matured fruit by 1776. Reason and research were replacing habit and dogma. In matters of faith, Hooker had quoted Augustine: "To refuse the conduct of the light of nature is not folly alone but accompanied by great impiety." In matters of government, Locke declared that a healthy body politic was achieved only by those who lived in *freedom under a law to which the people themselves had consented*. And if we would find premonitions of a later day, we need but read a paragraph from Chillingworth, one of the Restoration divines. "Take away this persecution, burning, cursing, damning of man for not subscribing the words of men as the words of God; let them leave claiming infallibility

163

that have no title to it, let them disclaim it in their actions."
He found inexcusable those who "do offer violence to other
men's consciences."

So was the colonial twig bent: to Reformation and Rebellion.

The good society was not seen to reside in absolute monarchy any more than in absolute dogma. From the overorder
of the Tudors and Stuarts, men burst into the overgrowth of
revolt, from forced conformity into nonconformity. The ac-
ceptances and rejections were clearly signalled and the cleav-
age was marked by a scaffold. The group urge sustained a
veritable army, the Model Army. And this same urge drove
the Puritans to America, as it drove autocracy from the
throne. So urgent was the desire for the good life that thousands undertook the hazards of the sea to establish it in a
free land.

The very familiarity to us still of the words of Milton or
Locke, our sure acceptance of what they won for their own
people and for us, the present timeliness of the elder and
grand phrases in behalf of liberality, all prove how unified
amid all its diversity our tradition is, how few the great urges
have been, how forthright the direction. It is no marvel that
the colonists remembered, and preferred revolution to an
abnegation of their liberties; rather it is a marvel that any
people forget, and that vigilance is necessary to preserve the
light of our tradition which should be as diurnal, sustained,
and free as the light of the sun.

5. Revolution

The seventeenth century, through two rebellions, one restoration, and the ultimate arrival (in 1689) of Willam and Mary, of the House of Orange, saw Parliament triumph in England.

Two revolutions, again, distinguish the eighteenth century: the American and the French. The earlier creative minds in France, almost more than in England, gave the formulas to the American patriots. And, to return the compliment, the success of the American Revolution did much to prompt the subsequent leaders of the French Revolution in matters of doctrine, practice, and, above all, hope.

5.

By 1760 the American tradition is strong enough to take wing on its own. It was nested largely in England; but, to us, its deepest meaning lies in the new plumage it acquired in a new land.

Because our tradition was different, so our own Revolution differed from the Rebellion in England or the Revolution in France. Both of these ended in dictatorship; ours did not because of a golden handful of men, many of them artists.

The truly articulate ones among the American Fathers—orators, pamphleteers, poets—Jefferson, Paine, Joel Barlow, Franklin, Freneau, John Adams, Patrick Henry—were "full men," if ever there were such; and reading maketh a full man. They clung to the same fundamental knowledges as their Puritan forebears, but there was much more. They were the children of the Age of Reason.

In the furniture of their minds stood the huge *commode* of Gibbon, packed with hatred of intolerance and of clericalism; the wardrobe of Montaigne, containing a similar intransigence; the luminous chandelier of Montesquieu, hung with the crystals of his *Lettres Persanes* and his *L'Esprit des Lois*. The *chaise percée* of Voltaire was there, too, with the

167

divan of Rousseau. Every one of these writers, each in his fashion, had been a classical scholar, and each recommended a return to the sobriety of the Roman republic or to the intellectual liberation of Greek democracy. In their works we find outspoken or implicit the germs of revolt from the social, political, religious standards they perceived around them. All this vigorous material—this mental baggage—was bequeathed to the American Fathers for their use and adornment. And the classic revival in architecture (which we see at Monticello), like the French *Directoire* furniture, was but a timely and concrete realization or visualization of the longing for republicanism and liberty.

From 1726, when he was thirty-two and went to England to imbibe English liberalism, to his death two years after 1776, Voltaire made war on the status quo with the most brilliant polemic quill that ever served the causes of demolition.

L'Infame, the object of Voltaire's particular acrimony, was not the Church: it was the "system": the hung-over feudalism and privilege which lingered so unsuitably in the Europe of the eighteenth century. Laws no longer were apt to the changed conditions of population, work, or education. The mass of people knew it; they hurt themselves daily over the discrepancies. Only the privileged would not see it. In behalf of the victims, Voltaire produced his most sympathetic work. His defenses of Calas, of Espinasse, and of many others who suffered from the injustice of that system, remain as witnesses to his more noble instincts—as *Candide* remains a living masterpiece. That he turned and twisted, with little dignity except when it was offended, that he accepted decorations from Frederick the Great and pensions from three monarchs, or ostentatiously went to Mass—these evidences of an almost

168

cynical levity fade, or even are accounted for, by the fact that he had been exiled half a dozen times before he was forty-five.

Voltaire's hands, like those of Jefferson, where upheld, his work supplemented, by the genius of a host of contemporaries. Among them was Condorcet, who envisioned a future cleaned of the hip disease due to inequality of rights and freedoms, so that nations and classes might walk without limping. Like Aquinas or, later, Jefferson, Condorcet saw that general education was the means, the only evolutionary means, of achieving that future. Fortunately for Condorcet, there was at that time in office, as minister of finance to Louis XVI, an economist, man of letters, and man of sound heart, Turgot, upon whose doctrines (published from 1750 on) both Adam Smith and Jefferson drew. Turgot, for thirteen years the intendant of Limoges, had seen the horrors of the poorest and most overtaxed corner of a France in which famine was by then the norm. Upon the already wretched fell the added burdens of *taille* and *corvée*. The nobility and the Church were largely exempt. Turgot presented to the king a plan for the national economy which sought to reduce taxes by spreading them, abolishing the privileged corporations (the closed guilds), taxing the three orders (nobility, church, and commons) alike, instituting free trade, and, insofar as possible, basing all taxation—here he was a precursor of Henry George —on a single tax on the land. America listened.

Almost all the men who were to preside at the birth of the United States were then young men, in search of a doctrine, a political and social and economic birth certificate. They listened, because France was the foremost doctrinaire nation. But Louis XVI turned a deaf ear, egged on by the ever-inept Marie Antoinette and the financiers and nobility. The Old Guard showed whatever long teeth it had left. Turgot fell in 1776, and Louis inherited Necker and the

169

French Revolution. The Revolution was not what they intended—D'Alembert, Voltaire, Condorcet, Turgot—nor was Napoleon. They failed, they thought, in their own day, only to succeed in the following century.

I have left to the last the most effective and most addled of the instigators of the French Revolution—the greatest artist and the greatest bounder, Jean Jacques Rousseau. In a curious way—not by a frontal attack but by the back stairs, as though he had introduced Bellona dressed as a kitchen maid—he was one of the most immediately effective men who ever lived. He borrowed from Locke and coined a phrase. To him we owe the popularity of the *Social Contract,* the right of the governed to live under a government to which they consent. He was not a clear political thinker, yet he made popular the concept that the will of the majority (often bemused but ultimately right) *is* government. To offset the sophistication of his day, he glorified—and I use the Holloywood word expressly—the savage, the naked, natural man. This glorification, too, produced its effects on remote frontiers, in Africa, Asia, or the Americas, where the emissaries of empire were either leading savage lives or encountering savages. In spots, he appeared to desire a form of nationalism, compounded of the natural instincts for brotherhood and for religion, which may have appealed to Hitler. (Hitler, we know, was a reader of another artist-concept-maker's works, Nietzsche's, and doubtless enjoyed that master's reference to "Christians, cows, women, and other democrats.") But Rousseau did grasp at the connection (or the disparity) between man the individual, and man of the herd group; and he saw that upon the free choice of this strange, sapient man must rest all stable government.

With these ideas, and many more, Rousseau impregnated a diversity of novels, operettas, confessions, open letters, and essays as odd and as numerous as his mistresses or his occupa-

170

tions—which included being secretary to the Greek archimandrite, apprentice to a notary, apprentice to an engraver, teacher of music, secretary to the French ambassador at Venice, contributor to the *Encyclopédie,* exile to England under the wing of James Boswell, and incurable vagabond. Where Condorcet and Adam Smith were read by one or two, Rousseau was devoured by thousands; and, thanks partly to Byron, his fervid popularity continued into the nineteenth century. There is no better example of a man whose philosophy was not cogent, whose education was scanty and character weak, and whose economy was disastrous, who yet by sheer artistry, by the power of his imagination, became the source, like a hot sulphur spring, of the glowing enthusiasm of at least three generations—the revolutionary and romantic generations who substituted for the crown of prerogative the cap of liberty.

The other Frenchmen, from André Chenier to Lamartine —artists all—who conceived, nourished, and sustained the revolutionary spirit in their own country, do not belong in this chapter. They came too late to effect our Revolution. But their effect on thought was still vibrant and transpontine in the nineteenth century—our next chapter. The few we have so briefly examined do belong; they belong firmly in our tradition, by themselves and by the evocative power they exerted on the American Fathers.

"The exertions of Locke, Hume, Gibbon, Voltaire, Rousseau," wrote Shelley, "in favor of oppressed and deluded humanity, are entitled to the gratitude of mankind." I would go further back even and more emphatically, to ask: Who shall say that the world was the same as it had always been, after *Piers Plowman,* after *Pilgrim's Progess,* after Montesquieu, after Tom Paine? What they wrote is written. It stands. It moved others who since have moved us. Thought

171

is the *primum mobile*. And these men were the "movers and shakers of the world forever, it seems."

The years from 1760 to 1800—like a screen upon which bright figures move—illuminate, perhaps more than any other forty years one could pick, the successive stages in the cycle of revolution. The documents are copious. And nowhere else can we see so plainly the workings of historic laws. Here come first the prophetic agitators, speaking for themselves; then the generality of people roused from complacence to make the bold comparisons between things as they are and things as they should be. Slowly a group urge is born. Then come the catalyzers, the orators and writers, putting into memorable and referable form the age-old and ever-new aspirations. Later still, the group urge, become vocal and insistent, finds or engenders its generals and politicians. Lastly the artists return to select the beneficent residue and to hand on to posterity the matters cordial to the tradition.

Before we name names, let us look, in a page or two, at the colonies. In what condition were they?

Partly from determination but more largely perhaps from the bounty of nature, America escaped the morass of pauperism and brutality into which England had fallen. Tenacious, Americans clung to their liberties and even more to their habits. They accepted implicitly their intention of occupying an equal position before the town council or the Lord's table. Indentured servants became free, bought land, and were masters soon in their own right. Few lacked land if they did not lack the energy to clear it. Prisons were as revolting as in England; but the frontier swallowed the offender more often than did the cell. All travelers took note of the highest standard of living they had ever seen. (In France there was famine and plague.) All noted the free bearing of the colonials. Schools and colleges appeared like mushrooms, since it was everyone's duty and privilege to be able to read the Bible. Provincial and cocky, surely—but not squalid. And as to moral temper, there was a conviction of the dignity of labor and of the dignity of the individual which illuminated all daily living. This is not an overly roseate picture; for, though there was much to deplore in ruthlessness and slavery, the varied reports do picture a wide-spread community the like of which was not to be found elsewhere. "Newness of spirit" was here. As George Fox, the Quaker, said after his conversion, "The whole earth has a new smell." And some of that Quaker serenity—as well as vast activity and no small dose of smugness—characterized the conversion of the rough yet bountiful coasts into the land of the free.

There were, of course, vestigial corruptions and a few new ones, like slavery, shockingly peculiar to the New World. In spite of the theories by which men hoped to live, many men found themselves living under a system which was at some variance from the doctrines of Wyclif or from the ideas of Milton or Bunyan. The state of democracy and of elections was, and long continued to be, quite similar in some respects to that we may see today in countries new to democracy and to elections. It is often as hazardous to force a blessing on the ignorant as to foist a curse. Democracy, the most complicated political system imaginable, does not establish iteslf comfortably overnight. Every known form of power, prestige, and prerogative is naturally arrayed against it. We expect "free elections" and secret ballots and decent order—none of which we ourselves have possessed for so very long, and yet we are the inheritors of the only tradition from which such blessings can spring.

The property qualification for voting in Virginia just before the Revolution was fifty pounds, and a man had to show property of a thousand pounds before he could hold office. A large part of the population was thus completely disenfranchised. A few wealthy families controlled the governor's council, or House of Burgesses, and neatly combined their economic, social, and political powers in a fixed privilege. By 1776, there were more than two hundred thousand salves, mostly in the South. Yet, in spite of the feudalism of society—against which there were most vigorous and often bloody protests—there was an ingrained sense of freedom which went far to nullify the meanness of class distinctions. Religious tolerance was granted in England in 1689, yet the Act of Toleration did not reach Virginia till sixty-six years later. Paradoxically, the retard was due to the fact that tolerance had been practiced in Virginia from its inception— connived at, rather—and why make a statute out of something that would inconvenience the orthodox Anglicans? The assumption of liberality is one of our traits; often our laws lag way behind our practice. Our labor movement has been less revolutionary than most because all workers assume they are "free and equal" and will blame any circumstance rather than admit a doubt of their primary assumption.

When the privileged classes pressed too far, the colonials of the frontier, the energetic ones, the ones with their "primitive" faith and independence, joined with the disenfranchised of the coast to protest their grievances, and especially to protest because, having no vote, they had no place to submit grievance. A dozen minor revolutions broke out—the Sons of Liberty, the Regulators, the Green Mountain Boys—and some ended in pitched battles. But, if nothing came immediately of these, other than the burning of a governor's mansion, in time many of the abuses were corrected. The habit of protest, however, was kept alive, and only the want of some more than local cause, some cause which would overleap local barriers, kept the colonies as orderly as in general they were. That want was supplied by England, an England which through a series of world-wide victories came into possession of a huge empire. The mother country proceeded to administer all of it, including her old colonies, on police-principles. We did not care for those principles.

Up to 1760, the colonies had been or had felt themselves to be part of the family, younger sons, but still sons. Now they were just help—as though all the colonials had suddenly become indentured of body and soul in the household of an empire whose benefits and inheritance were not for them. The contiguous lands of the west, into which every coastal state was pressing, from which came fur and food, in which lay the hope of the million or more frontiersmen who had left the mercantile centers and had fled from the royal governors, from the packed benches, the grip of the large landholders, from the carriage folk and slaveholders—these western lands were overnight declared closed. England would throw them not into the colonies but into her empire. The economic future of the colonies was suddenly snuffed out, as surely as it would have been had France won the French and Indian Wars. (That we were not forever confined to a coastal strip on the Atlantic, with a huge Latin empire at our backs, was due almost entirely to British resolve and British regulars. But that was in the 1750's; and twenty years later our gratitude was considerably diluted.) The Tidewater gentry saw eye to eye with the frontier on this, for the rich had speculated in those lands, and their economic future was also at stake. At the same time, England cracked down on all carriers with her trade regulations for the West Indies. And, in tightening every link of empire—in a search for all possible revenue or, more correctly, for all leaks in revenue—she added the crowning indignity of interfering with the illicit Rhode Island traffic in rum. The New England shipping interests felt as put upon as the Virginian tobacco planters.

Further, the landed gentry had controlled the local legis-

175

latures with, if little democracy, considerable equity and to the general prosperity. Agents of the Crown were now to supervise all legislation. The Parliament of England was declared superior to the legislatures of the colonies. Lastly, the great planters were all in debt to London; the long debit had grown to millions. At a future auspicious moment it would be observed that independence would cancel the debt. It was a tempting suggestion. Even so, for all the debts or the western lands or the taxes, few of the gentry would have moved (and they were long in moving) had they not been stirred intellectually and morally. The aristocrats of the Tidewater were latitudinarians, high-minded students of Locke and Milton and of the Protectorate. (Jefferson and John Adams salted their correspondence with allusions to the republics of antiquity, to Thucydides and Plutarch, and to the early writers who composed our tradition.) And just as the great families of England, the Percys and Cecils, have always led the people forward to social gains against the massed recalcitrance of the plutocrats, *nouveaux riches,* and yellow press, so Richard Henry Lee, Jefferson, Washington, Livingston, Hancock, from one end of the coastline to the other, sharpened their pens or drew their swords in defense of a liberal transformation, of a forward movement which would bring the greatest good to the greatest number. If liberty and order were to be restless bedfellows, if the yearning for republican forms had to be tempered by democratic processes, few boggled at utopia. I think we can say that their faith has been rewarded. Naturally, for their pains, many of the most high minded were called "traitors to their class." It is an old cant phrase, doubtless hurled at the first Roman official who became a Christian, still in use, and usually nauseating.

Certainly, economics played an important role in the American Revolution. But a purely economic interpretation would, by leaving out the nobler sentiments, omit a large part of the truth. The Revolution was sustained by the forces which have ever moved the world: the might of piety and heroism, of generosity and justice, the desire for liberation. He who writes of tradition may not shun a preoccupation with glowing, but not glittering, generalities. The American Revolution was so largely compounded of intellectual and moral resentment, and of spiritual and social hope, that the values outweighed the means, the spirit outweighed the facts.

II.

The first voices are modest; we cannot maintain truly that they display any art. But it was these *Vorspielers* who prefigured the grand chorus.

Roger Williams we have met before—the noblest of the early band. (He died in 1683.) Often we shall find the moral judgment preceding by years the overt act; but with Williams to believe was to act. He could not breathe in an atmosphere of falsity; and the exploitation of the Indian and the poisoned bigotry he encountered in Massachusetts allowed him no compromise. He moved. In Rhode Island he lived in harmony with his tolerant ideals, dealing justly and fatherly with the natives; and he ceased not to attack the narrowness and obduracy he loathed. Before Most Holy God, angels, and men—he wrote—any persecution for cause of conscience was a foul, black, and bloody thing: "that is but Machiavellism, and makes a religion but a cloak or stalking-horse to policy and the private ends of Jeroboam's crown and the priest's benefice."

It is cordial to our theories to find Williams, in some four lines enforcing his quotations from the Bible with a reference to a Renaissance Italian. What does Sewall, in 1700, call his tract, the first direct attack on slavery, but *The Selling of Joseph!* And he drives home his argument with a verse from Exodus: "He that stealeth a man and selleth him he shall surely die." Perhaps all is grist to the polemic mill. But it is important to note that the grain is constant: a mixture of Holy Writ and, most usually, a reference to Rome or Athens. Primary, of course, in a society which is itself developing in a new Promised Land, are the quotations from the Prophets.

How near to a direct quotation from Amos is Wise's injunction to civil man to "make the common good the mark of his aim." As early as 1717, John Wise of Ipswich, Massachusetts, resisted the arbitrary taxes imposed by Governor Andros, not because the taxes were onerous, as they doubtless were, but because "the natural equality amongst men (the just and natural prerogatives of human beings) must be duly favored" and because government was not designed to "give one man a prerogative to insult over another" but rather "to cultivate humanity and promote the happiness of all." Wise petitioned the government to reverse the Salem witchcraft convictions. He was one of the many men who were as horrified by the burnings then as we profess ourselves to be today. A fellow citizen, in Ipswich, the Reverend Nathaniel Ward, as early as 1644, had compiled the *Body of Liberties* for the colony's general court—a document which was a handy reference for all future patriots.

As in Cromwell's army, the Bible was the mightiest weapon in Continental saddlebags. Pulpit after pulpit bombarded the congregations with the mercurial word of God—used by one side to uphold God's anointed kings or by the other to consign to eternal damnation (as did the Reverend Jonathan Mayhew) those who did not resist tyranny. Mayhew was our first ecclesiastical rabble rouser; he went so far as to recommend that if the common good was not served, then it

178

was the citizens' duty incontinently to overturn the government.

More sympathetic perhaps was John Woolman, the Philadelphia Quaker, who, in his journal—here we are probably in the realm of art—tells how he was trapped by his employer into signing a bill of sale for an old Negro slave woman, and of his struggle with his remorseful conscience over the transaction. Like Williams, a century earlier, Woolman labored for fair play in the treatment of the Indians, and for a general amelioration of the conditions of the poor.

With James Otis and Sam Adams we cross the threshold of the Revolution. With Otis we also meet a first-class writer. As an astute lawyer, versed in Coke's *Reports,* he argued that only those with proper representation should be taxed (though the actual phrase "no taxation without representation" was probably first used by his friend, Sam Adams). As a member of the Massachusetts General Court, Otis was in a strategic position to champion the commercial rights of the colonies and to break a lance in behalf of natural law as well. Into the lists, even were the cause a small matter of coinage, he managed to flutter a banner whereon Locke and Montesquieu jostled Abraham and Isaac. Never can it be said too often: that the intellectual tradition maintains itself, in a vital essence two thousand years matured, through the words of those who spoke or wrote *memorably.* The unmemorable dies, unsung, unused. The quickening word remains, that Otis may take it from the lips of Locke, as we from the lips of Adams.

Probably more than any other man, Sam Adams, the incendiary, set the train that fired the Revolution. Where perhaps Tom Paine's pamphlets saved an army, Adams' surely created one. Like most of the Adamses, he was Harvard educated—and well educated. He wrote endlessly—for the newspapers, as founder of the committees of correspond-

179

ence which linked the separate states-to-be, as author of the *Massachusetts Resolves*. He may be said to have destroyed the noxious Stamp Act with the blast of his invective.* And a glance at any one of his tracts shows him reaching back for sustenance or precedent not only to the ubiquitous Locke but also to Zwingli, Roman law, Blackstone, the Bible—the whole peppered with Latin phrases and some verse. No need to question Sam Adams' importance (or notoriety). When Gage sent the troops to Lexington and Concord, it was not primarily to fire a shot heard round the world, but to lay by the heels two fellows called Adams and Hancock. Adams was a failure in business, a bungling tax collector; then a noisome goad and semioutlaw, the wily organizer of the Boston Tea Party; and finally, respectably, the Governor of Massachusetts. Withal something of an artist and the most endearing of the Adamses.

With his second cousin John we are nearing the heights, nearing our examplar of the artist-politician. We were secure in Wyclif, More, Milton—no doubt there of the art. For John Adams we may claim that, in young manhood, his *Dissertation on the Canon and Feudal Law,* and, in old age, his letters (mostly to his ancient enemy Jefferson) reveal him as a master craftsman, capable of holding a vision and of communicating it.

All these men wrote and spoke constantly of natural law. The meat of it had come from England, with some Continental sauce. This natural law may be difficult to define, but it is not only essentially easy *for us* to apprehend its significance, it is also imperative that we should, since we have accepted it in accepting our Declaration of Independence and the concept of inalienable rights. Natural law, for us (it would be quite different for Asiatics, Berbers, Solomon Is-

---

* Franklin was responsible for the repeal, but Adams for the agitation which demanded it.

landers, Eskimos, Bessarabians, or any who did not share our tradition) might be called the distillation of the humanitarian concepts of the Bible, of the early philosophers, and of the Church Fathers as presented or colored by Wyclif, Erasmus, More, Hooker, Milton, Locke, and Montesquieu, and as embodied in the increasingly liberating charters. In the seventeenth and eighteenth centuries it was fashionable to term "natural law" what we might incline today to call "social justice." It enjoyed various presentations, from the practical and hard-headed variants of Milton or Jefferson, to the literary extravagances of Rousseau which inspired Marie Antoinette to dress as a milkmaid. It lives vigorously today.

A brilliant exhortation to the observance of this natural law as well as a workable resumé of the tradition of liberality lies in the *Essay on Canon and Feudal Law* which John Adams wrote as a young lawyer, more than ten years before the revolution. "Let us study," he wrote, "the *law of nature;* search into the spirit of the British constitution; read the histories of ancient ages; contemplate the great examples of Greece and Rome; set before us the conduct of our own British ancestors who have defended for us the inherent rights of mankind against foreign and domestic tyrants and usurpers, against arbitrary kings and cruel priests; in short, against the gates of earth and hell. . . . Recollect the civil and religious principles and hopes and expectations which constantly supported and carried them through all hardships with patience and resignation. Let us recollect it was liberty, the hope of liberty for themselves and us and ours, which conquered all discouragements, dangers, trials. . . . Let us hear [from every pulpit] the danger of thralldom to our consciences from ignorance, extreme poverty, and dependence, in short, from civil and political slavery. . . . Let it be known . . . that many of our rights are inherent and essential, agreed

181

on as maxims, and established as preliminaries, even before a parliament existed."

Here, again, is the inquiry into dominion, the source and use of power. Here, too, is that search for the natural right to counterbalance the natural taboo. Since we accept, on the negative side, that we are *not* free to commit adultery, murder, or theft, to betray, embezzle, or lie, there must be positive rights that we may accept equally categorically and that we are free to enjoy. Jefferson called them "life, liberty and the pursuit of happiness," adding that "all men are created equal," and asserting the right of people to overturn their government if it failed to enhance their life, their liberty, or their pursuit of happiness. By 1792, Joel Barlow (in *Advice to the Privileged Orders*) recast one phrase to read: "all men are equal in their rights"; and today we would say, "all men are entitled to equal opportunities" and we would add, because of Lincoln, "without regard to race, color or creed." These truths were "self-evident" to the Fathers of our country. To question them, to delay their application, to dodge our personal responsibility of practicing them in our lives, to distort them into a license to set up internal secret police, racial cleavages, witch hunts, foreign monarchies, or imperial cartels may all be expedient, even advantageous, but such are not Americanism. They are something else, for better or worse. They are no more in our tradition than Benedict Arnold or Huey Long or Senator Joe McCarthy.

III.

If one were to choose summarily a dozen examples of the artist in politics—without regard to the American tradition— I suppose one could not go far wrong by beginning with Jeremiah, continuing with Demosthenes and Cicero, then leaping to Wyclif, More, and Milton. After Milton the names abound. Should we confine ourselves to those who held of-

fice, we would come shortly to the two most happily effective
men whose art and influence have never been questioned:
Franklin and Jefferson.

They are indeed so accepted and renowned that I shall
consider them here only as the two most gifted among a small
group of creative minds which shaped these United States
we know. Franklin, Washington, Jefferson, Hamilton, Madison—no five more dissimilar men of genius ever undertook
by combined, simultaneous effort such a colossal act of mid-
wifery.

There were six documents crucial to the birth: the Albany
Plan of confederation; any one of the separate state constitutions (Massachusetts, for instance, wherein John Adams'
hand is discerned); the Declaration of Independence; the
Constitution itself; the Bill of Rights; and *The Federalist*.
These are, to be sure, state papers, not usually (unless produced by Cicero or Milton) considered as works of art. But
if a style which is always lucid and cogent, and a fervor which
often achieves incandescence and drama, are characteristics
of art, we may accept them here. Certainly, the intent of
these papers was to procure the greatest good to the greatest
number and to embody the prophetic injunctions of liberty
and justice into an irrevocable way of life.

In 1754, at the age of forty-eight, Franklin submitted to a
colonial congress—assembled in Albany to deal with the problem of French-Indian attacks—his plan of union for the colonies. It was the first effective expression of the idea of
federation in America. Thirty-three years later, at the close
of the Constitutional Convention in Philadelphia, Franklin
folded his capable, aged hands over his paunch and told the
assembly how he had observed for weeks the red sun painted
on the back of the President's chair; and that he now knew

it was a rising and not a setting sun. Between the two gatherings, the Revolution was fought and won.

As a boy, with but two years of regular schooling, young Benjamin began to educate himself by reading Plutarch, Bunyan, and Locke. At the age of nineteen he wrote a "Dissertation on Liberty"; in 1790, the year of his death, he wrote, under the pen name of Historicus, a brilliant attack on slavery. (This in a letter to the Federal *Gazette,* containing a long, fictitious quotation from an Algerian dignitary on the necessity of making slaves out of any captured Christians—who else should wait on table?—all in Franklin's most caustic and exuberant manner, with the relish of a man of twenty!) I cite his first and last works to show how perennial was his liberality. Also because his letter on slavery was but the last of a series of parables of which, along with Swift, he was one of the greatest masters in English prose. He published a fake "Edict of the King of Prussia," suggesting that Prussia, having once colonized England with Jutes and Saxons, should levy the same taxes on her erstwhile colony as England was trying to levy in America. He edited a spurious edition of the Boston *Chronicle.* And he invented any number of verses from the Bible (which thoroughly nonplused practitioners of the "higher criticism") when necessary to drive home a point. Balzac, it seems, attributed to him the invention of "the lightning rod, the hoax, and the republic."

This genial man—in moments off from his duties as postmaster general, as professional printer, founder of the American Philosophical Society, fireman, Freemason, or as commissioner to a Catholic monarchy, France, which it was his job to convert to the cause of some remote Protestant revolutionaries—found time to write two masterpieces: his *Autobiography* and *Poor Richard's Almanac.* I doubt if one could name a score of American authors who had written lasting works and omit the name of Franklin.

It is curious, also, to note that the two most brilliant diplomatic achievements of the age—the enlistment of French aid and the purchase of Louisiana—were made by the two artists, indisputably artists, among the Founding Fathers, and not by the generals, the politicians, or the financiers. Not by Washington, Burr, or Hamilton.

Franklin did not invent the idea of federation which he took to Albany; he knew of the Greek instances from his Plutarch. There had been a dozen leagues, brave attempts to make workable the principles of *par inter pares*. But nobody evaluated "par" equally; and Athens, like Chronos, tended to eat her children. Franklin knew too, by much reading in French philosophy and history, that from the fourteenth century on there had been assiduous advocates of European federation. Henri IV (probably to circumvent the Holy Roman Emperor) toyed with the idea. But almost always heretofore, except in Switzerland, the performance had broken down before the rival concept of sovereignty or before the batteries of egotism. Albany was too soon; and the colonies were not then free entities. But at the Constitutional Convention the genius of the Founding Fathers achieved the unique triumph of giving lively and compatible form to a government founded in revolution. Federation was made vertebrate with union.

In spite of Franklin, whom they trusted, and of Hamilton, whom they suspected, and of Madison, whom they did not know, the generality did not embrace the union with avidity. However, the alternatives were worse: discrepant laws, interstate barriers, confusion in trade, particularly world trade; the inability of the several states to cope with their own problems—with such unjust conditions as provoked Shays' Rebellion in Massachusetts. And in 1788, the federal Constitution was adopted. Almost at once it was seen to be a standard "to which the wise and honest" could repair.

Forthwith the normal disjointures in the federal constitutional armor were observed—the age-old discrepancy or tug o' war between order and growth, between inertia and reform, between the ease of the coast and the rigor of the frontier, between centralized government and states' rights, between the Federalists and the Democratic-Republicans. And, conveniently but oversimply stated, between Hamilton and Jefferson.

Upcountry folk had borne the brunt of Indian warfare. England had properly tried to tax the colonies so that she could use the money to maintain the frontier forces. But the Indians and Indian warfare were far from colonial legislatures, equally far from the comfortable estates of those who ran the legislatures. The frontiersmen were left to fend for themselves, and being without representation could not make their protests effective. To them, the seaboard seemed effete, a mercantile agglomeration of established churches and intolerance, of people who, by owning slaves, themselves neither toiled nor spun but were busy exploiting their class differences; a place of venal justice, from which issued the collectors of quit rents but no easy money. They felt about the seaboard exactly as their Puritan ancestors or John Bunyan had felt about London folk. As the Jews marched with the Ark of the Covenant, so the upcountry people moved west with the tradition in their hearts—Barebones Parliamentarians a hundred years after the fact, sturdy, evangelical, radical, riotous. Mostly, they were Scotch-Irish Presbyterians, English and Welsh, German and Swiss Protestants. Ethan Allen, Patrick Henry, and Franklin were their heroes; but Jefferson they trusted also, and he made the bridge for them between coast country and back country. It was their pressure which kept the first state constitutions in the way of more, not less, liberality; it was the echo of their cry which brought Jefferson hastening home from France to help lay the fire of

186

the Bill of Rights upon the cold and classic altar of our Constitution.

The people of the coastline had a logical tendency to cherish the similarities with the mother country rather than the divergencies. Carriage folk are carriage folk everywhere. The rich quite naturally know each other because they are the only ones who can afford to entertain each other. (That is one reason why persons of a marked caste, like generals or bankers, have rarely met the right people. They have met only themselves.) Provincial awe and colonial deference lingered on in Boston, New York, Philadelphia, Washington, and Charleston quite long enough to disgust Henry Adams. Long before Henry Adams, James Fenimore Cooper, a good upcountry man, had observed his fellow countrymen in Europe bowing (as Dean Swift also had said) before the Duchesse d'Argent, Mme. de Grands Titres, and the Comtesse d'Orgueil, and he wrote, "whenever I felt in the mood to hear high monarchial and aristocratical doctrines blindly promulgated, I used to go to the nearest American legation." Even in their prolongation to the American "academies," such attitudes were pertinent to a very small group, pernicious only insofar as our painters and writers and musicians were warped to a European fashion, and utterly outside the great disposition of the American people. If Americanism has, by itself, any virtues, these must lie in the differences from other national traditions, habits, and customs. The Tidewater would have minimized these differences; the hinterland clung to them and was proud of them. The hinterland was where the frontier was, a few hundred miles from the coast in those days; but as the frontier pushed westward, for thousands of miles and through a hundred years till it ended on the Rio Grande, the Pacific, or the fringes of Canada, it held true to the claims, desires, and intentions which

187

brought the Green Mountain Boys under Ethan Allen thundering from their ranges to storm Ticonderoga.

All those gathered at Philadelphia were in agreement that this infant government, this experiment, should be designed to bring the good life to the country. But who should exercise dominion? And, since there was much talk of rights, what was to happen when two rights came into conflict? If there was truth in the feeling that our tradition was founded on the Bible, classical philosophy, English common law, and a generous mortar of folklore, then was it not the duty of our government to exercise an implemented solicitude and to protect human above property rights? In spite of the liberal and guiding words, from Wyclif's to Sam Adams', it was difficult for the Founding Fathers, with all their brains, to find the answers. Their answers, like ours today, were perforce often inconclusive, haphazard, and frequently paradoxical.

The champions of man—Jefferson, like the later Lincoln—appeared to have imposed their solutions, perhaps because of their energy, their magnetism, their moral worth, or the obvious inspiration of their prose. Yet the nineteenth century was to be the most rapacious century our civilization has seen. Perhaps after all the very diversity of the answers was what Americanism is. We can find Washington, the conservative estate owner, advocating socialism, or Sam Adams, the contemporary "bolshevist," in his old age trembling at the proletarian specter. Dickinson hoped the Senate would resemble the House of Lords as much as possible. Jefferson wanted the least possible government; Hamilton wanted all authority vested in the central government. Today, the Jeffersonians have taken to Hamiltonian methods. Marshall, and the later Webster, were all for property rights. At one moment, Hamilton, in behalf of sound money, wanted to lead an expensive and untried army to capture Louisiana; not long after, that dreaded, improvident Jacobin, Jefferson,

188

bought Louisiana in the greatest, most peaceful, financial bargain to which the United States have ever been a party. The freest people in the world clamored for government interference and protection, and received it in the Tariff Acts of 1789 and 1816. Prince Henry of Prussia was asked if he would accept the American throne. John Adams was hooted at as a monarchist. Of such was the republic of heaven on earth.

Granting for the moment that the very diversity of the answers was what Americanism is, we may even so observe a trend, more than a trend, a sustained effort to lay upon the government the charge of an "implemented solicitude," the obligation to interfere on behalf of the common man. The Founding Fathers were explicit on the subject.

As early as 1825, the German economist, Frederic List, came over to observe this young nation, so free from many of the ills of Europe, so endowed with ideals and immense expanses of free land. He found a new economy, owing something to Adam Smith here, to the physiocrats there, to the wishes of the landed gentry in one place, of the hinterland frontier folk in another, to the merchants on one hand, to the farmers on the other. Concurring with the trends he noted, and highly applauded by our native economists, he wrote, "Government has not only the right, but it is its duty, to promote everything which may increase the wealth and power of the nation, if this object cannot be effected by individuals." So far with Hamilton; the government in business, and by *obligation*. Tariffs and protection represented "the government in business" by *invitation*, the invitation of the interests. George Washington conceived of government ownership by *equitability*. "Would there be," he wrote in 1784 to Richard Henry Lee, with reference to the vast grant lands of the West, "would there be any impropriety in reserving the mines and minerals to the Public instead of to

189

the few knowing ones?" In the last hundred and fifty years a hundred compromises have been offered. The mines and minerals and forests went to the few knowing ones, under charters of laissez faire and grab, with what appeared to be a minimum of government interference. But noninterference was a not very pious illusion, since, along with special charters, state money, loans, and subsidies, the government gave twenty million acres to the Union Pacific and forty-four million acres to the Northern Pacific railroads. This was interference with a vengeance—some of which was wreaked upon our forests and rivers. Chief Justice Marshall put the federal government into business, this time *by law,* when he removed the river traffic of steamboats from the jurisdiction of the states, and, by his decision, prepared the way for the Interstate Commerce Commission.

None of this is as remote from the artist as it might appear. The artist may well ask himself if a government which from the start was so solicitous of manufacturers that it imposed one tariff (always a form of subsidy, let us remember) so stringent that Massachusetts and Connecticut contemplated secession, and which gave so lavishly to the railroads, why then should that government not be as solicitous of its national civility as of its sewage? Earlier, into the separate state constitutions, into the charter of the territories, it was written that public education was among the first duties of the government. In fact, Congress ordained that in the new territories certain lands be set aside, tax free, for the erection of schools. In 1790, in an address to Congress, Washington had admonished: "Nothing can better deserve your patronage than the promotion of science and literature." And he returned to the charge in his "Farewell Address" (which was written for him by Hamilton). John Adams felt that "the revenues of the State would be applied infinitely better" and more usefully, politically, in the diffusion of education

190

among all classes than in any other way. The Founding Fathers, each and all, thought it becoming that the government should foster the arts and sciences.

Particularly was this true of Jefferson. More than any other he besought the states to assume some responsibility for imponderables as well as for imposts. He wrote Madison how strongly he felt that the greatest safeguard to liberty was an educated electorate. As a patron of the arts he knew what illuminated patronage could mean; as a creative artist himself he knew all the hazards and disappointments of a craft. A lawyer, he founded the first professorship of law in America, at William and Mary. A scholar, he founded the first great library, at Monticello; and this library included the scores of such music as was available, which it was his delight to play with his friends. We do not know if he played the violin better than Frederick the Great played the flute. But we do know that both found exhilaration in ensemble playing. In some ways, Jefferson was the most extraordinary architect his age produced—his principal creations, which stand in all their loveliness now for us to admire, represent but a hundredth part of his activity.

That he was farseeing in many ways we know. We often forget that it was Jefferson who not only induced Virginia to cede to the Union her vast western territories but also wrote in the proviso that the Northwest should be free of slavery. This alone perhaps, later on, saved the cause of the North in the Civil War. To the end of his life, he clung to one profound attitude: "eternal hostility against every form of tyranny over the mind of man."

He was not present at the Constitutional Convention—neither he nor Adams nor Patrick Henry. In replacing them, Madison reached a height of enlightened steadfastness he never reached again, and Franklin brought all his ancient

191

and supple wisdom to the reconciliation of old order and new growth.

Between 1763 and 1826, a new link was added to the chain of our tradition, probably the most important American link so far. To the inherited links of reformation and rebellion we added that of revolution. We grew mightily, and, from 1763 to the establishment of the Constitution in 1789, we grew in disorder. The handful of men who instigated the disorder, and then in the happy magnitude of their various talents set up the first orderly and workable democracy, is enshrined in the center of our tradition: Washington with his cherry tree, Franklin with his kite, Jefferson with his documents and buildings, Tom Paine, Nathan Hale, Paul Jones, even the enemy André. Never have we had such a group of leaders, of elucidators, instigators, prophets, heroes and interpreters. Never has there been among us a more pronounced group urge than that which welcomed the Revolution, sustained its leaders, and did not relax till the new link was forged, till the desire for growth was appeased.

We rejected all those things which the Reformation and Rebellion in England had rejected. Now, by our Revolution, to our inherited rejections we added those of empire, monopoly, taxation without representation, the theory of Parliament or Congress being above law, and the evasions of an unwritten constitution. We reaffirmed our acceptance of those hard-won liberties embodied in the Bill of Rights. We accepted the implication that a democracy to be successful must be enlightened, and that enlightenment is achieved through wide education. The charter of the new Northwest Territory stated that "the means of education shall forever be encouraged." We accepted, almost accidentally, a two-party system which was borne of our knack for experimental accommodation, of our effort to achieve order without the sacrifice of real democracy or liberty.

Compromises, divergencies, inadequacies were many. Some of our reading would lead us to believe that the America of those days was, socially, a patchwork of ideologies varying from anarchy to monarchy, cross-stitched by a few patriots and numberless crooks. Henry Adams reviewed the period with something akin to despair. Even so, we did weather the storms of the Revolution and also the more difficult and later rages of liberty and success. The historian Ramsey could point to the "beneficial effects which have resulted from that expansion of the human mind" during the life of Jefferson. And we may rejoice that we were led by men, creative men, of energy and moral favor—men who, having love in their hearts, had spurs in their flanks.

IV.

We emerged from the Revolution with new forms installed and old rights affirmed. But both forms and rights had little meaning unless applied to or exercised for mankind in general. By close on two thousand years of philosophical and religious training, our best men were individualists, experimentalists, cosmopolites. Such characteristics mark the intellectual élite of the three most civilized ages known: of Pericles, Leonardo da Vinci, and Voltaire. It was this last age which our Founding Fathers adorned. By an astonishingly small number of brilliant men, our forms were installed and our rights affirmed. But these had to be acceptable to a like-minded people who, if in general of limited competence in high matters of jurisprudence or fiscal policy or international relations, would have been quick to detect a fraud.

Obviously, the Constitution and Bill of Rights appeared to the majority as works compatible with traditional desire and hence acceptable. Further, we know that no such government could have been set up if there had not been a meeting of minds or if the same moral values had not pertained for leaders and followers alike. In spite of sectarianism and skepticism, there is no doubt that by and large leaders and followers understood each other on a reverential plane.

The persistence with which natural law, God's law, right reason, or plain nature were invoked in all our eighteenth-century documents to account for our actions and justify our deeds—many of which demanded no justification, some of which did—has led many critics, particularly of the Latin school, to regard all those in the Anglo-Saxon tradition (for this seems to be an Anglo-Saxon trait) as hypocrites. It is true that we insist on pious slogans; but are they worse than bare-faced ones? The Founding Fathers were in truth thoroughly imbued with the Puritan strain. They were Bible readers, deep searchers into their consciences. Anyone who reads the letters of John Adams or John Quincy Adams, of Washington or Jefferson, feels at once that, though these men were far from perfect, rarely have their equals been seen for moral fervor. Such moral fervor was expected of them. They addressed men equally imbued with Puritan ideals. Only so was the great mass of people to be moved, only by rousing their sense of right and of fitness. It was a simpler age: one of Biblical right and wrong. The sciences of expediency, economic necessity, expansion, these had not been named or currently spread among the people. It was still essentially a moral age, when positive good or positive wickedness moved men, and when hope was a more potent force than fear. In spite of those who would underestimate the altruism of those days, we may be devoutly thankful that the honor for it, if not so great a practice of it, persists in our tradition.

I do not wish to imply that the eighteenth century or the turn of that century was of a more elevated nature than our own (I think perhaps it was, but that is not my point), that there were no tares amid the wheat, that there were more righteous men. But their world was smaller and men knew their leaders better. All classes of society were agreed on a concept of reverence for the Christian God. In those days, people believed; they did not just have beliefs. Also, colonial solidarity was not dead, nor that solidarity which binds minorities—the minority of dissenters, of revolutionaries, of agitators, of the persecuted. As to the sore spots, they were indeed abundant. We suffered from all the diseases which breed, precisely, in colonial minorities.

Our tradition was forced to digest the progressive extermination of the Indians and the brutal lawlessness of the frontier. The isolation of the early farms turned sturdy individualism into bitter loneliness, and physical isolation into moral and political isolation. The rare gatherings, even on the Sabbath, became orgies of escape. Hard life made hard characters. Competition divided men into the successful and the failing. Even so, the Puritan faith followed the frontier. The words of democracy and Christianity were inextricably mixed. The faith and zeal of the Pilgrim burned out in time, but new interpretations and incentives and urgent revivals quickened the spirit and lifted the hearts of the people in recurrent waves.

I know it is the fashion at present to consider economics as the primal cause of everything, from Crusades to Grand Remonstrances. We hear of the "man of historic determinism," a powerless molecule in some inevitable wave of the future, where not even the undertow is left to hazard.* Rather would I believe with the elder Henry James that "history is a divine drama, designed to educate man into self-knowledge and the knowledge of God." Forces and factors and chances there are—even some broad trends or urges

* "Events with which history is concerned have been determined by forces according to fixed laws" (Am. Historical Ass'n. 1905).

(ever dependent on the man of free will) which I have tried to formulate. But I prefer to believe that man's destiny is in his own keeping; or else let us throw democracy and Christianity out of the window and revert to the awful concepts of Oedipus Rex, to the Erinyes, and to moral nihilism.

"Economic man," like "dietary man," is nonsense. A man is no more what he eats than what he earns. The Spartans and Socrates ate the same food; Pontius Pilate and Jesus ate the same food. Let us remember—as we move on to consider briefly a final influence on our Founding Fathers—that Tom Paine did not write "These are the times that try men's pockets" but "These are the times that try men's souls." If he had written the former there would not have been a man left at Valley Forge to face the winter.

In 1739 George Whitefield came from England, bringing with him the new word and the new song of evangelism. His friend, Charles Wesley, had just written, "I know that my Redeemer liveth"; another friend, Isaac Watts, had just written, "Oh God, our help in ages past." These and other hymns Whitefield brought with him; and when his ministry of thirty years was done, from Georgia to Maine the hymns were household words. The Unitarians had been slowly grafting, in good works rather than in faith, the altruism of the Carpenter of Galilee into the marrow of our land. Some fervor, perhaps, was wanting; and this the eloquent, rabble-rousing Whitefield supplied. He found here the powerful if reactionary Jonathan Edwards. Together they carried the revival throughout the breadth of the country. "The Great Awakening" was their work, and that awakening touched the years of revolution and the men who led our Revolution. It touched the young colonies at a propitious moment, after the austere fervors of the Reformation had subsided into the laissez faire of mercantilism, and before the colonies had achieved an intellectual stature tough enough to dispense with a crude revivalism. If our Revolution did not follow the course of the French Revolution to the sterile throne of Reason but continued soberly in the religious tradition of the Puritans under God, it is in large measure due to the labors of the Unitarians and the intense if narrow mission of Whitefield and Edwards.*

In Virginia, a young man named Patrick Henry used to drive over with his mother to hear the great preacher. In Philadelphia, Benjamin Franklin listened to Whitefield and, calculating by square feet, decided that Whitefield's voice, so vibrant was it, could have reached thirty thousand people. Franklin would not be converted, but he was the preacher's friend for thirty years and followed with approving interest the enormous impetus given to education by The Great Awakening. From little beginnings in "Log College" went out the evangelists to found a hundred schools and colleges— Princeton, Hampden-Sidney, Washington and Jefferson, La-fayette. And when Whitefield was dead and Franklin was an old man over eighty, the acquaintance of thirty years may have come to Franklin's mind in a moment of despair. The Constitutional Convention was on the verge of collapse. Hot summer days in Philadelphia and hot tempers had almost wilted the gathering out of existence. There was bitter rivalry, discord, and acrimony. It was then that the old skeptic stood up. "The longer I live," said Franklin, "the more convincing proofs I see of this truth: that God governs in the affairs of men. And if a sparrow cannot fall to the ground without His notice, is it probable that an Empire can rise without His aid? We have been assured, sir, in the sacred writings that except the Lord build the house, they labor in

* Note D, *Bach*, page 302.

197

vain that built it. I firmly believe this; and I also believe that without His concurring aid we shall succeed in this political building no better than the builders of Babel." Franklin then asked the delegates to offer a prayer. From that moment, the Convention took up in wisdom the labors it had set down in wrath. A desire to cooperate came to the members. And from their prayer came the Constitution of the United States.

To pass successfully through a revolution and to emerge as a new nation required of leaders and followers alike a common faith and a common hope. The common hope was to establish an independent republic. The Constitution would not have been ratified if the authors of it had written what was incompatible with the popular desire, nor would the leaders have been followed, through war into peace, had they used a speech which eluded common understanding. This understanding, this knowing how a man used words and what was meant by them, was possible because there was a common faith—a faith based on the Christian Bible.

It is for this reason that the revival has historical importance, as the revivifying of a common morality, the recreation of an ancient solidarity which unified the country in a common cause, when sects and cliques and castes could so easily have split the land beyond any hope of concerted action.

The power of Methodism, Unitarianism, and of Congregationalism is something no Congressman neglects. In its heyday, it entered into political action, through Hannah More, Clarkson, Wilberforce, or John Howard, to abolish slavery in England, to relieve the prisoners and insane, to lift the new horrors of the industrial revolution and to secure equitable labor laws. It profoundly affected the men who framed our Constitution. And all through the nineteenth century it inspired our greatest writers, those writers (whom we turn

198

to next) who led the causes of abolition and reform, who kept the transcendental vision before their eyes, hitching their wagon to a star, to what Longfellow was to call "the star of the unconquered will."

6. The Artist in Politics

In 1780 France was embarked upon the spectacular seas of Napoleon's dream. England was digesting the loss of thirteen colonies and turning a frightened eye upon France. In America, the new nation took stock of itself. It looked to see how much of what "The Violent Men"— as the conservatives dubbed Adams and the other Fathers —had wrought would survive. Or how much the Old guard's "fidgets, whim, caprice, and vanity" (as John Adams said) would tarnish the bright hopes of the New World.

6.

I. *The Risorgimento*

The nineteenth century was more openly rebellious than the eighteenth, and the artists took a far more active part in the turbulence. The great romantics were outriders of revolution, and entirely conscious of the role. It was they who expressed the immanent despair of the great mass of people who felt cheated of the fruits of the past revolutions—fruits so successfully garnered, not by the people but by the proprietors and exploiters of the new-born Industrial Revolution. It was the artists who celebrated the shattered hopes and kindled the revolutionary fires afresh. Hearty as may have been the misunderstanding between the artists and intellectuals on the one hand and the masses on the other, still it is true and vastly important that in the nineteenth century the creative artists did enter the arena and present to the lions of tyranny the shining trident of liberty, fraternity, and equality.

The ubiquitous revolutions in the first half of the century were largely attempts to fulfil the promises of the earlier revolutions: the American and the French. Implicit in those promises had been the sudden notion of nationalism, which began as a desire to be free of foreign yokes; the memory of social justice, which was incompatible with privileged orders; and the hope of a more equitable distribution of opportunity.

Inevitably, the cry for freedom and justice (which we have followed since the days of the earliest prophets, heard now faintly, now loudly) rose against a world which, at least in Europe, was devoid of equilibrium. As a reaction to Napoleonic ideas and Napoleonic armies, the several monarchies had fallen so far backward that their collapse was imminent. They managed to survive 1830 and 1848; but by 1875 they succumbed to the popular resentments.

In some countries the urge was to be free of foreign overlords: in Greece, of the Turks; in Poland, of the Russians; in Italy and Hungary, of the Austrians. In some, notably England and America, the battle for social justice was fought under the banner of reform. Italy longed for unity; only so could the ancient ruptures of Guelph and Ghibelline be healed. Germany, too, was tired of a potpourri of princes and demanded a centralized and representative government.

France—which we shall look at more closely later, since most of the poets and painters and musicians who illustrate our theme circled around Paris—enjoyed a more complicated role of desires. Eventually, the multiplicity ended in disaster: a second empire and Sedan.

Though Napoleon I had codified the law, preserved or enlarged many of the rights conferred by the decrees of the Revolutionary Convention, and certainly inflated the French national ego, though he had promised freedom to Switzerland, Italy, Germany, and to any other country he desired to occupy, his fall was the signal for a revolution against all he had professed, the good with the bad. Louis XVIII, in 1815, climbed to his throne through a White Terror almost as copious in heads and as arbitrary as the Red Terror. Not only did the restored Bourbons bow slavishly to the foreign powers, but also at home they sought by every means to thrust France back into feudalism. Government ministers employed their time trying to revoke the social benefits of the Revolution, to reestablish the censorship, and to hand all education back to the clergy. Large stipends to former *émigrés* were neither popular nor financially easy. Finally, when two renegades, Polignac and Bourmont, were chosen to crush the liberal workshops, the people rose and drove the Bourbons into exile. Thanks to the intervention of the aged Lafayette, the July Days (1830) ended in an exchange of King Log for King Stork: the ineffable Louis Philippe.

All the European governments watched this overturn with apprehension and redoubled those repressive measures which usually defeat their own purpose. Heartened as the people were by the events of 1830, they were to wait eighteen years before a new and more powerful wave of popular resentment would lash the breakwaters of reaction, monopoly, corruption, foreign rule and wage slavery. And, in those years (1830–48) when the mob was sullenly suppressed, when the armies made great show but no campaigns, when governments pretended that all that had passed was merely an inexcusable breach of etiquette, the artists were busy promulgating the formulas, the charters—one might say, the rationale of resurgence—which, in the near future, were to be implemented by the armed forces of Garibaldi and Kossuth.

In Italy, this period was known as the *Risorgimento*. Its roots go back to 1797 when Napoleon drove out the Austrians and founded the Cisalpine republic. By 1798, he had turned Rome into a republic; in 1799 he reached Naples (where Sir William Hamilton and his beautiful Emma held ambassadorial court, with Lord Nelson, also courting) and accomplished the same feat there. Short-lived as were these unfortunately superficial upheavals, they taught the miserable people of Italy several lessons. The Austrians could be beaten. Furthermore, the sacred words of liberty which Napoleon used, the intensive dissemination of republican doctrine, the brief reforms in administration, all gave the Italians a taste for better things and an indication of how to achieve them. The people wanted only voices to explain their plight to the world (and to themselves) and to provide them with the heroic leadership, oratorical but indispensable, without which they would never have united in one cause.

A book, *Le Mie Prigioni*, by Silvio Pellico, an imprisoned conspirator, roused Europe to a belated interest in the sorrows of a country which Europe itself had for several centuries cheerfully exploited. And the contagious exaltation of a gifted patriot, Mazzini, furnished the rationale. He was as effective as Sam Adams, as stimulating as Tom Paine. And in Foscolo and Leopardi, the *Risorgimento* boasted far loftier poets than our Revolution could show. In place of correspondence committees, Mazzini used, criss-crossing the face of Europe, the Society of the Carbonari. If anyone prepared the way for Cavour and Garibaldi, and for his majesty Victor Emmanuel, that man was Mazzini.

It is difficult for us to realize that Italy, over the centuries, was a land of sorrows. "The population, ground down by preposterous taxes, ill-used as only the subjects of Spaniards, Turks, or Bourbons are handled, rose in blind exasperation against their oppressors." What John Addington Symonds wrote of the seventeenth century was true till the end of the nineteenth. Tossed and victimized among Hapsburgs, popes, kings of Sardinia, local grand dukes of foreign blood, between Spain and Holy Roman Empire, Italy was treated by the powers as an international pawn. To the Italians, it was tragedy. As Gladstone said: "The negation of God erected into a system of Government."

The desire for unity was not new. It had lain at the center of Dante's emotions five centuries earlier. No great poet ever worked so ceaselessly, but so disastrously at politics. Dante had seen the faction, Black and White, Guelph and Ghibelline, wreck the free-flowering commune of Florence, murder his friends, and drive him into exile. As prior of Florence, Dante had defied the pope; later, he urged his own party to avenge themselves on his native city, Florence. Everywhere, Dante failed except in the one way which he could not live to see. For five hundred years, the *Divine Comedy* nourished in generation after generation of readers the longing for union rather than faction, for cooperation rather than banditry.

This same longing suffused the work of two other major poets early in the nineteenth century. Ugo Foscolo and Leopardi wrote poignantly of the disgrace of Italy, of her stagnation and degradation, cast back as she was into a Dantesque limbo after brief hopes of liberty—a limbo, alas, where the greedy malefactors suffered no agony such as Dante would have visited upon them, but where the usurpers seemed to flourish mightily. It was Foscolo and Leopardi who roused the intellectuals. In no country is it more evident than in Italy that the intellectuals, the élite, were the instigators and sustainers of the revolution. More gifted as writers than our own "tidewater gentry," though less versed in liberal law or the processes of democracy, they were the architects of a new nation.

The Carbonari, far from being akin to the Black Hand, were a group of aristocrats, intellectuals, professors, liberals, banded in a common ideal of liberation from foreign rule. Indeed, Louis Napoleon and the King of Sardinia were at one time members. All over Europe the altruists found themselves linked with similar vociferous minorities which convention and Departments of State usually feel should be tolerated, often admired, but never encouraged. If the Society of the Carbonari was more theoretical than active, more genteel than inspired, it did establish a climate in which Mazzini could organize a dozen uprisings.

In 1831, he founded *La Giovane Italia.* Exiled, pursued, he scattered the seeds of revolt for twenty years. From France, from Switzerland, from England, while the death sentence hung over him in Italy, Mazzini poured out popular treatises. He founded journals; addressed open letters to various kings, to the pope, to Kossuth, to Alexis de Tocqueville. He ran an underground press. He returned under amnesty to become one of the Roman triumvirate (1849). We must agree with Carlyle who considered Mazzini a "man of genius and virtue" as well as a martyr. And we may rejoice that before his death in 1872, Mazzini saw Italy united and free, when Victor Emmanuel marched into Rome, the king's sovereign city at last. Mazzini did not rejoice wholly: he would have preferred a republic.

II. *The Laggard Muses*

We have seen the poet, the philosopher, the pamphleteer —artists of the pen—bravely carrying what Heine called the "sword and laurel of the liberator." But there seem to have been laggard muses. What of the painters and musicians before the nineteenth century? I think I can explain their absence and also show that they were not total abstainers. The inherent virtues like the canons of music do not lend themselves readily to the uses of propaganda. The painters and draftsmen, on the other hand, have frequently held the brush at the service of a cause—usually, but not always, the cause of glorifying a patron. Let us begin with them.

Since the day of the *graffiti* scribbled on the latrine walls of Pompeii to the last fresco by Rivera in Mexico City, the power of arresting the public eye has been amply proven. A disputatious curiosity has followed new techniques in painting with more notoriety than is accorded the other arts.

The play is over, the music evaporated, the book closed; but the painting remains, eternally abiding our question. It may tell a story or point a moral. It may be quietly and intensely subversive (as, in the manner of Dante, the Gothic renderings of the Dance of Death swept prostitutes and simoniacal prelates or ruthless kings pellmell into hell). It may sneer; and you cannot refute a sneer. The most you can do with paint is whitewash it.

Medieval painting, and for that matter, sculpture—witness the capitals at Vézelay and sundry choir stalls—was astonishingly free with the private lives of the clergy. And I rejoice to think, considering the thesis of this book, that at Chartres, in the noblest of the stained-glass windows, the apostles are depicted as carried on the shoulders of the Old Testament Prophets. To be sure, almost all the surviving painting from the Middle Ages is of a religious character, but the painters knew their prophets and did not suppress the social implications.

With the Renaissance, the painter was no longer limited to religious subjects. (Saint Sebastian was the entering wedge; he was a saint but could properly be depicted in the nude and so demonstrate his creator's skill with flesh tints.) By the seventeenth century, the classic tales were well established as a font of inspiration; and the often subversive heroes of antiquity were displayed on the walls of potentates who must have ignored the implications of their decors. Plutarch is hardly Mother Goose (though she had political implications in her day).

It would be exaggeration to class Veronese with the dissenters just because he was haled before the Inquisition to account for his sumptuous irreverences. Rubens was definitely in politics: he played ambassador for the Spanish power in the Netherlands. (And it is pleasant to record that, at the court of Charles I, Rubens dealt with an English negotiator who was also a painter: Sir Baltasar Gerbier.) Lucas Cranach, on the other hand, supported Luther with an attack on the papacy, and Holbein's iconoclastic *Masque of Death* can have brought little comfort to the vested interests.

It is, however, the caricaturists and dealers in comedy who by their wit and wits evaded the censor most effectively. The "brass hats" have ever been mortally afraid to attack them in proper fear of reprisal. We must digress here to consider the scathless ones, from Aristophanes to Low.

In general, the deft allusiveness of comedy has saved the skin of many an author who, had he written in obvious anger and high seriousness, would have been flayed by the authorities. Where Euripides was exiled for impiety, Aristophanes —who wrote a peace play, *Lysistrata,* in time of war—remained unscathed: * Euripides, however, had pleaded the enemy's cause. In the last fatal throes of her maritime empire, Athens, insatiable, drove the island of Melos to war. After a long siege, the island fell, its men were massacred and its women and children sold into slavery. The following spring, Euripides produced *The Trojan Women.* It is the heartbroken, desolate cry of conquered people unjustly attacked and butchered. Euripides flung the loathing in his soul before the Athenian audience; and, at the end, in Hecuba's great speech, proclaimed that only through the artist, such as himself, could absolution and healing be achieved. This was too much for the archons. It is not easy to indict a pungent comedy but the tragic mask is vulnerable.

The artists of the Middle Ages were given to caricature not only in sculpture; they possessed a nimble and critical wit in their plays and poetry. Wyclif and Langland addressed a people not unprepared for the more serious word. The

* When the demagog Cleon tried unsuccessfully to trap Aristophanes, the charge of usurpation of civic rights was hurled at the playright—much as today our courts use the charge of tax evasion to snare the elusive gangster.

Wandering Scholars were nobody's fools, though they had to sing for their suppers and watch their tongues accordingly. And Reynard the Fox was no respecter of persons.

In the medieval plays—the mysteries, moralities, and early comedies—an author might be as ribald as Aristophanes, might flick the burly burgher with quick steel, might even bring the evangelical stories into Nancy Goodbody's or Pére Patelin's kitchen, but there was no tampering with orthodoxy. If dogmatic heresy was at stake, there was a mound of preinquisitional brushwood heaped around it. However, in that golden age of Christianity the words of Christ were still orthodox. The gape of hell-mouth, the contrast between Dives and Lazarus, the story of the meek who shall inherit the earth, and the examples of him who should love his neighbor as himself—these represented not only sound doctrine but also still powerful truths. And into the pageant on the cathedral steps, the Church welcomed a homely restatement of the Gospel story.

Like *Piers Plowman*, the most moving of morality plays, *Everyman*, was sharply critical of society. Though the protest was made more in humility than in anger, still, by its very piety and directness it leveled every human to the naked child of God, shorn of trappings, requiring only Good Deeds to lead him heavenward. Not through the *superbia* of Hildebrand (Pope Gregory VII), but through the meekness of St. Francis lay the road to salvation.

As we return to more modern times, and before we reach Hogarth and Goya, we should consider those painters who somewhat occupied themselves with grotesque and caricature. Da Vinci and Dürer must be mentioned; Callot and Brueghel with emphasis, since their influence was far-reaching.

Pieter Brueghel was registered as a member of the artists' guild at Antwerp in 1551. Whereas his paintings now occupy (after centuries of disrespect) a place of honor in our mu-

211

seums, his engravings are less well known. Great works of art they are not, but they concern us because of their almost revolting indictment. As Erasmus had written in *Praise of Folly,* so Brueghel, with deadly burin, drew the follies of mankind, of his peasant neighbors in particular. His macaber phantasmagorias spare no one, neither the proud who love not God and ignore poverty, nor those who "make ready their arrow . . . to shoot privily at the upright in heart." The glutton is represented by a drunken fat monk; a cardinal's hat perches on a scarecrow. Mammon gets his deserts in "The battle of the money-pots and the strong-boxes." With these castigations, there are also engravings of the virtues, Hope, Faith, Prudence, and Charity, tending the afflicted. Even in the gentler engravings, Brueghel's horror of bigotry, superstition, corruption, leads him into an orgy of unsightly protest. We may turn away in disgust; but we cannot deny the power of the polemics.

More decorous (and wholly satisfactory as works of art) the engravings of Jacques Callot (1592–1635) so enchant us with their dexterity that we might overlook the implications. In the series of fairs, there is the pomp of coaches and façades, but the beggar on his crutch catches the emotional center of the picture. And in the Miseries of War, for realism, Callot was surpassed only by Goya. Callot had been employed by the sovereign of the Low Countries as also by Louis XIII to celebrate martial triumphs—sieges and charges. These too are splendid engravings. But for himself, drawn from the very fields of battle he was employed to glorify, Callot designed the series wherein war was shown as it appeared to the common soldier, the sordidness caught in a few trenchant strokes.

As we leave caricature and the grotesque, we might remind ourselves how great has been their influence. Certainly, from the Reformation, on through an unseemly and hilarious flourishing in the eighteenth century, caricature itself

212

was a mighty arm wielded against the pretenders of any faction. That sundry prelates, the first four Georges, or both Napoleons maintained their state at all is astonishing, considering the virulence of the pens that depicted them. By means of the daily press and the handbill (clandestine often, or printed in Holland) the caricaturists rallied the defense of the underdog: lunatics in Bedlam, the diseased and starved inhabitants of poorhouses, the victims of corruption in high places, or the slave. Gilroy and Rowlandson and Cruikshank (like the later Nast and Low) practiced the caustic arts of deflation and asepsis, and became as famous as they were effective.

When we come to Hogarth (1697–1764) we find an artist supreme, among Englishmen, in three categories: caricature, *genre,* and portraiture. He wanted Goya's imagination and Daumier's compassion to be master of them all. As a satirist, Hogarth had no equal; this we see best in his conversation pieces—he himself regarded them as "dramatic presentations" —the celebrated series of moralities: *A Harlot's Progress, A Rake's Progress, Marriage à la mode.* These he first painted, then engraved.

A generation later, Blake was to search, not about him, but far upward in a noble attempt to bring us a report of the heavenly host. The fashionable painters (of whom only Gainsborough is truly estimable) were to celebrate their Black Masses every hour on the hour, as their sitters—with faces rendered whiter and more masklike by applications of mercury—trooped in by appointment. But Hogarth, his eye as keen as Dean Swift's, looked about him and recorded life with passion, veracity, and grandeur. Into the market place, gin parlor, gambling house, Hogarth sought humanity; and he engraved his warm understanding of mortal weakness or strength as he engraved his disgust with all that was bloated or pretentious. In company with a few other great painters,

213

who also were storytellers, his intent was to elucidate, to interpret people to themselves. "Which being interpreted meaneth," as the Bible commentaries said. He was probably the greatest English painter, and—shepherding rakes and prostitutes—he labored on the side of the angels.

When Hogarth died, Goya was already eighteen. Unruly, as handy with a guitar as with a brush, given to brawling (the rival religious processions at Saragossa were apt for fisticuffs), Goya took off for Rome with a band of bullfighters. We hear of him again, back in Madrid in his thirtieth year, married to a court painter's daughter. During the 1770's he was busy with cartoons for the royal tapestries and advancing in royal favor. By 1794 he had seen through the court and its courtiers and, no longer in the mood of elegant persiflage that created the cartoons but sobered by the first advance into Spain of French Republican troops, he began *The Caprices*. These aquatints, in their macaber introspection, separated him not only from his own youth but also from the eighteenth century and its decorative rationalism. With *The Caprices*, Goya buried the young painter of the ravishing *Picnic* (in the Prado), all sunshine and parasols.

The royal family posed—three Spanish kings, one after another, the insatiable queen and her lover, Godoy. All the while, outside the palace, Napoleon's troops passed by. They had come as allies and remained as conquerors. After nearly ten years of occupation, of war with Portugal and England, Napoleon showed his hand. Murat was directed to depose the king and install Joseph Bonaparte in his stead. The Spaniards rose; there was the massacre of May 2, 1808. Goya's royal sitters had fled.

To Goya, the calamity was not of crowns but of a nation, not of generals but of a poor people. In his magnificent *Dos de Mayo* the French firing squad is silhouetted against the white shirts of the martyrs—the central figure hurling defiance at his murderers. Almost as companion pieces to this great canvas, Goya drew *The Disasters of War*. For compassion, horror and hatred these drawings have never been surpassed.

To be sure, centuries earlier, Rembrandt, like Callot, had perceived with humanitarian eye the dark values of man's agony. But Goya sank his gaze beyond humanity, like a plummet, to the ancient anarchs of cruelty and pride. In his portraits he did not so much pillory the royal family of Spain as putrify it—as though he had stung with some bloating poison. First he stripped the crowns from royalty, then the *panache* from war, and then mankind itself down to the haunted recesses of fear. If, gazing at his earlier pictures, one could hardly remain a monarchist, after surveying Goya's last works one would be close to anarchy of soul. The Inquisition was troubled and Goya died in exile.

Curiously enough, another painter—not nearly so great, yet fine enough—David—saw the Napoleonic generals in a different light. Strange, because David began as a thoroughgoing revolutionary. He had been a member of the Convention, and voted for the king's death; he, too, had had his quarrel with the Inquisition yet ultimately became president of the Convention. The virtues of the Stoic, the Roman republican virtues of Cato, were those most dear to the late eighteenth century, in America as in France. Everybody quoted Plutarch. For David, who had studied in Rome, it was entirely congenial to turn literature and marble into paint—though unhappy for his art. Brutus, Andromache, the Horatii flowed naturally from his brush. When the heroic subjects of the *cabinet de lecture* took shape before his eyes in revolution itself, he changed the toga into a *sans culotte* and produced the *Oath of the Tennis Court* and the *Death of Marat*. Later, David was to find much in Napoleon which was sympathetic: an end to the bloody rages of Robespierre, the warm slogans of liberation, the Romanesque pomps, the superb defense of France against the massed armies of the allies, reactionary and rapacious. David painted a canvas of the fervid young Napoleon leading the Republican troops toward Italy, a Leonidas in buskin. Not long after, he was appointed court painter.

The return of the Bourbons threw David into exile. He too returned to his early traditional manner and painted *Mars Disarmed by Venus,* probably not unaware that here was an analogy with the sad state of France, disarmed at the Restoration. Few painters have so successfully crystallized the political enthusiasms of a people or shown forth in visible splendor the triumph of acceptable doctrine. In the best sense, David was the propagandist both of the French Revolution and the Directorate. Though his painting is now out of fashion—except for a few superb portraits—it would be unwise to underestimate his powers in moving the people of his own day toward liberty and glory.

A younger contemporary of David's, the medalist David d'Angers, was eloquent in behalf of the possibilities of a democracy. Could the artist, he wrote a friend, be happy only under a royalist regime "which begins by asking him to relinquish his dignity, and which grants the man of genius favors only in a courtier's livery?" "Liberty possesses an immense expansive force. Despotism feels the need of corrupting men to dominate them." And that he owned a really democratic faith, like that of Jefferson whose portrait he made, is sustained by these further lines: "I concede to no jury of artists the right to admit or refuse the work of their colleagues. I want artists as well as authors to have their liberty of the press, and so prevent their falling victim to the passions and the fashion of the moment. I recognize but one judge for the artist: the public."

216

Let us take 1804 as a crucial date. We may confidently say that from then on, throughout the nineteenth century, the graphic artists supported the writers with battalions of canvas. Delacroix, of course; Daumier, with his special Muse, an off-spring of Amor and Atropos, whose unblinkered eye dissected the hypocrisies of a callous law and a corrupt legislature; * and Courbet, who was on the barricades during the Paris Commune. He it was who hauled on the rope that toppled the Colonne Vendôme, bringing down the statue of Napoleon into the iron railing where, all through the Second Empire the Bonapartists had reverently festooned their daily offering of Parma violets.

If we come late to music, finding it difficult to discern any musician, unless it be Mozart, who before Beethoven commented with any astringence upon the social fabric of his time, the ancient curse of anonymity is partly to blame. We do not know who wrote the tunes that plucked up dejected hearts or set rebellious feet to marching.†

But if I cannot find that Josquin des Pres was moved by the fall of Constantinople or that Palestrina bothered about the Peasants' War, my ill success is due largely to the fact that we know next to nothing personal about either composer. Neither was of sufficient importance to be mentioned in ambassadorial correspondence or in the accounts of the Fugger bank. Furthermore, unless coupled with the subversive word, music by itself is not actionable. A painting or a polemic are there for all to see; they can be hauled into

---

* Daumier, one of the giants, was imprisoned for the caricature of a pygmy: Louis Philippe.

† The *Marseillaise* is a happy exception.

court. A piece of music is too evanescent, too ambiguous to be haled before the inquisitors.*

I chose 1804 as a crucial date because in that year Beethoven was at work on *Fidelio*, a paean to liberty at a time when the mere subject was considered subversive. And that same year, when the liberal pretentions of the emperor were snuffed out under a papal crown, Beethoven deleted the dedication of the *Eroica* to Napoleon.

Long before 1804, the power of musicians to assist in the toppling of thrones had been quite effectively exerted. It was said that the song *Lilliburlero* (perhaps sung to a tune composed by Purcell) had helped to drive James II from his realm. And it is certain that Beaumarchais, with the subversive ribaldries of his *Barber*, shaved the royal pate of France. In this work, Mozart had a preponderant share, for Beaumarchais' play found its widest audience when transmuted into the greatest of all comic operas, *The Marriage of Figaro*. The French Revolution was blown in with a gale of laughter.

There are several reasons why we cannot make a list of musicians (before Mozart) comparable to the roster of writers and painters. Some of the reasons apply only to music, some to all the arts. Anonymity and ignorance are two of the reasons. Another would be that the artist was rarely a member of the ruling classes, and therefore in no position to assert and maintain notions unpalatable to the patrons. What the artist thought in private transpires on occasion, inadvertently almost, to reach our perceptions through the magnanimity and humanity of the work, as in the frescoes of Giotto.

There are further reasons for the apparent abstention of

* Cimarosa, the composer of *Il Matrimonio Segreto,* was cast into prison and sentenced to death for having welcomed the Napoleonic armies into Naples. Cimarosa's excursion into politics was too brief and ineffective to enter into our annals.

THE ARTIST IN POLITICS

musicians from politics; and I feel the word "apparent" is proper. But before we discuss them, I must make plain my use of the words involved. The whole of the Introduction to this book was given over to the *powers* of the artist. Great artists have used their power greatly, lesser artists less greatly —till we come to those artists who have abused the power and so do not figure in these pages. Artists may cut throats; Gesualdo murdered his wife and her lover (which, in the Renaissance, was less of an innovation than his harmonic progressions). But what interests us here is the altruistic power of elucidation and communication. There are other powers, some of them good, some bad. Material power is the most often corrupted. Most political power is sustained by compromise. Of course, many artists have compromised (Wagner would be a good example); all politicians must. It is material power which corrupts, as Acton pointed out—and he did not qualify his famous statement. So when I would write that art is creative and power destructive and that, in an emotional sense, the two are mortal enemies, I am pitting the purest aim of art against the lowest aim of power. Permissibly, I think: for art should be pure and material power almost inevitably cannot be. In an age of dictators, from Huey Long to Franco, the statement seems reasonable.

Any man, the artist included, may with propriety desire power (in the ordinary use of the word); an artist is alone in wanting to use that power on himself, on his art. Material power, except in the procuring of some comfort and much time to work, is of no use to him. Such power has come to a few of the artists we have observed, but usually with unhappy consequences. In the main artists have abjured or avoided it, not as the plague, but as something that in no way contributed to their art. Too often that art was at the mercy of a tyrant's whim for the artist to desire a share in tyranny.

Those forces which, in their bare state and during the length of history, have been antisocial have borne most heavily on art. They have carried different names at different periods: pirate, horde, tyrant, robber baron, priest caste, slaveholder, dictator.* These have been the rulers of the world, the contrivers. They are the ones who have "thrust our high things low" and created those wrongs out of which the artist has had to make "an everlasting music." They were the ones who wrested the despairing cry from Joan of Arc: "I tell you that they have sold and betrayed me." With the levers of ambition or fear, it was they who toppled Leonardo's equestrian statue before the troops of Louis XII; they who cast Phidias and Socrates into prison, hounded Shelley, exiled Victor Hugo and Thomas Mann, and shot Lorca against a wall.

One problem of the artist has been to reconcile his life as a social animal with an acute sensibility. The artist has no time for political power or the exercise of it. Yet he would not sink into an abstention as politically unwise as morally unworthy, because his career has been contracted or enlarged precisely by the political state of the world he lives in; and as his art has been contracted or enlarged, so have the expressions and expansions of the culture of his nation. Too often the artist, despite his gift of being articulate, has tried to float high above all mundane considerations—as indeed he does when the bomb explodes squarely beneath him, in his cellar.†

* To be sure pirates and dictators, once secure in their ill-gotten gains and respectable, have subsidized any artists who could add to their glory.

† Holding office is another matter. The Latin nations, far more than the Germanic or northern nations, have not, in the choice of ambassadors, clung as exclusively to enriched stockbrokers or executives of oil companies. Many a statesman and politician of high rank in Latin America won his first notability through being an excellent poet or novelist. His government made use of his gift, aware of the obvious fact that a man who is lucid and persuasive with his pen probably has a lucid and persuasive mind. Munoz

Until late, the cold shoulder which politics has usually offered the artist has often met with a glacial reciprocity. Yet the artist, more than any man, is affected by the conditions that surround him and, as much as any man, through his gift of presentation, could ameliorate those conditions and bend them to his need. His freedom and livelihood are perpetually at stake. A banker can flourish in any civilization that tolerates banks. Not so the artist or scientist. To flourish he must not be tolerated: he must be cherished. The source of the money that keeps him alive is of extreme importance to him. Essentially, he works not for himself but for others; the demands of those others have control over him, sometimes remote but always actual. And that control may be a contamination.

In spite of his need for serenity, or at least for the quiet essential to contemplation—the uninterrupted hours of gathering his thoughts—the artist has been forced to react, to protest. He has done so as an obligation, for agitation is provocative as well as inconvenient. Since perturbers are the mortal enemy of the status quo, their lot is not wrapped in velvet. Yet, more than all others, the agitator has advanced the world. His name is various: Akhnaton, Jesus, Rousseau, Samuel Adams. Even so, there have been times, such as the nineteenth century which we now examine, when the writers and musicians and painters strong in numbers and zeal, have manned the barricades of righteous anger and frequently achieved exile as a reward. And we might remember that the nineteenth century was amazingly appreciative of its artists, perhaps for the very reason that the artists did express a deep solicitude for the rest of mankind.

Marin of Puerto Rico, perhaps the leading Latin American statesman, achieved early acclaim as a poet. Paderewski was a brilliant example of the "artist in politics." *NOT SO —*

Throughout the nineteenth century, our State Department made enlightened use of artists as ambassadors—an abandoned practice.

No one would recommend that an artist throw down his tools and rush into politics; nor would an artist welcome the intrusion of politicians. No musician could relish having to bend to a new prudence every hour; and if that is temporarily the case today in Russia, Russian art will be in as sorry straits as Nazi art. On the contrary, freedom is the artist's essential—freedom and equity. For these two the artist should be vigilant, and, if need be, prepared to struggle. In the private realms not controlled by law or custom, but in that no-man's land which is a man's personal discretion, a realm where he is damned or saved by senses of value and obligation, his latitude of responsibility is enormous. The power of the artist over the multitude is no more to be neglected than the power of the multitude over the artist is to be abused.

III. *The Romantics*

Paris was the haven of all those whom the Bourbons or Louis Philippe did not themselves send into exile.

Chopin was there, in communion with the exiled Mickiewicz, the poet and agitator, the voice of Poland appealing to the nations from her partitioned agony. In 1830, the kingdom of Poland was reduced to a Russian province; in 1848 the last scrap of Poland fell to Austria. The next year, Chopin died. Charged with the perennial sorrows of his country, his frail genius had sublimated the greater part of his work into one national lamentation; but the strength of that exquisite sensibility could carry him only to the piano, not out into the arena. About him, many of his friends were on the barricades, and the woman he loved was their prophet.

Those barricades lay across Europe. In Italy, Mazzini was biding in prison, to escape later into France, where he founded the association of Young Europe and became the friend and biographer of George Sand. Manzoni, with poems, plays, and novels, was harassing the hated Austrian rule. It was for him that, years later, Verdi wrote the *Requiem*— Verdi, the good liberal, whose libretti, in their day, were chosen often with an eye to politics, and which the authorities sometimes had to warp into conformity. In Germany, Schumann was refusing to serve in the civic guard which the government called out to quell the Dresden revolution and was railing at all academic dominance and authoritarian stupidity. There in Germany we must pause before returning to Paris with Wagner.

The dying past and the burgeoning future meet, almost with a chuckle, in the account of the Duke of Württemberg who imprisoned the army doctor of the garrison at Stuttgart, young Herr Schiller, because he had skipped to a neighboring town to witness one of his own plays. Perhaps it was more than absence without leave, for *Die Raüber* and *Don Carlos* were loud with the cry for political and intellectual freedom. To the end, Schiller remained the outspoken pupil of Rousseau, and his last play, *Wilhelm Tell,* was the first to make the plain people of a land the hero, and to take the liberation of that people from tyranny as its majestic theme. For all the talk of liberty (which naturally had provoked an equally strong reaction from those whose prerogatives were endangered) Schiller's was an act of courage in those days. Particularly as he depended upon princes for his livelihood.

Wagner would never admit that he depended on anybody, though he made demands on everybody and accepted their munificence, including Ludwig's, with condescension if not with grace. He fancied himself a whole torchlight procession: defiant of existent regimes in politics, music, drama, as in family life. Where many an artist has been content to let his protest against coercion remain in the realm of personal

223

complaint, Wagner inflated every idea and emotion he possessed and exhibited them to the world.

In some haste, he left Dresden in 1849. He had been a young and successful *Hofkapellmeister;* yet he wrote a strong letter to the king in behalf of the downtrodden people and, with Bakunin, the philosophic anarchist, threw in his lot with the revolutionaries. The gesture cost him his job. He fled from the Dresden Opera in one direction (to find Liszt) while the king of Saxony fled in another. Prussian soldiery came and restored the king; Wagner prudently remained in exile, first to Paris, then mostly in Switzerland, whence he published a pamphlet entitled *Art and Revolution* and various other radical letters.*

In the main, it would seem that whatever agitations occupied him, Wagner's intention was to stir up the waters to propel his own barque. However, he could not but have seen the universal misery, the new servitude of the multitudes to an as yet uncontrolled machine. Bernard Shaw is certain that some of Wagner's social indignation was poured into the *Ring*—at least up to the point where he dropped all allegory and plumped for grand opera, in *Götterdämmerung. Das Rheingold* is then important philosophically if we agree with Shaw that the Nibelungen represented the new and present slaves of the machine. Their home was Manchester, too; and the appeasements and connivance of Wotan, to hold his empire *status in quo,* were the foreshadowings of later sons of Manchester.

Wagner made three trips to Paris during his lifetime: The

* When he hurried from Dresden, he was not unaccompanied. In his pocket was the score of *Lohengrin,* and with him was a young fellow named Heine. (No relation of the poet, this Heine achieved an otherwise distinguished career. From Wagner's side, he traveled to America, was made a general in our Civil War, and, by his marriage to a New England lady, became the grandfather of Putzi Hanfstaengl.)

first time at the age of twenty-six, with *Rienzi* in his pocket. The second was on his flight from Dresden. And the last, in 1861, when *Tannhäuser* was whistled off the stage. By then, Wagner's revolutionary fires had burned down. The burgeoning power of a centralized Germany was something Wagner could use. And he lived long enough to see the Bismarck-Wotans and the Krupp-Alberichs in the saddle. Bakunin was in prison.

Undoubtedly, at this time, one of the most extraordinary artists in France was Lamartine. Extraordinary in that he was one of the finest French poets yet a vain and foolish politician. At first a royalist he became a revolutionary whose eloquence revived the principles of 1830. By 1848 he was minister for foreign affairs and one of the five members of the Executive Committee of the new republic. Though he was not fitted for administrative posts and failed in office; though his poetry declined in favor even during his lifetime, yet for some memorable years he was the high-minded orator of the new order and his words crossed the ocean to become the bible of the Latin American reformers.

Eighteen forty-eight, more than 1830, had repercussions the world over. In Chile, an ardent disciple of Lamartine, Francisco Bilbao, organized the *Sociedad de Igualidad*. From the Argentine to Mexico the popular cry went up for a reform of the social order. As usual, once the armed idealists had freed their lands from the despotism of Spanish viceroys, the people saw the administrative, the military, and the ecclesiastic—in short, the expedient and lucrative—plums snatched by oligarchs whose unscrupulousness was matched only by the skill of their contrivances. From the moment when the Bolivars and San Martins had accomplished their liberations, the landowners moved back and the social gains briefly won were withdrawn in the name of "order" and nationalism.*

In France it was the same. Lamartine, like Victor Hugo, was a moderate republican: he quelled the mob by his eloquence one minute and the next lost the support of the bourgeoisie when he attacked monopolies, tried to reform the finances or extend the franchise and ameliorate the lot of the workers. The left and the right repudiated him. Liberty became the privilege to oppress; the trumpets of freedom from foreign yoke became the brass of nationalism. Where the romantics would have a republic of moral values rather than of clericalism, of idealism rather than expediency, of justice supported by power, the opposition, of left or right, sought only to possess and to exploit. The immediate catastrophe was the election of Louis Napoleon as president. "When the conspiring forces of clerical venality and political prostitution had placed a putative Bonaparte in power attained by perjury after perjury and supported by massacre after massacre," as Swinburne wrote, the political hour of the poets was over. Hugo went into an exile of twenty years. The suppression of any beneficent socialism opened the door to the ultimate Marx; the seizure of power for the purposes of nationalistic and personal glorification showed the inevitable way to Hitler.

The poets of an earlier day had aspired to a similar altruism.

It is true that we are called a democracy because the administration is in the hands of the many and not of the few. But while the law secures equal justice to all alike in their private disputes, the claim of excellence is also recognized; and when a citizen is in any way distinguished, he is preferred to the public service, not as a matter of privilege but

* James Fenimore Cooper and William Cullen Bryant were among the most ardent supporters of the revolutions in South America.

as the reward of merit. Neither is poverty a bar, but a man may benefit his country whatever be the obscurity of his condition. There is no exclusiveness in our public life. . . . We are lovers of the beautiful, yet simple in our tastes. . . . To avow poverty with us is no disgrace; the true disgrace is in doing nothing to avoid it. . . . We alone regard a man who takes no interest in public affairs, not as a harmless, but as a useless, character. . . .

Such was Pericles' vision of Athens.* And it is probably a pity that the realization of that vision has not been more permanently entrusted to the artists. Certainly Pericles was more "practical" than the oligarchs who overreached themselves; Jefferson more reasonable than Aaron Burr; Lamartine and Hugo more truly prophetic of the future than Louis Napoleon.

However, the creative élan of the artists, from 1830 to 1850, announced and disseminated the ideas and ideals by which we now profess to live, or, at least, to hope. And, as we look at Paris in those years, we must realize that the artists themselves had not the foresight to despair.

Delacroix had painted a huge canvas, in 1826, depicting *Greece Lamenting on the Ruins of Missolonghi* and, what is more, exhibited it, at a modest entrance fee, for the benefit of the patriots. Liszt was writing in the *Gazette Musicale,* "Away with you, carriage trade; be off, Aristos of the Stock Exchange; the artist who feels the dignity and grandeur of his mission has nothing to say to you. . . ." Thus was the thumb blithely at the nose. It was safe to lament the lost liberties of Greece or to lampoon the terrible Turk, even if one gave him rather Bourbonesque features. Theophile Gautier wore a pink waistcoat for the opening night of *Hernani,* to show his sympathy with a playwright whose

* *Thucydides,* Jowett, tr.

works were generally frowned upon by the court because of the unflattering light they cast on royalty. The subject and the waistcoat caused a splendid riot.

Berlioz, of course, found himself continually at war with directors, with critics, with the public. His view of bureaucracy could be summed up in Barthe's verse:

> Rien pour l'auteur de la musique.
> Pour l'auteur du poéme, rien . . .
> Le frivole obtient tout:
> L'or, les cordons, la crosse.
> Rameau dut aller à pied—
> Les directeurs en carrosse.

If Berlioz did not throw his hat over the mill, he did throw his music into the fight. He arranged melodies for the revolutionaries—indicating choral passages not for the conventional soprano, alto, tenor or bass, but for "everything that has a voice, a heart, and blood in its veins"—and wrote his great *Requiem* for those who fell. (The death of reactionaries never seems particularly provocative of noble music.) Actually, Berlioz was an artistic reformer, not so much a social revolutionary as one who wished to drive the money changers from his temple.

Curiously enough one of the artistic catalysts of the romantic-revolutionary ferment was Franz Liszt, whose republican ardor was rooted in a large altruism and Christian piety rather than in the egocentric mysticism of Wagner. His ardor was also stimulated by a close companionship with the founders or students of European socialism, Saint-Simon, Lamennais, and Comte, whose doctrines or systems were to find their way into every home through the later novels of George Sand.

In the 1820's, the prodigious young Franz was smarting

228

from the condescension of the Esterhazys and from the wrath of the Comte de Saint-Crique who had ejected him by the back door. His own immediate, phenomenal success on the concert platform or in the salon did not in any way lessen his apprehension of the disequilibrium of society, the incredible misery of the people, the insolent neglect or the meager rewards of the gifted leaders of science and art. Indeed, his own success propelled him to an eminence from which he could observe with freedom and clarity the backs (and backyards) of a society prostrate at his feet. And against that *a posteriori* and shocking spectacle—of a world divided into a few lonely men of talent, a ruling caste that appeared, by the Bourbon restoration, to have lost none of its powers or pretensions, and the great mass of people who had achieved some liberty in politics only to be reincarcerated by the machine—Liszt sought a weapon of protest. He sought it first, and always, in the effort to ameliorate; but, not being a writer or orator or a man of practical power, he was increasingly aware of his impotence. He sought that weapon through his own, peculiar talent, and through the example of his own life. One of his early, revolutionary pieces bears the motto, "Live working or die fighting," which was the slogan of the striking workers of Lyons.

Actually, by his very heterogeneous curiosity, Liszt achieved a vicarious effectiveness of which he was largely unaware. His warmth of heart precipitated what his brain could not command. And, more curiously, he achieved his effect through a woman, George Sand, whose lover he never was, a woman not given to taking practical advice.

The young pianist-composer met the young novelist, *la femme la plus 'forte' (dans le sens biblique)*, as he called her, through Alfred de Musset, who took him to her salon, in October 1834. All three, at that first meeting, eyed each other with some skepticism, some awareness of future rivalry or infringement. Though Liszt and George Sand were never lovers, she considered the possibilities. "Could I have fallen in love with him, out of anger, I would have done so," she wrote. "But I couldn't. I should hate to like spinach because, if I liked it I should eat it, *et je ne puis pas le souffrir.*" Already, in *Valentine,* George Sand had published a novel dear to the son of Adam Liszt, the erstwhile keeper of a princely sheepfold. There, the novelist had drawn the acid portrait of a fatuous nobility in contrast to that of the young genius of humble origin: the aristocracy of talent. For all her contempt for that of birth, Sand, conforming to the prejudices of her day, saw no happy ending and had to let the genius die. After meeting Liszt, and fortified by his example, the lady of high degree, Fiamma, heroine of her next romance, *Simon,* rejected the marquis to marry Simon, in whose veins ran not the liquefaction of coronets but the red blood of talent. George Sand's debt to Liszt was to be even greater.

At that time—of which Liszt wrote, "The Kings depart, but God remains and the people stir"—the Encyclopedic criticisms of the eighteenth century were beginning to be assembled or warped into political theories. Upon the foundations of the Encyclopedists, of Voltaire, and of the French and American revolutions, the thoughtful were attempting to build anew. Among the first was Saint-Simon (1760–1825) who desired a socialist government entirely in the hands of the eminent: the artists, the scientists, the industrialists. That was but a hundred and fifty years ago; and these last twenty years have shown that Saint-Simon's program was not all compound of idle imaginings. His aim "to reward each according to his merit" has a contemporary ring. And his practical assurance that the chief preoccupation of sound politics should be "the moral, intellectual, and physical amelioration of the people, the most numerous and the poorest" is not unsound doctrine today. A man of far greater system, Comte,

230

decrusted the robust core of Saint-Simon from its elabora-
tions and set the firm structure of socialism against which
the subsequent Owen and George and Marx have leaned. If
their attitude seems now to partake of the inclination of the
Tower of Pisa, it was not so in those times. Between Saint-
Simon and Comte came the Abbé Lamennais, more sympathetic and eloquent, more spiritually imaginative than the
theorists, to whose benign and fluid Christian socialism Liszt
responded immediately. In Lamennais' trilogy of powers,
with science and industry, the creative artist was to have preponderance as the prophet of God. To this political creed,
Liszt could give his whole enthusiasm.

Lamennais was one of the most attractive figures of the
period, in his personal influence not unlike the Abbé Dimnet
or Jacques Maritain today. Lamennais had been the darling
of the Church, only to break with the hierarchy over his
antipathy toward monarchical intrigues, and by publishing
his *Paroles d'un Croyant.* Less than a month later he met
Liszt. To him, Liszt could turn from the discouragement
with which he viewed his fellow artists, such as were sunk in
their convenient indifference to any social or spiritual problems at the lucrative behest of their patrons. From Lamennais, Listz received a rationale of art, of the artist's duty as
the interpreter and elucidator of social justice. After all,
Fra Angelico could not have conceived of painting except
for "the cause"—and who shall say that his art suffered
thereby? From Lamennais, also, the musician learned the
temperate balance and communion between art and religion,
between which, heretofore, Liszt's soul had been torn. And
it was to the Abbé, to one of his delicious and inspiring eve-
nings, that Liszt conducted George Sand, exhausted and
empty from the violent aftermath of her life with Musset
and ready for a spiritual awakening, a new release of energy.
This she found, immediately, in the immense fecundity of

231

a doctrine which considered artists the anointed prophets of humanity. Only, to teach the people one had to know them; to know, one had to love. Here was a discipline under which she and all her friends could live effectively. Under this banner, all the dissenters could march: Victor Hugo (the stormy voice of France, as Tennyson called him), Lamartine, Berlioz, Heine, Béranger; Bakunin, too, who refused to return to Russia and be a party to the oppression of Poland; and Nourrit, who had seen his own singing of "Amour Sacré de la Patrie," in *La Muette* at the Opera in Brussels, loose the revolutionaries of 1830.

From that day on, George Sand bent her talent to these doctrines of early socialism. From her pen came a spate of novels which affected her generation as powerfully as the writings of Wells or Shaw affected the turn of our century. They were the heralds of a now-accepted cause and have lost their force today. They have even dragged her earlier, less didactic work, into unmerited neglect. Yet because of them our world is different; certain liberties are more surely ours. Without Liszt, she might have floundered on brilliantly, obsessed by herself, wracked between God, love, friendship and good works. With Liszt as one of her guides, she became the gadfly of prerogative.*

In 1804, Shelley and Byron were at school; Wordsworth met Sir Walter Scott in the Highlands, and Blake, the first great English Romantic, was at the height of his powers. Blake † had brought out his *Songs of Innocence* in 1787; with them a wholly new spirit permeated our literature—at least, a spirit that had been long deprived of flight. Now

* Note E, *George Sand*, page 303.

† Blake was arrested for sedition, in 1803, and released. "Poets," said his lawyer, "are likely to be exempt from angry passions."

again the world could be refreshed by the tart herbs of plain speech instead of the florid bouquets of the preceding fifty years (gaudy and inane, Wordsworth called them). And with this more natural vocabulary went a spirit intent upon seeing Rousseau's natural man with a new understanding.

Freedom and justice, rather than correctness and acceptance, again become the province of the poet. Again, the incandescence of the sonnet, like a speck of radium, glows in Wordsworth, Byron, Tennyson, Swinburne, Rossetti, sending out a searing radiance upon the dark subjugation of Switzerland, the tyranny that flung Bonnivard into a damp vault, the heel of Islam upon Montenegro, and the persecution of the Jews. And when Wordsworth would praise this same sonnet form, this various, small instrument, he turns back to the blind dissenter, who, sightless, also knew the eternal spirit of the chainless mind.

> and when a damp
> Fell round the path of Milton, in his hand
> The Thing became a trumpet. . . .

How slowly does the word break forth from a stuttering tongue, from a mouth all mealy with substitution. The pastoral lockjaw that had so often afflicted letters—the preoccupation with long-dead kings or, if the eye glanced near, with however exquisite rosebuds—staggers the mind. We have only to look at the literature loosed by the late revolutions to realize what new and vital salt entered into our daily bread. That salt was sprinkled by the poets even more profusely than by the prose writers, by the spirits of altruism and sensibility and not by the "priests and perceptors whose position and authority is assured by the social system of which they are an integral part. Nothing is simpler to demonstrate than the dependency, in every age, of the official codes of morality on the class interests of those who possess the economic power. The only individuals who protest against injustices—or who make their protest vocal—are in effect the poets and artists of each age, who to the extent that they rely on their imaginative capacities and powers, despise and reject the acquisitive materialism of men of action." *

It may be said, with more elision than chronology, that the ten days that really shook the world were from July 4 to July 14: from the Declaration of Independence to the fall of the Bastille—though separated by thirteen years and by the Atlantic. The American and the French revolutions released those qualities of imagination without which compassion and intensity are impossible. Burke, a true Romantic, and the anti-Jacobins—overcome by the current red scare—had much to say and said it admirably. But they dealt with the past; the future belonged to Wordsworth, Byron, Shelley, to the Americans, and, much later, to Ruskin.

As a matter of fact, two Americans were of great significance to the liberation of thought. Tom Paine's *The Rights of Man* and Joel Barlow's *Advice to the Privileged Orders* resulted in a proscription by the English government and a precipitate flight to France for both writers. But their works lived on in England, provocative and fecund.†

The "morning of reason rising upon the world," which Paine foresaw, was greeted by William Godwin, louder if not more cogently than by any other Englishman. We shall look at his *Political Justice* later; he must be mentioned here because of his progeny, of the loins and of the spirit. Godwin married Mary Wollstonecraft and, after her death, he married Mrs. Clairmont. His daughter by Mary became the wife of

Predicated on what would happen to Fr. Rev.

---

* *The Philosophy of Modern Art,* Herbert Read, 1950.
† "True, Tom and Joel now no more
    Can overturn a nation. . . ."
            —*Boston Monthly Anthology,* March 1807.

Shelley, his Clairmont stepdaughter became the mistress of Byron. Blake illustrated some of Mary Wollstonecraft's books; Dr. Johnson had commended her. If the Liberal Party had a direct tutor, it was Godwin; and it was he who instructed the left wing of the Whigs (*los Liberales,* as Southey dubbed them) in a philosophic radicalism which was to color all nineteenth-century thought.

Perhaps Godwin's greatest pupil was Wordsworth, whose genius seemed to diminish as the poet left the inspiring humanitarianism of Godwin for the less active haven of pietism and tradition. But for twenty young years, Wordsworth set his lips to the trumpet that once Milton blew, and that has not been blown so nobly since.

With all the clearer spirits of the time, Wordsworth welcomed the French Revolution. Like Jefferson and Barlow, he was deeply troubled by the excesses of the Terror, yet clung to the new-won liberties, perhaps secured, surely only temporarily drowned in blood. Napoleon, too, at the start, seemed a liberator. Then, shatteringly the emperor appeared as the Gargantuan eater of communes, of countries, of a continent, and then, as one who finally would reach across the channel. The great curve of hope, of disillusion, rose and fell like a rainbow, to strike the firm ground of fortitude at the end, in Wordsworth's finest sonnets. A score of years of British history are in them and also, in some of them, a score of lines to sustain a nation for a thousand years.

In the first hopeful months of the French Revolution, Wordsworth was often on the continent during vacations from Cambridge.

> Europe at that time was thrilled with joy,
> France standing on the top of golden hours
> And human nature seeming born again.

Glory and hope to newborn Liberty!
Hail to the mighty projects of the time!

Bliss was it in that dawn to be alive
And to be young was very Heaven!

So did the world wear the beauty of promise. In the rude men who had made the revolution, Wordsworth found "self-sacrifice the firmest" and "works of love and freedom." But very soon the conservatives in England took fright, confused by "danger which they fear and honor which they understand not"; and soon that fear congealed at home into an attack begotten by impudence on a cloud of prejudice which would last for thirty years. Wellington was typical: glorious abroad, in England an obstinate, upcomprehending, cruel autocrat.

In prose and in poetry, Wordsworth proclaimed his faith in liberty; hailing the liberation of mankind, welcoming the early freedoms conferred by the French armies; then bewailing the lost liberties of those whom Napoleon abandoned; then, seeing the last refuge of liberty in England alone, summoning a heroic courage in his countrymen. Wordsworth's was not a solitary voice. Coleridge was beside him. In Parliament, Fox boldly rebuked those who, in revulsion from the passing excess of the French Revolution, would put all in prison who disagreed with them.

In 1797 Fox, speaking on Reform, said:

We are compelled to own that it [democracy] gives a power of which no other form of government is capable. Why? Because it incorporates every man with the State; because it arouses everything that belongs to the soul as well as to the body of man; because it makes every individual feel that he is fighting for himself and not for another; that it is his own cause, his own safety, his own concern, his own dignity on the face of the earth . . . which he has to maintain. . . .

236

Who that reads the history of the Persian War . . . does not find in this principle the key to all the wonders which were achieved at Thermopylae and elsewhere, and of which the recent and marvelous acts of the French people are frequent examples? . . . How long is it since we were told in this house that France was a blank in the map of Europe and that she lay an easy prey to any power that might be disposed to divide and plunder her? Yet we see that, by the mere force and spirit of this principle, France has brought all Europe to her feet. Without disguising the vices of France—without overlooking the horrors that have been committed and that have tarnished the glory of the Revolution—it cannot be denied that they have exemplified the doctrine that if you wish for power you must look to liberty."

The martyrdoms of Venice, of Switzerland, of Spain received their beatification at Wordsworth's hands. When Napoleon sold Venice back to the Austrians in a deal as treacherous as expedient, Wordsworth lamented the fall of the Venetian Republic in a lasting epitaph.

> Once did She hold the gorgeous east in fee;
> And was the safeguard of the west: the worth
> Of Venice did not fall below her birth,
> Venice, the eldest Child of Liberty.
> She was a maiden City, bright and free;
> No guile seduced, no force could violate;
> And, when she took unto herself a Mate,
> She must espouse the everlasting Sea.
> And what if she had seen those glories fade,
> Those titles vanish, and that strength decay;
> Yet shall some tribute of regret be paid
> When her long life hath reached its final day:
> Men are we, and must grieve when even the Shade
> Of that which once was great is passed away.

And when Toussaint L'Ouverture was left to die in one of Napoleon's prisons, Wordsworth cried the shame to a horrified world; for Toussaint had been pure in purpose, he had believed in France's abolition of slavery in 1793, he had aided the French, and now he was lured to France by promises of honor and given chains not of gold but of iron.

> Toussaint, the most unhappy man of men!
> Whether the whistling Rustic tend his plough,
> Within thy hearing, or thy head be now
> Pillowed in some deep dungeon's careless den;—
> O miserable Chieftain! Where and when
> Wilt thou find patience! Yet die not; do thou
> Wear rather in thy bonds a cheerful brow:
> Though fallen thyself, never to rise again,
> Live and take comfort. Thou hast left behind
> Powers that will work for thee; air, earth, and skies;
> There's not a breathing of the common wind
> That will forget thee; thou has great allies;
> They friends are exultations, agonies,
> And love, and man's unconquerable mind.

In taking leave, for a moment only, of Wordsworth, we must not forget that he was the laureate of England and that his words had weight. No columnist-commentator today holds such a commanding position. Nor has that command been held since then, except possibly briefly by Kipling.

Of the other great romantic poets who knew Wordsworth, two concern us deeply: Byron and Shelley. Byron also write his finest verse in praise of liberty, in outraged protest at tyranny of any kind. But, of all his works, let us choose those unwritten ones he lived in Greece. His dying struck a mighty blow. The grave of a hero is the heart of a nation. There, too, tradition takes its roots.

Byron's maiden speech in the House of Lords had been

made in behalf of the weavers in newly mechanized mills. Many workers felt that the machines were a death knell to all manual labor. Stupidly, but not unreasonably, some laborers, in a frenzy of fear, broke up some of the machines. The government as governments must, considering property more sacred than life, asked for capital punishment to deal with the situation. Byron's speech was brilliant and sincere and widely noted. Today, we may wish that Byron's humanitarian eloquence had not been withdrawn from the august House. But, by temperament, he was ill at ease in active politics; he preferred to skirmish from the edge of the forest. In political satire, rather than in parliamentary harangues, lay his genius; and the skill with which he pilloried his enemies, most of whom were in office and one even on the throne, did not comport with convention nor even with prolonged residence in England.

In Italy he became the champion of liberty. Not only were his works translated at once into most of the European languages (Byron himself was fluent in several), but also he championed the patriots in ways more akin to his buccaneering temperament than in making speeches. He smuggled arms; he raised and gave huge sums; he dressed like the native chieftains; and he was universally admired. Austria was still supreme in Italy. And in return for Byron's having written of the foreign yoke as ". . . a mass of never dying ill: The Plague, the Prince, the Stranger, and the Sword," Austrian police for years kept Byron (and Shelly) under surveillance. Secretly, he was elected chief of the *Americani,* a branch of the Carbonari.*

The uprising in Italy did not materialize. The time was not ripe. But for many years, the Greeks had badgered their Turkish overlords with some success. Magnificently, Byron

* At this time, Stendhal was driven from Lombardy as an undesirable alien.

had sung ancient Greece. He would now pay his debt to living Greece. Arms, money, a chartered boat—and, in late 1823, Byron sailed to join the insurgents. The short sojourn in Greece was enough for him to reconcile factions, to prove what a disinterested and astute leader he could be, and to center the eyes of the world on one small peninsula. When he died, the lament of Greece became a world cry. There were more practical reasons, but the popularity of the cause was almost certainly due to Byron. The result—practical and poetic—was that England lent her arms and sea captains; and within four years of Byron's death, the dream of liberation was made a reality at the battle of Navarino.

The superb effort of Wordsworth to rally the ancient virtues of his people for the defense of England bereft the poet, after Waterloo, of the energy to return to his earlier enthusiasms. The torch of liberty was carried briefly by Byron, more perhaps an intellectual brigand than an apostle. Shelley was born to the sacred fire of dissent. In the brief ten years between the publication (at the age of twenty) of his *Address to the Irish People* and his death in 1822, Shelley pursued his vision of spiritual and social freedom, ever sought the light poured "from Hope's immortal urn." Godwin and Godwin's daughter did much to teach him a dialectic; but his genius alone threw around the dry bones of theory a quickening mantle of idealism.

Even at the university, he could not accept an established Church which, through the Bishop of Llandaff, could applaud a God who ordained that there should be rich and poor, and that superfluity and penury were properly distributed. A God who condoned the most cruel penal laws, who allowed disabled soldiers to rot, who led Ireland to the verge of famine, could be no true God; and Shelley set himself to find, above the ecclesiastical God, the true fountain of justice and love. The extraordinary intellectual inquisitiveness of the ancient

240

Greeks, questioning the very stars in their courses, had foundered on the rocks of theology. Shelley, a true child of Greece, yet aware of Christian ethics, sought a Platonic resolution which, like a chord resolved in some ultimate harmony, would present a new Prometheus-Christ to an eagle-devoured world.

Toward the end of *Prometheus Unbound,* the Spirit of the Hour peers into the future.

> And behold, thrones were kingless, and men walked
> One with the other even as spirits do;
> None fawned, none trampled. . . .
>
> None talked that common, false, cold, hollow talk
> Which makes the heart deny the *yes* it breathes . . .

A note by Mary Shelley explains in a few lines the poet's hope. As in most of his poems, the philosophic intent is couched in allegory. "He followed certain classical authorities in figuring Saturn as the good principle, Jupiter the usurping evil one, and Prometheus as the regenerator, who, unable to bring mankind back to primitive ignorance, used knowledge as a weapon to defeat evil by leading mankind beyond the state wherein they are sinless through ignorance, to that in which they are virtuous through wisdom." Such is the possible world proclaimed by Demogorgon:

> To suffer woes which Hope thinks infinite;
> To forgive wrongs darker than death or night;
>   To defy Power, which seems omnipotent;
> To love and bear; to hope till Hope creates
> From its own wreck the thing it contemplates:
>   Neither to change, nor falter, nor repent;
> This like thy glory, Titan! is to be
> Good, great and joyous, beautiful and free;
> This is alone Life, Joy, Empire, and Victory!

241

No man so filled with compassion, with dissent from conventional cannons of acceptance, with a true ardor for social justice, could overlook the plight of ordinary mankind in those post-Napoleonic days: the worker in thrall to the machine, the poor laws an outrage, prisons the abomination of desolation, politics a glittering shambles. Shelley wrote some satires which, though often without point today (when Castlereagh, the prime minister, and George, the prince regent, have lost their interest for us), in those years pierced with the barb of Aristophanes. One or two we shall examine in the next section; for Shelley was a true reformer, of all the poets the most dedicated. Effective too; for his voice was one of the most far-reaching,* preparing, in the wilderness of reaction, the way for 1830 and 1848. Within ten years of his death, the Reform Bill was passed, slavery was abolished in the English Colonies, the Bourbons had decamped from France, Greece was on the road to Freedom.

IV. *Reform*

Before we consider the artists who, if they appreciated it or not, profoundly affected the cause of reform, let us look at what it was that seemed, in their time, to need reforming. Reform, in the usual connotations of the word, concerns the generality of people. The masses, in general, are workers; and throughout the nineteenth century the reformers tried to ameliorate the conditions of work—labor's rights, its standing before the law, its ability to achieve the good life. Since time immemorial, laborers in the same trade have banded together, because, for close on three thousand years, labor's one power has been union. And, lest we feel that we are roving from our proper field, let us here remind ourselves

---

* He was not unknown in his day. There were literary debates in the universities on the question of his superiority to Byron, for instance.

that not only Socrates and Dante but also each of the Twelve Apostles was a member of a labor organization.*

The labor unions of today are a logical extension of practices and traditions which have their roots in prehistoric times. To avoid a close, though brief, scrutiny of the main problem of the vast majority of people is to flee from the sword only to hide in the scabbard. First, let us for the moment accept that guilds and unions were and are the same thing; the names given in different times and different ages to labor organizations. There were variants in the classic world, as there are today. (*Palliata* or *togata,* mystery or morality, *comedia del arte,* Javanese *tcharita,* or "noble tragedie," all are dramas, stage plays. *Eranos, thiasos, collegium, phratry,* guild, all are unions.) Emphases vary according to the enemy; protection, like the camouflage of the chameleon, accommodates itself to a background. In the nineteenth century, along with a customary concern for wages and prices, the unions encountered the peculiar hazards of a machine age, among which were the tools, too costly to be owned by the worker.

Toward the end of the eighteenth century in Europe, there were three kinds of guilds. The merchant guilds resembled the boards of directors of our present oil companies and banks, and were endowed with private monopolies and privileges. The craft guilds, as the name implies, controlled under special license the manufactures, and by the fifteenth century (as in Florence) ran the local communities of most of the free towns. The third guild was that of the journeymen, loosely organized, often itinerant, yet the direct ancestor of our present unions.

Already by 1500, the autocratic methods of both merchant and craft guilds had caused complaint. Somewhat to liberalize

* Note F, *Labor Unions,* page 304.

the monopolies, Henry III, in 1581, extended the franchise to all branches of mechanical industry. In France, the restraints and exclusions practiced by the guilds were so destructive of economic health among the people, that even the Third Estate, in 1614, demanded their abolition. All through the seventeenth century, laws were passed to free industry from the aging and ingrown guilds. Finally, in the interests of the plain workingman, the French physiocrats and also Adam Smith asserted the right of every man to labor. "It is one of the first duties of justice to free those whose only property is their skill from limitations arbitrarily imposed." To find a slogan of our CIO used *against* the guilds is a strange turn of the wheel. Privilege, monopoly, and reaction reached their logical conclusion. In 1776, Turgot abolished the guilds in France. Prussia followed suit. England, in 1800, fell over backward by passing the Combination Acts which forbade all, even future, labor organizations, thereby implementing injustice more flagrantly than the guilds had ever done. Fair wages, tolerable conditions, reasonable protection —all those things which, not being bestowed, as one would expect, have to be demanded, with power behind the demand —disappeared. Judge Sylvester, "Bloody Black Jack," earned his sobriquet in savage sentences, and labor achieved a new list of martyrs. Labor faced the nineteenth century in both Europe and America without any protection whatever. Laissez faire and exploitation had free rein.

By 1820, the condition of the majority of people was at a nadir we today can hardly bear to contemplate. Servants, of course, were lodged in unheated mansards and were if possible more uncleanly than their masters. The laborer in any field was wholly at the mercy of his employer. Many farmers lived in thatched cottages where the one room must suffice for a family of eleven, and received as a weekly wage the sum of ten shillings. In an angony of dying handicrafts, England was filled with pauper apprentices.

Not only were the workers caught between the two millstones of new machine and illiberal law; now their children were caught too. A child of six could handle bobbins in a factory, a child of eight could work in the mines that produced the coal that made the power to turn the wheels. Children were *impressed* into serfdom—for it was little else. "From children thus trained up to constant labor," wrote one worthy, "we may venture to hope the lowering of its price." It was not till 1840—the time of the Chartists and their apologists, whom we shall consider—that the first act was conceived to rescue the children, and so rescue the future of England. Also in that year, the first laws were passed to protect the miners; before then, as though still classed with animals, it was not even required that a death in the mines be reported.

Since the laboring man, artisan or agricultural laborer, had no court to which to appeal, his one recourse was to some group demonstration, where like as not the mounted military would appear and trample upon or fire a volley into the assembly. The Peterloo Massacre, the Tolpuddle arrests, and the Chartist fiasco were but scattered incidents in a mass reaction to intolerable laws.

The laws, for their part, were also reactions—against anything which might cause the few to lose their prerogatives. Besides the Combination Acts of 1800, there was a temporary suspension of habeas corpus, an act against "unlawful oaths," a Treason Act and a renewal of enclosure laws which robbed the villagers of their land—so great was the panic at the thought of a reviving unionism.

Two cases in America explain the fear of unions and the necessity for them. The Cordwainers of New York called "a general strike against the Masters" in 1809. In the lawsuit which followed, a curious judgment was made: that if a group of men got together *for* something, then the group constituted a society, tolerable before the law; if, however, the group got together *against* something, then it constituted a conspiracy! Since the masters had used coercion by locking out the strikers, the strikers in turn had coerced the non-members. For that, they were condemned.

Three years previously, there had been a great trial in Philadelphia of the Journeymen Boot and Shoemakers, the result of an indictment for "Combination and Conspiracy," because of a strike to raise wages. The court report bears the motto, "It is better that the law be known and certain than that the law be right." There had been a mass meeting—and the men had armed themselves against attack—to declare their right either to a raise in wages or to stop work. All this "to the great prejudice of the masters employing them." First, they were charged with unlawful assembly. Then, it was wisely pronounced that the strikers were not being prosecuted because they had, by raising wages, also raised prices, since—as the bench pointed out—no buyer need buy at a price which did not suit him. (The court did not observe that it was the master and not the journeyman who raised the price.) Lastly fines were imposed because the strikers had combined to coerce all shoemakers into a raise. In other words, the closed shop was the point at issue. It had been the crucial point in the uprising of the journeymen in 1600, in Magdeburg.

By the time of the Philadelphia strike, the law that a laborer *had* to work was obsolete. He could, with legal countenance, lay down his tools and sit idle—and payless—if he so desired, without undergoing the lash or a term of not exceeding a month in prison, as theretofore. What irked was the mass aspect; and obviously so, for if one man lays down his tools, no great cause is won, no principle established, no

246

wage scale altered, no trade incommoded. Whereas, if all workers lay down their tools, then indeed the particular work (say of building a cathedral) does not get done at all. Then, the masters must bargain, and the doors are open to who knows what pernicious winds of change. The struggle is between the power of mass and the power of money. And scab labor is just as subversive of the one as counterfeit coin is of the other. Both are surreptitious drains on either capital.

These then were, in brief summary, the problems that confronted England and America, and such were the miseries which many of the poets and pamphleteers sought to end. For their pains the writers were naturally accused of stirring up class trouble because they had pointed unerringly to the causes thereof.

Two books were published before the turn of the century, and became at once the testaments of a new hope. *A Vindication of the Rights of Women* was brought out by Mary Wollstonecraft in 1792; in 1793, Godwin published his *Political Justice*. Mrs. Wollstonecraft's title explains the nature of her protest against having her sex classed with children and idiots. Godwin, harking back to Locke, Rousseau, Jefferson, and Bentham, propounded a radical philosophy which recommended a wide popular education, a minimum of government (even to the abolition of marriage laws), a reliance on reason and enlightened self-interest, and the amiable benevolence of a "pantisocratic" society. In arriving at his not very viable conclusions, Godwin perforce pointed out the glaring faults of Georgian England. His excoriations more than his doctrines opened the eyes of those poets who made incandescent what Godwin had left inert.

By 1793, Wordsworth had already fenced with Burke. Skirmishing with that great parliamentarian was to be a long avocation for the Romantics. Though Burke himself was a Romantic and often was the accepted political philosopher of the Romantic movement, though he too was definitely a remarkable artist, his orderly and often inflexible conservatism alienated the men whose political theories were more nebulous and emotional than solidly practicable. Expressing the loftiest sentiments with sincerity and wide comprehension, Burke was in the forefront of the "liberators" in his great speeches on the conciliation of the American colonies. As much as to anyone, America owes to him the accommodating latitude that characterized the ultimate peace treaty with England. He was ever against the king's faction and court cliques. The moral indignation he displayed in his speeches against Warren Hastings set a magnificent standard of colonial government, in justice and humanity.

But, from its inception, Burke took umbrage at the French Revolution—before his fears were fully justified, and while the Godwins and Wordsworths were hailing the rising sun of liberty across the channel. Burke feared the effect of French revolutionary ideas on the people of England, as he dreaded manhood suffrage or parliamentary reform. He hated violence and lawlessness anywhere. He believed in government by a territorial aristocracy and in sound commerce. Violence drove him into frenzy—and rather than face the facts pertaining to England's seizure of India, he had to "draw a sacred veil" over those unpleasant days and accept India as a gift over which England was privileged to rule with justice. Even Lord Morley admits that Burke was both prejudiced and ignorant concerning the French Revolution. Burke had thought that a little give and take would mend matters. But, said Morley, "it was only by revolutionary methods . . . that the knot could be cut. . . . There was not a single chamber in the old fabric that was not crumbling and tottering." In general, the Romantics looked upon the French

248

Revolution with hope; Burke, with despair. Burke ended by losing many of his friends, but even his enemies respected him; and all knew him for one of the greatest masters of the word.

In the 1790's, Wordsworth was at work on a poem, *Guilt and Sorrow,* dealing with the destitute widow of a soldier, the miseries of war, the horrors of the penal code, and the crushing of the poor. Curious that in this and in his poetry on Spain, Wordsworth should walk so closely with Goya. His sonnet, written in London, September 1802, not only has the temper of Godwinism but also bears embedded within it at least two couplets still in our language and our thought.

That same year, Wordsworth's sister quotes him as saying that, after a perusal of Milton's sonnets, "I took fire, if I may be allowed to say so, and produced three sonnets the same afternoon, the first I ever wrote, except an irregular one at school." Let me give two of them entire.

> O Friend! I know not which way I must look
> For comfort, being, as I am, opprest,
> To think that now our life is only drest
> For show; mean handy-work of craftsman, cook,
> Or groom!—We must run glittering like a brook
> In the open sunshine, or we are unblest:
> The wealthiest man among us is the best:
> No grandeur now in nature or in book
> Delights us. Rapine, avarice, expense,
> This is idolatry; and these we adore:
> Plain living and high thinking are no more:
> The homely beauty of the good old cause
> Is gone; our peace, our fearful innocence,
> And pure religion breathing household laws.

> Milton! Thou shouldst be living at this hour:
> England hath need of thee: she is a fen
>   Of stagnant waters: altar, sword, and pen,

Fireside, the heroic wealth of hall and bower,
Have forfeited their ancient English dower
Of inward happiness. We are selfish men:
Oh! raise us up, return to us again;
And give us manners, virtue, freedom, power.
Thy soul was like a Star, and dwelt apart:
Thou hadst a voice whose sound was like the sea,
Pure as the naked heavens, majestic, free;
So didst thou travel on life's common way
In cheerful godliness; and yet thy heart
The lowliest duties on herself did lay.

At much the same period, Coleridge (living near the Wordsworths at the time) wrote:

We have offended, oh, my countrymen;
We have offended very grievously,
And been most tyrannous. From east to west
A groan of accusation pierces Heaven!
The wretched plead against us; multitudes
Countless and vehement, the sons of God
Our brethren.

Another splendid vindication of humanity deserves mention here as in some ways it struck the most modern note. In an *Essay on the Poor-Law Amendment Bill,* Wordsworth wrote, ". . . it follows that the right of the state to require the services of its members, even to the jeopardizing of their lives in the common-defense, establishes a right in the people —not to be gainsaid by utilitarians and economists—to public support when, from any cause, they may be unable to support themselves." In other words, if a nation has the right to demand of its citizens that they die heroically in its defense, that nation has the obligation to see to it that the citizenry live decently at other times.

250

Hard upon these poems and essays came the first poetry of young Shelley, the disciple of Godwin, the friend of Wordsworth and Coleridge, of Lamb and Byron. The very images which distinguish Shelley as a lyricist are those of a man made instantly wretched by all corruption and misery; a man so earnest that he must needs express his concern in prose or poetry. Being far in advance of his day, Shelley remains (more even than Victor Hugo) the highest prophet of the new era.

In 1817, Shelley wrote a *Proposal to Reform the Vote*, attacking the unrepresentative character of the House. "Perhaps," he cried, "the people choose to be enslaved," to be degraded, ignorant, and famished. He knew there was no choice, but only the impositions of a corrupt government. Unionism, as we have seen, had collapsed. The paternal solicitude lightly brushed into Elizabethan Poor Laws—even that had gone. Manchester was Golconda; English manufacturers were supplying the world, and nothing must interfere. Three labor organizers were executed and buried at the same time that Queen Charlotte died. Shelley's *Address to the People on the Death of Queen Charlotte* is one of the most moving pieces of pamphleteering we have. "Let us follow the corpse of British Liberty slowly and reverentially to its tomb," wrote Shelley; and, so writing, drew an apocalyptic contrast between the two funeral processions, one to the limepits and one to the Abbey.

Fortified by his deep knowledge of the past and with a sure prophetic sense, Shelley (like Ibsen and Shaw), was ever fascinated by the drama as a vehicle of protest. "The drama," he wrote, "being that form under which a greater number of modes of expression of poetry are susceptible of being combined than any other, the connection of poetry and social good is more observable in the drama than in whatever other form." In a travesty of *Oedipus Tyrannus* called *Swellfoot the Tyrant,* Shelley wrote a devastating play upon the subject

251

of that same pathetic Queen Charlotte and her monstrous
George IV, first gentleman of Europe. The tyrant is surrounded by swine, his "kingly paunch swells like a sail before
a favoring breeze." The king cannot have been more pleased
by this indirect attack than by the lines directly addressed to
his Prime Minister, Castlereagh.

> Corpses are cold in the tomb,
> Stones on the pavement are dumb.
> Abortions are dead in the womb
> And their mothers look pale—like the white shore
> Of Albion, free no more.

Or the impression of the last years of George III.

> An old, mad, blind, despised, and dying king,—
> Princes, the dregs of their dull race, who flow
> Through public scorn—mud from a muddy spring—
> Rulers who neither see, nor feel, nor know
> But leech-like to their fainting country cling,
> Till they drop, blind in blood, without a blow,—
> A people starved . . .

We may wonder how effective the romantic poets were in
England. A speech in the House, we know, has turned the
tide here, a pamphlet (like Paine's *Common Sense*) has turned
it there. Oratory and prose are surely immediate in their
effect. But by their very nature, speech and pamphlet are
ephemeral. Poetry is not so. There are fashions, to be sure.
Yet the fair and fervid word, the luminous poem, the work
of art—these things live. They cannot be destroyed. Like
Shelley's heart, in the funeral pyre on the beach, they refuse
to turn to ashes.

"How often a single thought has given a different form
to whole centuries; and how individual men have, by their

252

expressions, imprinted a stamp upon their age which has operated beneficially upon succeeding generations," wrote Goethe.*

· And what Anatole France said of Zola is true also of Shelley. "He was a moment of the conscience of mankind."

I have mentioned the Tolpuddle martyrs and the Chartist movement. The Tolpuddle affair was flagrant: six men, countrymen of good standing, in 1834, were accused of having held a meeting for the purposes of forming a union among the local farmers in Dorset. Several men had been hanged for the same offense in the preceeding years; these six were merely chained in the hulks (floating prisons) driven into prison ships, and transported to Australia. So cruel was the sentence, so utterly unworthy were the legal proceedings, that the case could not be stifled but roused a wind that beat upon ministries and parliaments till the "martyrs" were released.†

The story of Chartism must be briefly told; it is of interest to us because, like the weavers' strike of Wyclif's time, the resistance of a small group epitomized a larger struggle. There is particular interest because, being the only movement of this kind in the first half of the nineteenth century, it caught the attention of all those who had the imagination to apprehend the cast of intolerable conditions and the talent to express their indignation. (Chartism was also the parent of the Populist movement in America.) Shelley saw the beginnings; Ruskin lived to see the end. Coleridge, Southy, Disraeli, Carlyle, Kingsley, Dickens, each in varying measure

* Eckerman, March 11, 1828.

† When G. B. Shaw was asked to write a commemorative piece for a book on the Tolpuddle affair, he answered "I am afraid I cannot say anything in praise of the Dorchester martyrs. Martyrs are a nuisance to Labor movements. The business of a labor man is not to suffer but to make other people suffer until they make him reasonably comfortable."

protested, their voices carrying behind powerful or parliamentary doors through which the feeble wail of undernourishment could not penetrate.

To possess a document—the doctrine was hoary with complexities, but the desire was simple enough: the procurement of a decent life for a human being—the wretched workers drew up a People's Charter in 1838. Their demands seem eminently reasonable to us: manhood suffrage, the ballot, annual parliaments, the abolition of property qualifications for the members of Parliament, the payment for those members, and equal electoral districts. From such a liberalized government, once established, the workers hoped that laws would issue putting a term to such customs as those whereby an employer might dismiss all his workers at once, yet whereby a striker was punished if he tried to better his lot, and an organizer was deported or executed. Robert Owen led one wing for reform along doctrinaire lines; the Working Men's Association led the other. From the beginning of the century, for forty years—under the aggravation of more repressive laws or ineffectual reforms—the agitations of despair mounted. There were mass meetings and speeches, petitions, publications, arrests, and riots. Finally, with aid from Glasgow, Manchester and other manufacturing centers, plans were formed for a monster parade to carry the Charter to Parliament, together with a petition signed by six million people. In great alarm the government posted the police and the military (Prince Louis Napoleon was one of the volunteer constabulary), and forbade the meeting. Instead of half a million marchers, only some fifty thousand, separated and scattered by the soldiery under the Duke of Wellington, moved here and there, uncertain, hopeless.

This was the year 1848, when Continental Europe was plagued with revolution. On the May day that the Chartist movement collapsed, young John Ruskin, aged twenty-nine, was married. Already he had published *Modern Painters*. Within ten years he had published *The Stones of Venice*, *The Seven Lamps of Architecture*, and most of that criticism of art which has assured his immortality in spite of the prunes and prisms that jostled in his thinking. His interest in craft brought him to the craftsman, and inevitably to the plight of both craft and craftsman. By 1860, Ruskin became an apostle of social reform, a political economist, a founder of socialist and cooperative farms, shops, mills, even museums. In *Sesame and Lilies, Time and Tide,* and a half dozen other books, as in innumerable lectures and articles, Ruskin expounded his theories. And in his sermons were some weighty stones that he did not hesitate to hurl at convention or hypocrisy where he found them. More clearly than anyone before or since, he saw the interdependence of art with craft; the impossibility of one being healthy, the other sick; the true, exhuberant relation between politics and art. He saw clearly what the Industrial Revolution had been doing to mankind and, as a man and an artist, he hit and hit where it hurt.

Four lectures, published in 1862 under the title *Unto This Last,* encountered the deepest hostility. Today, the book is respected as a valid and essentially sound inquiry into the sources of wealth. Emotionally, *Unto This Last* is a plea for common honesty. And it is far more readable than the works of Mill or Ricardo, in whom Ruskin could find little truth. It is, in fact, brilliantly written, simple, and engaging. Public honesty should include honest labeling and advertisement—an injunction incorporated decades later in our pure food laws. Labor, to survive, must be organized "under honest captains." * And to raise up generations of healthy and skilful workers, government-sponsored trade schools were indispen-

* Presumably, under honest captains of industry and honest labor leaders.

sable. From trade school to government workshop, competing with private manufacture. And, at the end, homes for the aged and destitute. All this eminently practical rationale for a healthy body-politic was imbued with Ruskin's prophetic sense of values. His quarrel with political science was that it did not take into account the true mainsprings of men's wants and actions: ethical, or emotional, considerations. "No human actions were ever intended by the Maker of men to be guided by balances of expediency but by balances of justice."

In another lecture in the mercantile capital of the world, home town of the Chamberlains, Ruskin announced, "Here we sit in Manchester, hard at work, very properly making comforters for our cousins all over the world." But he led his audience further: "Our cities are a wilderness of spinning wheels instead of palaces; yet the people have not clothes" (*The Future of England*). And he could thrust with acid humor. He devised a statute of Britannia of the Market "who may have . . . a partridge for her crest, typical at once of her courage in fighting for noble ideas and of her interest in game, and round its neck the inscription in golden letters, *Perdix fovit quae non peperit*. ('As the partridge, fostering what she brought not forth, so he that getteth riches not by right shall leave them in the midst of his day, and at his end shall be a fool.' Jeremiah, XVII.) Then, for her spear, she might have a weaver's beam; and on her shield, instead of her Cross, the Milanese boar, semifleeced . . . and her corslet of leather folded over her heart in the shape of a purse, with thirty slits in it for . . . money to go in at."

He was a far better political economist than some of his contemporaries allowed. His aversion to science and to economists in general, or the Gothic-revival quality of some of his advocacies, should not blind us to the encompassing accuracy of his vision. Ruskin attacked, in political economy, what he was among the first to call, laissez faire. What he had to say about war, in a bellicose era—just after the Crimea—has not lost its pungency. He would have no truck with the few nabobs who urged "peasant millions into gladiatorial war." And with a sharply practical eye he saw through the false opulence of society, of a people so ignorant of their real interests and so concerned with nothing else.

He expressed his sympathy with the revolutionaries of 1848 and with the dark passage of Ireland. Before he died he had given his considerable inherited wealth away, all of it—living solely on the remunerations of his own work—for he disapproved of interest money. And he left us one thought which should be remembered: that discipline and interference lie at the very root of all human progress or power.*

The transit of Chartism—its rise and fall, its errors as well as its aspirations—was the school, not only of Ruskin and Carlyle (who disapproved), but of almost every artist living at the time. No man could look out of his window or conduct his affairs in England or America (for the American scene followed closely on the British) in those years without his eye meeting the insecurity, the disequilibrium of society. The poet, Thomas Hood, transmuting the sordid world about him, touched pity and anger with the pure fire of his poetry and added *The Song of the Shirt* to the chorus of bitter resentment. Far more notable than Markham's *The Man with the Hoe,* Hood's song became immediately the minor charter of the reform movement. In one of his first speeches, the young Disraeli defended the Chartists. In his novels, *Coningsby* and *Sybil,* Disraeli advanced the rights of the factory workers over a spent oligarchy he was himself one day to rule. Disraeli, like Ruskin, took up the plight of Ireland, strove for better corn laws and refused to hand the keys of government to the locks of Manchester.

* *Political Economy,* Article I. The truth of this has been apprehended by many groups, from the early Church to the communists.

The insidious fallacy of child labor was but one of the many grievances which roused the artists. He who said "Suffer little children to come unto Me" was closer in spirit to the pagan Shelley than to those bishops who regularly vetoed the anti-slavery bills. Like Hood, Elizabeth Barret Browning wrote some of her most moving poetry to free the children. And of course Dickens, as in *Oliver Twist,* was laying bare the plight of those degraded beyond endurance. Through his enormous popularity, Dickens, more than any other novelist, roused public opinion to effective remonstrance. Schools, sanitation, the prison, and machine shop, in all their horror, were woven into his pictures of ordinary life—in *Bleak House, Hard Times,* and many more. Charles Kingsley, the poet and novelist, gentle Canon of Westminster, deep in the disciplines of Christian socialism, he too upheld the cause of Chartism— one which seemed to peter out so feebly yet which more than served the turn of justice and fair living because these artists would not let it down. The cause had taught them, in brute practice, and died; by their labors, they made it live again and come to fulfilment.

We have considered slavery, up to the Renaissance, in its effect upon the artists. The slow death of that dragon begins in the Houses of Parliament and ends with the last battle of the Civil War in America.

In the year of our Lord 1713, one hundred and ninety-two slaveships plied their loathsome trade out of London, Bristol, and Lancaster. (Oh, not that our good New Englanders were blameless. The bottoms out of Salem were not all for cod and china.) If England led the traffic, it is but fair to state that she also led the opposition.

In 1671, George Fox, founder of the Society of Friends, the Quakers, deemed it incompatible with the dignity of one human being to own another or to deal in flesh. Twenty-five years later, the brethren of Pennsylvania formed the first association against the slave traffic; this was the forerunner of the Pennsylvania Society of which Franklin was president. But nonconformist associations are apt to be on the fringes of government as well as of society. Governmental England did nothing for one hundred and one years except hand down the excellent decision that a slave whose foot touched the soil of the British isles should be free. (Not only Britons never should be slaves.)

A few divines, many of the artists—Pope, Cowper, Sterne, to name but a few—joined the condemnation which the Quakers had continued to express. In 1787, the Committee for Abolition of the Slave Traffic was formed by men whose names it is good to record: William Wilberforce; Granville Sharp, the leader; and Thomas Clarkson who, the year before, had written his university thesis on *Slavery and the Commerce of the Human Species.* Throughout the nineties, these men submitted petitions to Parliament, sometimes winning in the House, ever defeated by the lords and Bishops. It was not till Charles James Fox came to office that the bill was passed, in 1807.

French agitation had followed the same course. Under the presidency of Condorcet the *Sociètè des Amis des Noirs* was founded in 1788, with the help of Mirabeau and Lafayette. Abruptly, three years later, the French Revolution, true to its own principles, gave equal rights for Negro citizens. But this, handsome as it seems, was all directed except in revolutionary France against the slave traffic only. In all the colonies, save Denmark's, the institution of slavery itself, as in our South, continued unmolested. Again Wilberforce petitioned Parliament; but the mere suggestion so outraged the planters in the colonies that the colonial governors did not dare pursue the matter. It was not till 1833 that Wilberforce carried the day, and the abolition of slavery (with indemnity to the planters) was decreed for Britain and her possessions. Colonial France followed suit. The Argentine had honorably accomplished it before anyone else, in 1813. The United States was the last among civilized nations to make amends.

In the earliest New England documents we find that a certain sum was regularly paid to trappers for a fur, but "niggers and injuns" got half price. Washington himself, though he deplored the peculiar institution, owned slaves. Indeed, it comes as something of a shock to realize that for much less than a third of the time which has elapsed since the first colony was founded has America been free of the curse of slavery.

We need not go deeply here into the political aspects of Southern Slavery. As a schism which precipitated a civil war, it was compounded of economic necessity, economic fallacy, a clinging to agrarianism, a jealousy of northern industry, and so a jealous insistence on states' rights, a reasonable dislike of tariffs, and a thoroughly muddled adherence to whatever part of Jefferson's concepts seemed to enrich a planter. Enough Southerners were liberal minded, enough were convinced that slavery was uneconomical to have permitted of the emancipation of the slaves, right after the Revolution, had the nation commanded enough money to indemnify the owners, as England had. But by 1860, the pattern was shot with counterthreads of nullification and sectional rancors and obstinacies. A last and crucial test lay in the virgin acres of the new territories, the new states. To prevent the westward-pushing planter from taking his slaves with him was something the South would not tolerate; to impose slavery on a free soil was something the North would not permit. Slavery where slavery had always been was possible, but to extend it was abomination. At the cost of the most shattering war we

260

have experienced, the curse was removed from us. By the Thirteenth, Fourteenth, and Fifteenth amendments, the Negro was officially authorized to be what he is not yet: completely free.

Certainly, a man from Mars might be excused for concluding that discrimination and slavery were not only our general custom but very much in our tradition. We know he would be wrong. *A tradition can tolerate the ignoble but not what is known to be ignoble.* And ever since Jesus and Paul spoke to the Mediterranean world, we have known that bondage was ignoble. Hundreds of years of slavery have been our habit; emancipation is in our tradition.

"The demon of reform has a secret door into the heart of every law-maker, of every inhabitant of every city," said Emerson. Less sweepingly, I think it can be said that very many of the artists of the midcentury—the time of the Civil War—were reformers at heart, and almost all were Abolitionists. From James Fenimore Cooper and Bryant to Longfellow and Mark Twain, this would hold true. And of Harriet Beecher Stowe it can safely be written that her book was as great an implement for the Northern cause as was the army of the Potomac.

An "army marches on its stomach"; but it is recruited through a different organ: the seat of the emotions. Men will not march till they are roused; and they are roused by what they can believe. If they fight to keep the barbarians from the door, or to exterminate those who hold different religious beliefs and who should be sent back to the Devil whence they came, or to protect the life-giving trade routes, all this has been made clear to them (in slogans and propaganda, if you will); and cogency of thought and eloquence of expression alone can be convincing, moving, rousing. It took all that had

261

been written, said, and sung during the days between Voltaire and André Chénier to give a marching faith to the armies of Republican France so that they would follow Napoleon over the Alps to confer "liberty" on Italian soil. "First the singers, then the doers, and then again the bards to sing what has been done."

It took, quite reasonably, people of peculiar sensitiveness to perceive the gap between things as they were and things as they might be, between man's increasing mastery over nature and his prolonged insufficiency before his own kind. It took men who had the gift of expression to unroll this picture before the public and, by exhortation, make mankind uncomfortable, uncomfortable as long as there were slaves. Slaves in irons, or slaves of the machine age.

In the 1830's, when Jackson was President, Cooper was writing *The American Democrat,* a searching inquiry into the growth or decline of the principles and hopes which animated the Founding Fathers. Like Franklin and Jefferson, Cooper considered slavery a gruesome mockery in a land which called itself a democracy. Cooper's *Leatherstocking Tales* had brought him an immense audience (in Europe as well) and *The American Democrat* was read by his far-flung admirers.

William Cullen Bryant, as editor of the New York *Evening Post,* also commanded a wide attention. He saw what the new world should promise:

> . . . freedom at thy gates and rest
> For earth's down-trodden and opprest,
> A shelter for the hunted head,
> For the starved laborer toil and bread.

As a truly religious poet, Bryant could entertain hope while observing matters which might otherwise make him despair.

When sentence was passed (1836) on "twenty men who had determined not to work" and upon whom was laid a staggering fine, Bryant wrote:

What was their offence? They had committed the crime of unanimously declining to go to work at the wage offered them by their masters. They had said to one another, "Let us come out from the meanness and misery of our caste. Let us begin to do what every order more privileged and more honored is doing every day . . . We may be wrong, but we cannot help believing that we might do much if we were true brothers to each other, and would resolve not to sell the only thing which is our own, the cunning of our hands, for less than it is worth . . ."

Bryant then quotes from the legal proceedings.

" 'Self-created societies,' says Judge Edwards, 'are unknown to the constitution and laws, and will not be permitted to rear their crest and extend their baneful influence over any portion of the community.' "

"What nonsense is this!" continues Bryant. "Gather up then and sweep to the penitentiary all those who are confederated to carry on any business or trade in concert, by fixed rules, and see how many men you would have at large in this city."

And when the Reverend Elijah P. Lovejoy, the abolitionist editor, was killed by a mob in Missouri, along with the employees who vainly tried to keep Lovejoy's presses from destruction, Bryant wrote in an editorial,

The right to discuss freely and openly, by speech, by the pen, by the press, all political questions, and to examine and animadvert upon all political institutions, is a right so clear and certain, so interwoven with our other liberties, so neces-

263

sary, in fact, to their existence, that without it we must fall at once into despotism or anarchy.

That few people today read Cooper, Bryant, Dana, or Garrison—and they were not great writers—in no way lessens their importance in their own day. Perhaps, more than any poet of the time, Whittier led the crusade against slavery. The fire in his verses is still warm; of all the minor poets he is still the most moving. In *Stanzas of the Times* (1835) he hurled his bolt at a proslavery gang, who in a meeting at Fanueil Hall, had clamored for a suppression of free speech "lest it should endanger the foundation of commercial society."

1.   Is this the land our fathers loved,
            The freedom which they toiled to win?
        Is this the soil whereon they moved?
            Are these the graves they slumber in?
        Are we the sons by whom are borne
            The mantles which the dead have worn?

2.   And shall we crouch above these graves
            With craven soul and fettered lip?
        Yoke in with marked and branded slaves,
            And tremble at the driver's whip?
        Bend to the earth our pliant knees
            And speak but as our masters please?

4.   Of human skulls that shrine was made
            Round which the priests of Mexico
        Before their loathsome idol prayed:
            Is freedom's altar fashioned so?
        And must we yield to Freedom's God,
            As offering meet, the negro's blood?

When the clergy, in Charleston, gathered to bless a proslavery meeting, the Quaker poet could not be silent.

1.   Just God! and these are they
       Who minister at thine altar, God of Right!
       Men who their hands with prayer and blessing lay
         On Israel's Ark of light!

2.   What! preach and kidnap men?
       Give thanks, and rob thy own afflicted poor?
       Talk of thy glorious liberty, and then
         Bolt hard the captive's door?

4.   Pilate and Herod, friends.
       Chief priests and rulers, as of old, combine.
       Just God and holy! is that church, which lends
         Strength to the spoiler, thine?

6.   Feed fat, ye locusts, feed!
       And, in your tasselled pulpits, thank the Lord
       That, from the toiling bondman's utter need,
         Ye pile your own full board.

For the twenty-five years preceeding the proclamation of emancipation, Whittier poured out his righteous indignation in words that burned with the intenseness and effectiveness of Amos or Jeremiah.

In those years, as the thunderclouds of the Civil War gathered, there was fought another war, the war with Mexico, of brief duration and dubious origin. The poets we are considering did not take more kindly to the coercion of a neighboring country than to that of slaves or workers. For the inevitable war to end slavery, Emerson could enlist the Church Militant.

       So nigh is grandeur to our dust,
       So near is God to man,
       When Duty whispers low, *Thou must,*
       The Youth replies, *I can.*

But for aggrandizement, military prowess, the compulsion of others, Emerson had no sympathy. He loved freedom of the mind and retained his own at the cost of his benefice; he loved freedom of the man, and spoke against slavery. Montesquieu wrote. "Countries are well-cultivated, not as they are fertile, but as they are free." And Emerson quoted the phrase, in his essay on Civilization, and carried the thought further: "the highest proof of civility is that the whole public action of the State is directed on securing the greatest good of the greatest number."

In the *Ode to Channing,* Emerson wrote:

> But who is he that prates
> Of the culture of mankind,
> Of better arts and life?
> Go, blindworm, go,
> Behold the famous States
> Harrying Mexico
> With rifles and with knife!
> Or who, with accent bolder,
> Dare praise the freedom-loving mountaineer?
> I found by thee, O rushing Contoocook!
> And in thy valleys, Agiochook!
> The jackals of the Negro-holder.

Emerson received John Brown, that angry man of God, willingly at his house. They were welcome there who believed in the cooperative living together, in one world, of the decent in heart. Emerson's gift was to touch common things and remove them from the commonplace and, by so doing, give to mankind a spiritual perspective. He desired to lead men's minds into equilibrium, hoping that society would slowly follow, out of the disjointure of a ruthless age. Like Thoreau, he sought to establish a true harmony between the common welfare in a democracy and the will of

the individual, between selfishness and self-reliance, between
the "natural man" of Rousseau and the elect of Calvin. In
short, between growth and order. The problem of our democratic tradition as a whole was thus the problem of every
thoughtful individual. Emerson's own answer to the problem
was spiritual magnanimity, the practice of which was unfortunately beyond the capabilities of most people. Melville
was beset by the same problem, but his answer, like Haw-
thorne's, was dark: man's will broke before the forces of evil,
of nature, or upon the sharp edges of the social framework.
Fundamentally optimistic, directly fired by Emerson, Walt
Whitman announced a credo of "adhesiveness," brotherly
love, cooperative living.

He saw about him a society which was notable for its
pride in know-how, ribbing the country with rails at the
same time that the rich entrepreneurs were cornering those
railroads, as well as cornering oil, steel, tobacco, or sugar,
taking credit for an expansion which was really due to Government handouts, to the engineers, mechanics, and laborers,
thereby removing from the common people—the herd of employees—the true incentives for pride. In contrast to such a
society, Whitman sang of a society where democracy would
be actually practiced; he sang of a society such as the makers
of our tradition longed for. The promised land, the patri-
archs called it; Sir Thomas More called it *Utopia*. Up to the
end of the Civil War, much of Whitman's poetry is instinct
with hope, hope in the traditional American democratic
ways. As he saw those ways corrupted, he wrote more vehe-
mently of what might yet be when America outgrew the
complacency he saw about him. American democracy was
the "grand experiment," but how grossly exploited!

In *Democratic Vistas*—a small book much admired by Emerson—Whitman's dismay all but extinguishes his natural
optimism. (But he could write even of despair with gusto.) "I

would alarm and caution," he writes. There is "hollowness of heart, here in the United States. . . . Genuine belief seems to have left us . . . we live in an atmosphere of hypocrisy. . . . The official services of America . . . are saturated with corruption, bribery, falsehood, maladministration . . . with little or no soul." The Grant administration was not a dainty spectacle. Observing that era, Henry Adams felt impelled to write that "the moral law expired, like the Constitution." To Whitman, the embryo democracy was still asleep in the womb of Time.

If Whitman could agree with Adams, he was totally devoid of the besetting ennui that hamstrung Adams as a public figure. Walt could lament that "our New World democracy . . . is so far . . . an almost complete failure in its social aspects." But he could welcome the "clash and airing" of diverse opinions as the breath of democracy. And he did cling to his enthusiasm and hope. "I want the people," he said to Traubel, "the mass . . . men, women and children . . . to have what belongs to them; not a part of it, not most of it, but all of it."

Walt hoped that America could, probably would, "surmount the gorgeous history of feudalism" to achieve her destiny in a "pervading atmosphere of beautiful manners," but he was well aware that she might end as "the most tremendous failure of time," and when he looked about him, he saw the atmosphere more like "a sort of dry and flat Sahara." That there was need of more, much more, traditional "compaction and moral identity"—such solidarity as comports with an effective group urge—Whitman clearly saw. Of that urge he hoped to be the prophet. He hoped to breathe into the United States—and how he had cherished the Union, one and indivisible!—the breath "recuperative of sane and heroic life." He probably never realized that he was not, in his own day, the prophet of the common man.

Poetry was for women, in that grubbing age, and Longfellow filled the bill. But Whitman speaks directly to the twentieth century, while Longfellow, Lowell, and Whittier, powerful in their day, champions too, each one of them, murmur in the past. Whitman speaks thus directly to us, his unseen future, largely because he saw so fervently into his own present. He had hopes of us, seeing little about his own time that was comforting.

Melville mirrored the aching fact more truly. But if Whitman like Melville could be disgusted, he could not be disenchanted, for Whitman had faith in the tradition and a profound understanding of it. He felt, as Swift had felt, not so amazed to find men wicked as to find them unashamed.

Emerson, too surveyed the scene with sorrow. "The ways of trade," he felt, "are grown selfish to the borders of theft, and supple to the borders of fraud." Wendell Phillips, in Boston, felt that the ways of society were as callous as those of trade. He was hounded by the mob for his antislavery speeches, his works in behalf of women; and he was blackballed out of his club. In Stockbridge, Theodore Sedgwick wrote, "We are accused of exciting the evil passions of the poor against the rich. I would destroy those evil passions . . . by destroying poverty itself. To admit that the poor exist in sufficient numbers . . . to cause alarm to the rich is the severest censure that could be passed on all our boasted institutions." (Sedgwick might have reminded his readers that in the falling Roman Empire, it was considered ill-advised to take a census lest the slaves learn how greatly they outnumbered the free.)

Crass and wanton as those days undoubtedly were, shocked as were the decent in heart by the spectacle, even so the chorus of voices, rising in protest, grew to proportions that would soon change the face of the land. Incited by the artists, implemented by the ballots of the workers, a reformation of the social structure took shape, in the emancipation of the Negroes and in the emancipation of labor. The crusaders themselves saw the dawn; and Emerson could say "The astonished muse finds thousands at her side." Garrison had cried, "Urge me not to use moderation in a cause like the present! I am in earnest. I will not equivocate—I will not excuse—I will not retreat a single inch—AND I WILL BE HEARD." And he was heard.

Lincoln's was the last great voice of the period. "Labor is prior to and independent of capital. Capital is only the fruit of labor, and could never have existed if labor had not first existed," he said. In him lay the genius of our tradition. And his hands were upheld and the cause carried beyond his death by many helpers. Lone wolves, like Whitman; strayed angels, like Emerson; small talents greatly fired, like Mrs. Stowe's.

Platform, Bill of Rights, Humble Remonstrance, Charter —these have been the usually anonymous and traditional reminders to the forgetful in office that the people have not forgotten what their prophets have said. With such in their hand, the nobles came to Runnymede, the people followed Wat Tyler to London, the Model Army approached Parliament, the colonies petitioned the King, or the French advanced with their revolutionary Declaration of Rights. And each charter, each a written epitome of the group urge, harked back to the signed word, to the word of Wyclif, Milton, Locke, John Adams, or Jefferson.

This is a traditional pattern of reform or reformation which it is well to remember. First, a voice crying in the wilderness; then, perhaps long after, the group, taking up the cry; next, for the most part, failure; other prophetic voices keeping the cause alive; at last, accomplishment. Then comes the resting on the oars, the gliding, the imperceptible drifting back in forgetfulness or false security. And so it is all to do over again; but it is begun again each time at a higher level. At least we must hope so. By and large, this is the pattern of nineteenth-century reform, as of all enlightenment, in England and America; and we may see it plainly in the histories of the Chartist movement in England and the Populist movement in America. The Republican platform of 1912, embodied all the demands with which, not long before, the Populists had frightened the gentry.

The time is yet far when social justice needs no more sustaining. But the difference between its existence in 1800 and its movement in 1900 is all the difference between a half-dead body and one nimble on crutches. How far we have come and how far remains to go is summed up in Lowes Dickinson's definition. "Social Justice is the plea of the many against the few, of the nation against the class, of mankind against the nation, of the future against the present."

Before we leave the nineteenth century, let us review one or two broad aspects of it.

The Civil War was fought by large armies; it freed thousands of slaves. The labor movement concerned the amelioration of life for the majority of people. These were mass movements, led by a few generals or labor leaders and sustained by the creative artists. We may ask ourselves where such mass movements fit into a tradition so largely concerned with the individual man or individual incident.

In the first place, only such things remain in a tradition as enjoy the approbation of the people at large. Then it could be pointed out that the army of the Potomac is as firmly in our tradition as General McClellan, the Eleven Thousand Virgins of Cologne as Saint Ursula. But that would be a careless answer, for without doubt tradition does spring from the individual and, in the main, concerns individuals.

271

The proper answer is that we should make again the comparison between tradition and religion, and that we should ask ourselves what effect the masses have on religion, if we would know what effect the masses have on tradition. Tradition was made for the masses and is preserved by the masses. Who shall say that the more Christians there are the more the Church suffers? Would there be fewer saints, fewer prelates, fewer houses of worship, if the number of Christians trebled? Indeed, so also the greater the number of those who imbibe it the more potent is the stream of a tradition. Since there is no exclusiveness in tradition, it is purely accident if a hero issues from the loins of the élite. Johnny Appleseed, Daniel Boone, Nathan Hale, even Lincoln, these—as far as popular knowledge goes—might be parthenogenetic.

On the other hand, solicitude for the collectivity was and is very firmly set in our tradition. Federalist policy had been explicit; that geography, general education, common law (its clarification and equity), economic interests, the general welfare, as well as armaments, foreign policy, and taxes, were the proper concern of the government. John Quincy Adams had tried to go further. He declared that Congress should employ labor directly on public works, such as roads and canals and harbors, and that, to ensure these benefits to the people, the western lands, forests, and minerals should be held in trust for the nation. Adams and most of the Founding Fathers before him believed that the government should actively foster the sciences and arts as part of the education of the young republic. It was considered by Lincoln that man's first duty was "to improve not only his own condition but to assist in ameliorating mankind."

At the turn of the century, the Populists and Progressives brought again to the notice of politicians these fundamental tenets, but it was not till a financial panic had conducted nearly a quarter of the nation to the verge of destitution that any sustained solicitude of this kind was permitted the government. No one in the twentieth century (except a socialist or a communist) has dared to advance some of the theories of Hamilton and Adams, who died in a happy state of ignorance of the words socialism and communism. In short, what is now called government interference in some quarters and wise planning in others, was a commonplace to our forefathers.

The force of group urges depends not only upon the validity of the doctrine but upon the number of the believers. We cannot have pursued our study this far without realizing that truth and mass are the essential elements in the progressive unfolding of the story of our tradition. John the Baptist and Jesus spoke to the multitude; and it was the multitude, not the Pharisees or proconsuls, who remembered. Upon the death of Jesus, the multitude became a handful; but within three hundred years, the handful had become again so great a mass that the symbol of Christianity obscured the sky even for the Emperor Constantine, as he fought at Milvian Bridge. The prophet announces; the mass acts. What then of the false prophet? His power depends, as does that of the true prophet, upon how much his doctrine responds to the wishes of the mass. The wishes of the masses depend upon their conception of the good life, upon their tradition. If we believe in the American tradition we can point with trust to the past, to the group urges we have examined, and on the strength of the record it seems to me we may look with hope to the future. There have been corrupt leaders; on the whole they have been supported by the power of the few rather than by the respect of the many. It was the mass which supported Jackson, and which through blood and tears, shed not in the patriotic frenzy of war but through long, sordid years of grinding work, brought labor to its feet. Whether, in reviewing the nineteenth century, we discuss abolition or reform,

273

we find that what the artist-prophets announced the masses enacted. The pronouncement is not enough. The doctrine is incubated in the masses; and when it is great within them, the masses move. Welfare is a growth, not an imposition. Therefore, since group urges follow the tradition, and since we believe in our tradition, we cannot fear the search of the masses for more headroom, more education, and more liberty.

This book indicates to me that there is a contradiction in the American tradition — we place so much emphasis (idealistically) on individuality and the individual in society & yet we can also talk about the "common good" which in order to achieve, some individuals must sacrifice private interests to public need.
Is there any reconcil

Conclusion: The Tradition, and The Beneficent Residue

I.

Heritage is something inherited; tradition is something handed over or on. Heritage is a collection, motley and fortuitous; a tradition is selective. The Rockies and Sierras from south to north are part of the American heritage, but the peaks and passes that illuminate our tradition are those that have some personal cast, some reflection of the heroism of Pike or Donner. The selection, the art of memorializing, these are the province of artists who are ever turning the inheritances of indiscriminate time into a timeless testament: the beneficent residue of history.*

Tradition is to our habits and customs what religion is to our morals. The happy garden, the paradise of our tradition, is a place where everyone is free, heroic, and honest—or at least astute—as heaven is an enclosure to which those of sound morals may repair. Tradition is the ark of the people's covenant with themselves. A thousand metaphors will suit

---

* Note G, *Tradition versus Heritage,* page 308.

it, as a thousand will suit religion, since it is in the nature of a metaphor itself. It stands, rooted in everyday life, for an ideal of conduct and so also for an ideal of existence. Like religion, tradition is composed of well-grounded hopes, heroism, whitewash, and the picturesque.

No people would admit that their national tradition was squalid or slovenly. Few people have been able to stomach the cad-hero, as I consider Siegfried, and few religions have comfortably digested the cad-god. We may wonder what diluted devotion could underlie Sophocles' orisons since he considered that "Ares is blind and with unseeing eyes set in a swine's face stirs up all to evil." Our tradition, like our heaven, is something we wish to keep admirable, for we judge ourselves and somewhat flatter ourselves therein. However short of the mark the state of civilization may be, a nation, like any individual, asks to be judged by its purest aspirations as well as by its less exalted accomplishments. Therefore tradition can be no middle-of-the-road affair: its heroes are oversize and it swells with altruism and pride. Paul Bunyan, like King Arthur, is a magnitude. In short, tradition is a glorious compendium of desirable ends. Properly so, for if tradition is to contain the living word of guidance and courage, it comes not in disgrace or as an echo from the dark behind us but as a rainbow that leads us on.

Tradition is more than the sum of habit and custom. These two are the necessary cogs of our daily living; they tend to keep us in the safe but the same place. Though habit and custom prevent us from slipping backward, they do not of themselves urge us forward. By them we are firmly held, in spite of modernity; and much of what we call progress is but the retention of that grip. What may seem inventive and new in our day often turns out to be a device to keep us as comfortable in habit as were our grandparents. In 1803, the year Emerson was born, people climbed with ease to their top floors. Today, an express elevator must carry us to the top of a skyscraper, not as a marvel but as a necessity, not to add to our culture or civility but to answer an ancient problem of levitation newly complicated by the use of structural steel. No one is the wiser, wiser than Emerson, for having been whisked up to the sixtieth floor and brought down again. The new invention has merely allowed us to continue in our habit of visiting the garret.

In general, we conduct our lives as the transmitters and transmuters of the life which has been handed down to us. We find that the composition of our daily bread has altered little since it was coupled with circuses or miraculous fish. We find that our habits and customs also have changed less than we like to think. Even so, they change, however slowly, and they change for the better because tradition, like the moon upon a tide, exerts a steady and ever-growing pull. Tradition itself is ever growing, even at the expense of habit and custom, or rather because tradition may feed on what our convenience has sloughed off.

For example, we no longer travel by sailing vessel. Few people today would know the difference between a bark and a brig; yet the full-rigged ship, in its stateliness, stays in our tradition, from the anonymous trader to the *Bonhomme Richard,* preserved in story and song, models and pictures. Sometimes the converse is true. As a thing may be preserved in our tradition though custom has renounced it, so also a thing may cease to be material for tradition, once it has crept into our habit. As we accustom ourselves to flying, the wonder and unusualness of such locomotion depart; we begin to take it for granted. What remains in our tradition is the miracle of Kitty Hawk. In the days of Langley and the Wrights, flying was not common, rather a dream come true, a magnitude, a first venture toward one of man's desires.

This is not to say that habit and custom are at odds with

tradition. The three are complementary. Like the religious instinct, habit and custom have been with us since civilizations began. But religions arise with some primal incarnation and grow with succeeding prophets and enlightened acts, and the same is true of tradition. There come extraordinary periods when habit and custom seem to catch up with the ideal, to transcend themselves for a brief moment into tradition, as it were. These moments of increase occur when the gap between actual circumstances and the ideal is too great and demands to be shortened, they occur when the complacent cog of habit has been slipped. They occur when we realize that our habit changes less than we like to think; and when people suddenly decide that "less than we like to think" is not enough. From that moment of dissatisfaction springs the movement forward in the direction of traditional aspiration.

Certainly, the habits of most North Americans were severely disrupted in 1773. Young gentlemen of Boston, instead of playing cards, drinking, or courting, daubed themselves with nut juice and spent an evening destroying government property, in the form of tea, down by the docks. Middle-aged men of letters wrote incendiary articles and rode horseback up and down the seaboard, attending correspondence committee meetings. Farmers neglected their crops and ladies stored guns instead of cider in their cellars. Some of the "quality" whom the year before it had been a delight to honor, were now the recipients of cat-calls and rocks. Custom was standing on its head, but tradition was having a field day.

As there is a continuity to custom which might be called one aspect of civilization, there is also a continuity to the hopes of a people, regarding their civilization, which is a large part if not the whole of tradition. It is the continuity of an endless, growing chain of idealism, one composed of short and long links, to which a link is added every time there is a break. These "breaks" occur at those moments and places

278

where men attempt to make the pattern of their habits corre-
spond to the pattern of an ideal existence. More often than
not, when somebody deplores "a break in our tradition," he
is deploring some shift in the comfort of his habits; probably,
at that moment, tradition is in the process of consolidating
gains and forging a new link. Such was the new link begun
in 1763 and well advanced by the time of the Boston Tea
Party.

For a break to occur, several elements are necessary: the
prophet first and then the leader (Samuel Adams and then
George Washington, let us say); the urge of a people for
change; the state or circumstance of a civilization—an invention or discovery, an example from abroad, or the logical
extension into practice of slowly accumulated ideas. Above
all a sense that the direction of the new movement is one
compatible with tradition and that, in moving, man is but
proceeding where tradition impels. For our purposes, it is
the sense of direction which is most potent, for if the movement is not in the line of traditional aspiration it is a sport,
an aberration, and probably short lived. Since the choice of
direction is a voluntary act, there is here the essential implication of rejection and acceptance. As might be expected, it
is almost always a person or a small group that makes that
choice.

Throughout this book we have recognized the artists who
have made that choice: men of gifts and vision sufficiently
sound and persuasive to engender or lead a movement. Naturally, the artist does not deliberately elect to increase the
tradition; actual choice lies with the people at large. Of
Longfellow, *Hiawatha* and *Evangeline* seem to have entered
our gallery of immortals. America has selected from Lowell
the visionary Sir Launfal and also that precursor of Mr.
Dooley, *The Bigelow Papers*. Both these poets consciously
put their pens at the service of abolition and reform. The

279

immediate pamphlet, having done its work, has found oblivion. But the courageous, elevated, and moving passages, in prose or verse, have found immortality in our tradition.

Whatever the adjective used, of elevation or heroism, some radiance is imperative for, apparently, tradition has a nose for the impious. We would not have it otherwise, or tradition would become a contradictory and bedraggled patchwork. It is of little consequence that "tradition" can no more be precisely defined than "the good." We know in our hearts "whatsoever things are true," honest, just, pure, lovely, and of good report. People do not entrust to their tradition what seems unlovely to them. Even success is not of itself acceptable to tradition. The little ships that ran to and from Dunkirk in the waters of defeat have their glory with those that scattered the Armada, and of our own tawdry war with Mexico we have safeguarded only the memory of a few unsuccessful men who died in the little Alamo. From our railroad era, Casey Jones, crushed to death in his engine cab, still lives in a tradition which has long since spewed Jay Gould out of its mouth. It could not be otherwise with a compendium of desirable ends.

What then is the desirable end to which some things tend, and so are acceptable, and to which others run counter, and so are rejected? The answer would be colored, in particular instances, by the peoples whose traditions were under discussion; and since we are at this moment considering *any* tradition, it might be safe to say that the desired end of a people's, any people's, aspirations is the good life. Tradition is of the people, popular; and no benefit which appeared to be limited to the few or was impossible for the many would be considered eligible. No one has given thought to the social background of the men who died in the Alamo; their courage alone commends them to a people who believe that cowardice has no part in the ultimate, utopian good society. There can

280

be little exclusiveness in matters of salvation; and the saving graces of life on earth are the desiderata of tradition, as the saving grace of life after death is the promise of religion. Tradition, like religion, is not a respecter of persons.

From their literature and historic behavior, we assume that the traditions of the Greeks, Romans, Chinese, Persians, Balinese, Spaniards, and others differed or differ greatly from ours. However, among civilized people, the anathemas are curiously similar and invariable. Murder, theft, cowardice, cruelty; the wanton wife, the brutal father; disloyalty to man and disrespect to the gods; these are universally condemned. The turncoat is not welcome; a turncoat has a dirty lining on both sides. Condemnation has its roots in those primitive instincts which have always sought to protect the family and the tribe. Guilty ones are remembered as examples to be avoided; such do not linger in tradition. The doors of the good society, of the Happy Hunting Ground, of Valhalla are closed to them. On the objectionable vices, most civilized societies are agreed. It is in the emphases on virtue that traditions vary. The desirable end will differ as the temperament of the aspirants differ. Just as the hell of Arctic peoples is a place of ice and not one of flames, so the heaven of a nautical people is different from that of pastoral folk. To the Chinese, the good society requires heroes endowed with good manners and with natures capable of profound philosophical concepts; the supreme virtue of the Greek hero was valor. If there was a strong penchant in the national consciousness of the Romans, I should be inclined to name it "legality," as I might use the word "sanctity" for the Spaniards. Whatever the names given to the divergencies, it is obvious that the accumulation of national aspirations which forms a tradition must vary with the nature and temperament of different peoples. But if the notions concerning the good life are variable, the desire for it is a constant.

In general, the good society, which shall produce the good life, has two major concerns: order and growth. From the desire for order has come the concept of government, with its companion problem: who shall have the right to govern his fellows and exercise dominion? From the desire for growth has come the concept of freedom, with its companion problem: how shall the individual grow, yet not grow out of bounds or to the detriment of society? Both of these posits and problems lead to a distant goal where they must one day meet in reconciliation and solution, a goal where the balance between human rights and property rights and spiritual rights is truly and equitably held.

This was the equilibrium taught by the Prophets of Israel, by the Greeks in many profound maxims, by Jesus who would have us render unto Caesar those things which are Caesar's, and unto God those things which are God's. It was the imbalances of society that Wyclif, Milton, Jefferson, Whitman pointed out to the generality of men and which roused that generality to immortal and traditional longings.

The good life, then, is the desirable end to which tradition both tends and beckons. We have seen how tradition, is not to be confused with habit or custom. Tradition deals with happy magnitudes and things as we should like them to be; tradition grows by a series of climaxes. It adds to the links of its chain at those moments when people break with their habitual comfort to follow anxious, latent impulses toward a reconciliation of actuality and aspiration. These "breaks" imply the presence of prophets, poets, and elucidators who, having put forth the idea in a form which all may apprehend, are responsible for the break as they also are responsible for whatever is accepted or rejected. And lastly we have seen that the basis for election lies almost entirely in one question: does the man, the deed, the idea, tend to promote the good life?

These, then, are the essential phenomena or laws of any tradition.

As tacit, as implicit, as life itself, tradition is rarely considered except when interrupted. Only some sudden taking-off jars us into reconsideration and reappraisal. Yet we should be constant in our mindfulness, for tradition is the blood-stream of a civilization. It shows through the skin in the complexion and color of our lives, and it feeds the heart of our body politic. Dark reactions are undertaken in its name, whereas above all things it must be cumulative, interpretive, growing. When not traduced, tradition is the fertility-logic of our progress. The general laws we have examined should apply to the tradition of any people—and I think we shall find that they do; but general laws are remote and unsatisfactory. Our business is with our own tradition: to see how it obeys the general laws, to observe with more interest the local and nourishing peculiarities. So observing, we should come by a salutary glimpse of ourselves, and, in the light of what we find our tradition to be, a guide for our present conduct and aspirations.

II.

Far more truly than the Greeks could say of themselves and their land, we may say to ourselves, "America is the name of a culture, not a race." Our culture we can observe as directly as we can observe people, in our systems of law and business, in our schools and our jails, our books or our buildings, our food or our pleasures. Tradition is not so observable nor even so tangible. We may observe people but not life itself. Like life, tradition lies *behind* the manifestations of whatever civility we own, a spark, an impulse forward, a push from the past. We cannot suddenly look about us and point at it. We may learn what it is only by studying its his-

283

tory and thus deducing what is its present state. We move as we think; and much of our thinking is colored by tradition. It is logical to suppose that the direction of our exit from today is straitly conditioned by the direction of our entrance into yesterday.

The foundations of the American tradition, historically and spiritually, rest solidly on the Old and New Testaments; on Greek and Roman philosophy—these loosely compounded with the Bible in Catholic Humanism; on English liberal thought and common law, somewhat on French Rationalism or Enlightenment. They rest most vividly on a series of historical and mythical events (like that of George Washington and the cherry tree) which have been interpreted in the spirit of the tradition and so become both source and recipient of traditional strength; and they rest also upon the writings and lives of certain men and women.

Reflected in the temper of our tradition, we shall find certain definite national characteristics: a predilection for liberty, an itch to experiment, a habit of dissent, the will to autonomy, acquisitive and mimetic talents, public spirit, and a respect for, if not a steady practice of, tolerance.

We rise in the morning, conduct ourselves during the day and go to bed at night according to certain acquired habits wherein we conform to the custom of our kind. We give all working people one day of rest a week; we remit debts; we intend to deal fairly with others as we would be dealt by; we observe ten commandments; we claim that our word is as good as our bond; we do not indulge in incest; we drink, but in moderation; we do not sell our children into bondage— and all because from morning to night, in small and great things, our tradition is rooted in both the Old and the New Testaments. Otherwise we might abstain totally from alcohol, as should the Muslim, or consider it worthy to rob the

284

unbeliever. We do not share our wives, like the Eskimos, nor kill off the excess of people, like the Spartans, nor expose unwanted children, like some Orientals. We are not superior; we are different.

We use knowingly for our own devices the words and concepts of Greek philosophy, as we use their mathematics or the Arabic signs. Our Christianity is tempered, altered, enriched, and sometimes confused by the wisdom of the Church Fathers. The Orient in a thousand ways has touched us. Roman law was the basis of canon law, and as such the basis of legal custom for close on fifteen hundred years. All this is our tradition, in its early stages; this we share with all Christian peoples. Yet all Christendom is not today exactly like us. Our tradition is part of the world tradition, but it has its local options.

Chief among these is liberality. Other nations have liberality in their tradition, notably the English, the French, the Scandinavians, and the Italians, but perhaps none with our peculiar emphasis. Our history, our frontiers and our fights have helped to make it so. In other countries the liberal spirit has perhaps been slightly curbed to a more academic tradition or to one where empire or caste or faith took precedence. It is not that other peoples have thought less about freedom, but that in our short history, we have thought so much. The proportion is unusual, even if we remember that for the all-important first hundred and fifty years our tradition was identical with the British. Though we learned how to think from the British, it is what we have thought since we parted from them that gives special character to the American tradition. It is not minimizing our debt to say that the American tradition is most truly itself when it is most conspicuously different from its progenitors, and most un-American when it follows the temper of old English mercantilism, empire, or monarchy, or adheres to the maintenance of a star chamber. The heart of the tradition of the British Isles has also been freedom, but the free men began to cross the Atlantic into exile in 1620, and, by 1763, whatever the heart remained, certainly the sinews of England were tautened to the building of an empire. In the seventeenth century, England underwent two revolutions; by 1763 the torch of revolution had crossed the ocean to kindle fresh altars in the New World. For a hundred years—through Jefferson and Jackson and Lincoln—till the end of our Civil War, our preoccupation was with liberty, with more room in which to be free. Luckily, our expansion, achieved almost entirely by conquering natural hazards rather than subject peoples, escaped many of the corruptions usual to aggrandizement. It was saved by embracing the often uncouth virtues of the frontier.

The good society does not mean for us exactly what it is for others. We prefer growth to order: we tolerate government but we long for freedom. We want little control over our actions, and most properly none over our thoughts. Today, as a people, we desire a real equality of opportunity —a wicket to be entered only with the help of that general education so dear to the heart of Jefferson. And, as opportunity should be equal between persons, so also it must be equal between nations. If such equalities are to be just, the balance must be true. The word "liberality" covers the temper of this desire, and in this manner I use it.

Such things may not be demonstrated mathematically, but they may be devoutly expressed. "The spirit of liberty is the spirit which is not too sure that it is right. The spirit of liberty is the spirit which seeks to understand the minds of other men and women. The spirit of liberty is the spirit which weighs their interests alongside its own without bias. The spirit of liberty remembers that not even a sparrow falls to earth unheeded. The spirit of liberty is the spirit of Him, who, near two thousand years ago, taught mankind a lesson it has never learned, but has never quite forgotten: that there may be a kingdom where the least shall be heard and considered side by side with the greatest." *

After those portions in our tradition which are of grace, of divine authority, we honor most and cling to most personally certain man-given gifts—gifts which, at heart, are but the implementation of our moral laws and which make the cherished difference today between the acceptance and the rejection of Judge Hand's words. That difference is liberality. It is a frame of mind from which sprang Whitman and Emerson and Melville; Shelley and Shaw; Erasmus and Montesquieu and Mazzini; Hooker and Locke and Jefferson. That this spirit is honored today is the hope of the world.

III.

From the earliest prophets to our own times, we have observed certain "signs," in the apparent motion of our history, where the body politic seems to have paused as in a zodiacal progress. Our path has traversed the ecliptic of Reformation and Rebellion, in England, of Revolution and Reform, in America. These four R's, each representative of an overturn, are the climaxes of our historical narrative, the storerooms of our heritage, and the fountains of our tradition.

Each overturn was undertaken and consummated within the framework of a pattern which appears to be constant. By the spoken and written word, the prophet, poet, and orator have pointed to the disequilibrium of the times, crystallized in great measure the nature of contemporary afflictions, and indicated a way of life more compatible with traditional hopes. Slowly the group urge takes shape. The "cause" being

* Judge Learned Hand, 1944.

formulated, like-minded men gather, the men of vision and talent proclaim and exhort. Sooner or later, when action is possible, active leaders appear—generals, men of politics or merely of ambition. When the urge has spent itself—with much achieved, much lost, much yet to do—the artists are necessary once again to elucidate, to explain what has happened, and to winnow with the winds of just perception and genius the permanently valid from the ephemeral.

This winnowing is the process by which the beneficent residue of history becomes the body of tradition. The creative ardor of the artist has a double value: it is of immediate usefulness and urgency for its own time and also, by its contemporary authenticity, of truth for the future. As the artist-prophet has been the tutor of his own time, so he becomes the interpreter of his own time to future ages. We may therefore say that art is the free individual expression of the collective aspiration.

The creative act of the poets and prophets is, by its generation, a new thing. "Newness of spirit" is within. The accretion of each fresh element keeps the tradition ever new itself. What is stale, exclusive, conforming, does not lodge comfortably in the tradition, for the poets who made it—from the prophet Amos to Walt Whitman—were dissenters. In their pastures were few Sacred Cows (usually discovered to be the offspring of the Calf of Gold). Not one of our artists took refuge in the easy corruptions of silence. Dissent lies in the marrow of our tradition; passive acquiescence and conformity were never in the minds of the artists who framed it.

The seal of the State of New York, like the "banner with the strange device," bears the motto *Excelsior,* a gift from Longfellow. High, ever higher! And *Novus Ordo Seclorum* is engraved upon the Great Seal of the United States. Nothing in our tradition is static. Essentially an act of faith, tradition, like religion, will grow as the spirit and imagination of man grow, and as the successive incarnations of the prophetic spirit accummulate from generation to generation.

Dante defined the good life, the *vita felice,* as one where the potential intellect of every man was made actual. Long before, St. Augustine—in tracing the word "republic" to its Roman origin in *Res Populi*—defined the *populus* as "a body of rational persons united by harmonious participation in the things it likes." This sounds curiously fluid, but it will stand scrutiny. As a definition, it implies freedom for the masses, a genial freedom not unlike the warm solidarity desired for the people by Whitman. These are not the counsels of an impossible perfection. The further the target the higher you aim. The great ends are hard to define, of course. There are no exact definitions for the good life, for tradition, for democracy (there are a dozen forms of democracy in practice today), nor is there a definition for mother love. Yet, no matter how much the experimental psychologist may reduce mother love to a glandular reaction, still mother love acts as we expect it to in the overwhelming majority of cases. The good life is of the spirit, and therein hard to define; but the road to it is practical. Jacques Maritain, ambassador to the Vatican, would lead us to that good life through evangelic love, but he points explicitly also to those who lead, who are the heroes of the temporal struggle, "scientists like Pasteur or Washington Carver, poets like Walt Whitman, Hugo, or Peguy, pioneers of social justice, who give themselves to the government and illumination of their brothers' lives and who can know no rest as long as their brothers are in enslavement and misery."

289

The good life is not for one set or sort of people but for all mankind. Our tradition, being so largely preoccupied with freedom, with the release of all man's capabilities for growth, embraces the world, without provinciality or coercion. We may frighten the stranger when we deviate from the way; but those in the farthest island of the Antipodes could not take fright at the offer of federation instead of empire, of equity rather than exploitation, of brotherly love rather than segregation. In our tradition, as in our religion, all men are considered individually as free spirit, and in the mass as equal children of God. A federation of the world is implicit in the logic of the tradition, as the peace of the world was the first premise of the Prophets when they described the good society "Come ye," cried Isaiah," and let us go to the mountain of the Lord. And he shall judge among the nations and shall rebuke many people. And they shall beat their swords into plowshares and their spears into pruning hooks; nation shall not lift up sword against nation, neither shall they learn war any more." Our habit may be war, but our tradition is peace.

The good life, then, is the goal of our traditional desires. We have observed the growth and growing pains of that tradition through new links—links compatible with the spirit of our charters—added in moments of exuberance. Moments when the dissenting and reformative words have been pronounced, when the creative artists have given form to a popular but inchoate longing.

History, habit, heritage are with us, but they are not identical with tradition. As saints are the elect of God, so tradition is the elect of man. It has been chosen, especially, for commemoration. It has been sanctified by the mass of people. But the choosing has been done by artists who, in remembered words or pictures, have set the beneficent residue in the nation's heart.

There is no end to a tradition till all things perish. But,

290

reaching ever higher toward the goal of a good society, we do advance toward the goal posts only to find them the entrance to another field. Like religion, tradition leads us on perpetually to a new grace.

NOTES

These notes have two reasons for being inserted here, neither of which is for the display of erudition.

I do not believe in the genetic fallacy: that the proof of a pudding is in the cook's pedigree. Yet, in this book, the historical background has been of immense importance. And there are several places where the historical material needs to run over, as one might say, beyond the cupful of a chapter. There are, also, instances where I feel that the reader might like more substantiating information than can be contained in a disfiguring footnote.

The second reason is that some of the subjects touched upon, such as patronage, spill over the century mark, where I have tried to stop; and these notes are a bringing up to date of such material. In bringing the schedule up to our times I have not hesitated to let my prejudices enter, strongly even; an exuberance which I tried to avoid in the body of the book.

NOTE A   *Science*

The problem of science—that is, science as an urgent problem in everyday life—is barely a hundred years old. Galileo had shocked the Church, but daily life was little affected by the heliocentric novelty. Darwin was the first to broach a scientific theory that could really change society in its manner of looking at itself; but I much doubt if a man regards his family or his work today in a light any different from that of the ordinary man in 1800.

The incalculable benefits which science has bestowed upon us are ever present in the gratitude of anyone who snaps on an electric light rather than search for flint and tinder, or who, because of divine anesthesia, can face the dentist calmly. But, because life has been prolonged, we may ask if thereby it is better; or if the ice-cube is cooler than the old chunk? In other words, has science affected our emotions about ourselves? Or has science, with extreme and terrifying logic, in ever increasing abundance, handed gadgets of the year A.D. 3000 to a man whose brain is today no larger than a troglodyte's?

Perhaps the modern age is yet too young; perhaps the quantum theory bears too indirectly upon the human heart—a heart which seeks primarily for values. It seems to me that only when science affects men's thoughts about men or about the emotional world in which men live and beyond which they yearn, only then may science enrich tradition.

The rotation of the earth is part of our common knowledge or learning, not of our tradition. Some of the noblest (and most "scientific") recorded thoughts as well as the major premises of our tradition were adumbrated in the brains of men who were content that the sun should move around the earth. Galileo Galilei is in our tradition not because he helped destroy the Ptolemaic system but because he was a persecuted man and because he said something: *e pur si muove.* (He may not have said it but he should have. It is our tradition that he did.)

NOTE B   *Patronage*

So great are the problems today, so great the income of great nations, so great the possibilities and resources, that the line between public and private patronage hardly exists, or if it exists, it is cross-hatched with divided responsibility.

294

In so far as anything is tax free, just so far is it government subsidized. Church property is the ancient example. The majority of hospitals are supported by the city or the state as well as by the citizenry. The same is true of schools, colleges, universities, libraries, research centers, laboratories, (astronomical, chemical, etc.). The percentage of such institutions still supported solely by the private patron is infinitesimal. I think we may say that today a mixed subvention, part tax-exemption, part direct state aid, part private donation, supports almost all our nonprofit-making enterprises. The exceptions would be the research laboratories of the larger commercial corporations: yet, in these, the effort is industrial and competitive rather than cultural. Much gain results, but it is apt to be patented. Of the tax-free institutions the most encompassing are the foundations. Their protection and help is cast not only over the present-day Galileos, Newtons, da Vincis, Ambroise Parés, or Harveys, but also over the whole province of science, sociology, medicine, art, geodetics, and almost anything you can think of.

There is about some of the foundations perhaps more sanitation than therapy. Like the large corporations—the Standard Oil, the Catholic Church, or the government—the Foundations suffer from excessive bureaucracy. They tend to develop a peculiar type of mind: that of the administrator. He is as wary of creative people as he is delighted with the slightest gadget. He is devoted to bookkeeping and respectability. The foundation boards, almost all, are interlocking, and their pulse beats in a bank. Yet, in spite of all the pedantry and reaction inherent in such unwieldy corporations, the roster of their accomplishment is quite disarming to the curious investigator.

In Chapter II, we saw the ancestry of the marchant-prince who, in the last century, replaced the ducal patron. His enormous fortune came, not from a landed inheritance, but from the exploitation of frontiers and new traderoutes and newly discovered mines, and from the exploitation of frontiersmen, traders and miners. There are those who will agree with Daniel Webster that these financial barons based their activities on the principles "of human freedom and human knowledge." There are others who, after scanning the pages of Gustavus Myers *(The History of the Great American Fortunes)*, will feel that the never-contested record is revolting. Whatever the origin, the fortunes were made; and what is of interest to us is the disposition of the moneys and the reasons for that disposition.

It would be captious to insist that by the time a fortune was of great size the financier was probably of an age when the advent of death demanded careful consideration; and that some millionaires, unmindful of hell fire, bought horses or yachts while others, aware of the needle's eye, endowed institutions. It would be far more just to acknowledge that the financiers were plain men, industrious and lucky, who could not and did not wish to escape their traditions. North America was not El Dorado. The pioneers had come to settle, not for gold but for freedom. English liberalism was in the background, behind Jefferson or any of the revolutionary purists (Robespierre or Mazzini or Bolivar); and it was interwoven with the customs of those who left the New England town meeting in a covered wagon. The frontier itself was a "free for all." And the man who made a lucky strike, despite his dogged grasping, was not thereby rendered insensible. He wanted to give back to the frontier part of what it had given him. Austerity and obligation were in the tradition. Primogeniture and monopoly were not. In an effort to regain a simple equilibrium, I fancy, the men who are called the "robber barons" began to give their wealth back to the people who had created it.

There is one final resemblance between the ducal patron and the financier-patron. As we noted, the duke and the prelate were lavish with what were after all state funds. The financiers of the nineteenth century in large measure dispensed fortunes that had been made out of the state itself, out of the very soil of the state. There is certainly no human or divine law which recommends that a few astute men should have wrecked our forests or squandered our minerals for the benefit of one corporation or another. I have, however, never considered, as some do, that the words conservation and socialism were identical. And it is well to remember that so conservative a landowner as George Washington, in a letter of December 14, 1784, to Richard H. Lee, President of the Senate, asked, "Would there be any impropriety in reserving . . . the mines and minerals . . . to the Public instead of to the few knowing ones?"

Lastly, to end our catalogue, we may recall briefly a noble experiment to recapture the age old and high tradition slowly accumulated through centuries of Temples of Solomon, Colosseums, Hanging Gardens of Babylon, colleges at Oxford, autostradas, Pantheons, or palaces.

In 1930, in the United States, there was no vision and few apples; and the people perished. Between fifteen and twenty millions were unemployed. The government was faced with the alternative of dispensing a dole or inventing "made-work." Wisely, it laid emphasis upon made-work (the theory and procedure of WPA) to create the needed employment to keep people in those employments where they could best use their special skill and aptitudes, and to secure works which would be of permanent benefit to the country at large.

We are accustomed to having the civic authorities attend to our sewage, our police, our roads, our canals, our water supply, often our heat and light, most schools and insane asylums, some subways, and we think no worse of ourselves therefor. Yet enormous objection to the WPA came from precisely that group of men who had with such a lavish hand lent money to Germany between 1920 and 1940—money which Germany used for civic improvements, made-work, so that, not hampered by unemployment, she out-stripped her neighbors. The Nazis could well point out how much they had improved their country, how much they had done for the people, on our money, at the same time that they quietly reserved German taxes to build up a military machine with which to destroy us and those very financiers who so blithely contributed the cash. The obtuseness of those who cried out against the WPA was neatly balanced by their gullibility.

Some historians have indulged their fancy by picking out the single most civilizing event in the history of the United States. Many have chosen the opening of the Erie Canal. It did join East and West, thereby bringing wealth to millions and, through security, hastening the advent of an ultimate leisure and civility.

But I would put the brief span of the Federal Arts Projects in first place. They brought, in music, in the arts, in the crafts, in books, in drama, in design, in friendly cultural gatherings, in all the amenities of living, for the first time, to countless men and women lost in sparse communities or stifled in congested areas, to all the underprivileged, a knowledge and practice of those values which alone have raised men out of brutish and predatory habits; those values which spell enlightenment and upon which rest the hopes of democracy.

Through the art projects the country really came of age. We learned to know ourselves, our neighbors and our history. To the projects we owe the first admirable series of handbooks on our own land, its rivers and forests, people and lore. In the *Index of American Design,* we were given a record, inestimably precious, of the pattern of our ways and a document which, for the first time, we may offer in comparison to the great records of older countries. From the work shops poured nearly two thousand mural paintings to enliven the drabness of our public buildings. (And, while some were poor and many criticized, the majority were excellent; and the mere arousing of criticism, the stimulation of concern for unaccustomed things, was valuable.) Four thousand pieces of sculpture were called into existence; and, during one period, four million people a month (people who before then had never been able to hear such music at all) attended symphony concerts. There was a revival of the small local theaters, which the movies had gone a long way toward extinguishing and, in so doing, had nearly extinguished the very springs of dramatic writing and the profession of acting. After twenty years of the most brilliant theater in the world, the New York stage had declined with startling rapidity; and the notable productions of the Theater Arts Projects not only enlivened the metropolis but brought to the country far and wide the excitement and provocation to thought of which only the serious drama is capable. And, for the first time, the pent-up artistic energies of the Negro race, relegated before then largely to minstrel shows, assumed a natural and merited eminence.

Above all, the projects made possible, logical and agreeable the assemblage of neighbors together, in the community centers, wherein they met, learning to learn and to create, side by side, in tolerance and understanding. The whole atmosphere of the country was raised, expanded. In mutual discovery and in recreation, the ancient separations of ignorance and prejudice began to crumble. For ignorance and prejudice and rancour are but moral, amoral rather, and emotional currents; they can, like half-gods, be replaced, and only so, by stronger, more wholesome ones.

Theoretically, the board of directors of the Federal Arts Projects was the American people. In practice, it was composed of the most gifted specialists, certainly the most altruistic and inventive, in the various professions. I cannot explain why the level of excellence was so far above that of the old haphazard private or competitive designs. Perhaps it was because so much of our rising talent was on relief or close to needing it; perhaps because the overseers were young, not competing nor skimping, but designing their best, freely, for their country.* Yet I cannot move about our land without being constantly made aware, upon investigation, that if my eye delights in some new school or courthouse, some magnificently simplified viaduct, some bridge —such as the Whitestone, of unusual elegance and ingenuity— my eye is delighted by a scion of the WPA. I am aware, too, that the decorations, in fresco, sculpture or mosaic were from the shops of the Federal Arts Projects.

Here, the horse was squarely in front of the cart. Whereas overendowed boards or schools or conservatories may say, "We have the money, how shall we spend it?" the Projects were forced to say, "We have the talent; how can we bring it to fruitfulness."

For once, the Congress of the United States confessed, reluctantly, that man does not live by bread alone. Before long, they sat in halls designed for them by WPA, drove along roads built by WPA. Then the gentlemen of Congress kicked against the pricks. The motorroads did not lead to Damascus. The ancient provinciality was winning the day when the return of war and

* Fourteen out of the eighteen young painters whose works were shown at a remarkable exhibit in 1942 at the Museum of Modern Art had been sponsored at one time or another by the Federal Arts Project.

of employment ended the emergency. But the rest of the world had come to look and to learn. All Latin America watched the experiment: an experiment in that nationalism which is a co-operation and not a self-glorification, in the discovery and evaluation of talent, if only the talent of being a responsive neighbor. England also watched, and adapted many of the practices of WPA to her wartime uses. Apparently, nations do not seriously consider their spiritual welfare problems nor collect their moral garbage except when rudely awakened by a financial crash or a bomb. And then, when the crisis is over, the politicians with their insecurity before imponderables (and forgetting that both Hitler and Mussolini climbed to popularity on the promise, and often the performance, of just such cultural improvements as we have noted) turn to more customary pork-barrels, and condemn without knowledge or due appraisal such Projects, one after another.

Happily, in England the Council for the Encouragement of Music and the Arts (CEMA) has survived handsomely. The advisability of taking "the best to the most," of planting widespread civic centers, of formulating a national art policy, of taking Shakespeare to the countryside—all part of CEMA's program—is not limited to a time of catastrophe. The British experience, in sorrow, solved many problems which may now lead to joy. Rather than allow itself to collapse, the London Philharmonic reformed itself as a cooperative body, admitting as shareholders only the players themselves. The Theatre Royal in Bristol was acquired by CEMA and is now an active center for all the arts. Is there anything unbecoming to the days of peace, to the freedom of the individual, in this?

For the moment, we have in the United States rejected even the memory of WPA. Yet from others who took up where we left off we shall ourselves take back the theory and the practice of national, governmental, responsibility for the culture of the land, in science and art and adult education—not as relief but as release.

Patronage should be a wise solicitude. It was a form of that solicitude which the Church exercised in its most glorious moment—the cherishing and fostering of all the impulses that are

300

lovely in man—in the days before the Church relinquished her right to oversee the "just price" and before she tolerated two moralities, the private and the business morality. That time is gone. The state, really, if only to adorn and house itself, has not lost the tradition, however great may be the ignorance of any Congressman, however much he may cry "interference." As a state should see to it that no man starves, so it should see to the imponderables, "that men may pursue their studies in peace of mind, without the dust of poverty on their foreheads, nor in the lap of their virtue."

NOTE C   *Chaucer*

Chaucer, who was well bred and passed his life as a courtier, was a felicitous judge of his neighbors. Four quotations from Coghill's remarkable translation of *The Canterbury Tales* ("The Pardoner's Tale," "The Summoner's Tale," and the "Wife of Bath's Tale") leave no doubt about Chaucer's ecclesiastical and social perceptions:

> One thing I should have mentioned in my tale,
> Dear people. I've some relics in my bale
> And pardons to, as full and fine I hope
> As any in England, given me by the Pope.
> If there be one among you that is willing
> To have my absolution, for a shilling
> Devoutly given, come!

> Dearly beloved, God forgive your sin
> And keep you from the vice of avarice!
> My holy pardon frees you all of this,
> Provided that you make the right approaches,
> That is with sterling, rings, or silver brooches.
> Bow down your heads under this holy bull!
> Come on, you women, offer up your wool!
> I'll write your name into my ledger; so!
> Into the bliss of Heaven you shall go.

"Satan," the angel said, "has got a tail
As broad or broader than a carrack sail.
Hold up thy tail, thou Satan!" then said he,
"Show forth thine arse and let the friar see,
The nest ordained for friars in this place!"

"Just now," she said, "you spoke of gentle birth,
Such as descends from ancient wealth and worth.
If that's the claim you make for gentlemen
Such arrogance is hardly worth a hen.
Whoever loves to work for virtuous ends,
Public and private, and who most intends
To do what deeds of gentleness he can,
Take him to be the greatest gentleman.

"Gentility is only the renown
For bounty that your fathers' handed down;
Quite foreign to your person, not your own;
Gentility must come from God alone.
That we are gentle comes to us by grace
And by no means is it bequeathed with place."

NOTE D   *Bach*

If John Gay, with *The Beggar's Opera,* was delighting a few
capitals, the profounder and more copious Bach was pouring out
to a more lasting audience, in motet, cantata, and oratorio, the
evangelical exhortation.

From all the world goes up the cry of woe.
The guilty shrink with fear
Lest their dishonour presently appear
And men consumed with lust of gold
Untimely in the grave grow cold.

(Cantata 25, 1731.)

Bach was perfectly aware of the conditions around him, of the pigmies who controlled all his waking hours, of the prejudice and insolence which was so soon to crush Mozart, of those circumstances the alteration of which would before long turn his Europe upside down. He was aware of the prophetic texts he set so magnificently for his choirs to sing. Through him, the Reformation continued to work, and through him it lives mightily for us.

If in Bach's day fewer people could hear his music than now; if the same is true of Handel's *Messiah* (1742); still, that was the age which produced these great and reverent works. They were not produced in a void, but for audiences to whom such music spoke directly, enrichingly. They concern us now not just because they were to the taste of those remote days but because they expressed, as much as it can be expressed in music, the moral side of our tradition which is with us still. There are today at least forty-two million Protestant churchgoers in the United States. Every Sunday in the year, the congregations join in singing the hymns of Luther and Wesley and Watts. Surely, the "Rock of Ages" is as firmly imbedded in our tradition as, engraved, it was firmly affixed to the walls of the gentry, along with an engraving of Oliver Cromwell, in the Old South.

NOTE E

George Sand

Une Soirée chez Georges Sand
Eminence grise d'une époque—
Vos Richelieus? Mais, c'étaient tous les Grands!
Vous balanciez habile comme un phoque
Le Monde Romantique; à vos pieds
S'étalait un tapis hardi de plan:
D'Amours volants, de gloire et de chagrin—
Un tapis dont la trame était Musset,
Dont le reflet charmant était Chopin.
Vos Richelieus? Mais, c'étaient tous les Grands.
Eminence Grisette,
Georges Sand!

Qui voyons nous ce soir dans vos salons?
Vous renversez, Madame, l'ordre antique:
Quoi, pour une Muse neuf Apollons?
Que voyons nous? L'époque Romantique.

Voici la douce Anglaise qui fut si bonne
(Dit-on) pour d'Orsay, Lady Blessington;
La divine Mars plûtot comme Avril;
Ingres avec son style (toujours ce style!
Pointe sèche, mais point de sécheresse);
Vigny, brûlant de sa froide ivresse;
Delacroix, redécouvrant Rubens—O,
Voilà le plus grand maître du pinceau!

De sa main gauche, la belle d'Agoult
Tient la main de Liszt, sous un oeil jaloux
Craignant les talons-rouges et les pianos
A queues; plus loin Balzac; puis Berlioz
(Queen Mab en crinoline le confond
Dans un flot merveilleux de nouveaux sons);
Flaubert, sournois et guettant Salammbô;
Voilà, écarlate comme un clairon
Coupant les conversations en sourdines,
Le gilet flamboyant du cher Theo;
Et voici le vieux cygne, Lamartine.

Ils y sont tous, jeunes, beaux et ardents,
    Chez vous, Muse et Musette,
      Georges Sand!

NOTE F   *Labor Unions*

From shards and bits of inscription, from thank offerings and
tombstones, from laws and lawsuits, from Bronze Age villages
which appear to have been inhabited by fellow cooperatives of
one trade, we may surmise the existence of trade unions as far
back as 2000 B.C. We know definitely that, by 500 B.C., the institution was general in the Mediterranean basin and as far east
as India.

A miners' strike may well have lost the Peloponnesian War for Athens; the enormous number of unionized slaves and freedmen probably hastened in Rome the advent of the imperial dictatorship; the almost exact confluence and intermixture of the early Christian Church and the labor movement, for mutual protection, certainly altered the face of Europe; and the much later medieval guilds in the north met contemporary monarchies on an equal footing.

The bronzecasters of Luristan, the potters of Tanagra, the mosaic-makers of Byzantium, like the fishermen of Galilee or the trumpeters of Caesar, all belonged to craft unions. So too the architects, statuaries, money changers, ship designers, painters, engravers, jewelers.

From the records we may fairly reconstruct the Graeco-Roman union. It was democratically run, with elected officers: a president (male), a guardian (female) and a treasurer. There were also a stewardess and several trustees, a lawyer, a religious manager and a priest. One of the primary duties of the lawyer was to keep a defensive check on wages. He did not have to burden his abacus with any great sums of addition—a semislave or freedman earning up to fifteen cents a day, an architect (such as Polias, the designer of the temple of Minerva) receiving a drachma or seventeen cents a day.

The purpose of the union was manifold:

Through annual dues, to secure a fund out of which members might be given care when sick, and decently buried when dead. We cannot, today, with prompt registration at birth, and with a department of sanitation to see that we do not rot where we fall, have any idea what it meant to live without a name and die graveless as a dog. Yet that was the fate of millions in the antique world. Muratori (Thesaur. Vet. Inscr. 523) quotes a typical inscription: "Sacred to the holy ashes of T. Sillius and T. Liberius Priscus, president of the woodworkers union and five years' magistrate with the brotherhood of cloth-fullers; and to the memory of Clavidia his free wife, matron of the brotherhood."

To band together for purposes of protection and, if worst came to worst, of striking. From the body, once formed, delegates could be chosen who would plead before archons and tribunes and generals and governors. It was too much to ask that the delegates plead for headroom in which a miner might stand and not work a ten-hour shift (the length of time his lamp would burn) flat on his back. Too much to ask that foreign labor should not be expected to make bricks without straw. (Could Moses have been a union organizer? The conjecture would fit well with his killing the Egyptian foreman.) But there were infringements which might be pled; and each union had its lawyer.

To have, perhaps above all, some sort of corporate worship, often with its own temple and priest, practically its own sect. We do not, I think, realize to what extent religious rites were then a matter of caste. We presume instinctively that peoples who have left us such magnificent temples—at Paestum or Karnak, Athens, or Rome—people whose literature is bathed in familiarity with so many gods, must have gathered in huge crowds, fraternally, to worship in joy. We are rarely reminded (at school or at college) that the temples and the rites, the very gods themselves, were reserved to the free citizen. It was believed, by free and bond alike, that any happiness in afterlife (and how much more was a slave entitled to long for that happiness than his master!) was conditioned by a knowledge of some *Open Sesame,* some, what I must call, inside dope. (The thought persists to this day). Just as bathing in the blood of a bull was felt to impart some of his courage and strength, so the contact with a god's statue or a god's priest in an intimate ceremony, a mystery, at which the great passwords were uttered, conferred upon the congregation the right to enter the realms of the blessed. What more natural than that the laborers should, through union, make unto themselves their own mysteries?

Perhaps this use of the word mystery is cognate to the Latin word *magister.* Whatever its root, long before the Renascence it had taken on three meanings, one of which concerns us. It meant the usual mystification of the magician or the holy enigma of the churches; it meant also the religious plays. And, in its third meaning, the word mystery meant just, plain *craft. Arts et mystéres* was interchangeable with *Arts et Métiers.* A Mystery

306

being thus a craft was also a craft guild, and as such is spoken of by Hakluyt and Shakespeare. In 1500, the "Mysterie of the Barber Surgeons of London" referred not to their unsanitary ministrations but solely to their union.

The subtle equations between the mystery of the church and the mystery of the workshop are of great significance. That Jesus was a carpenter carried a meaning of vital importance to his contemporaries and to the early Christians, far beyond its value as a simple accounting of His formative years. It meant to millions of workers the world over that He was "one of them." He was born in a manger, and humble shepherds recognized Him first. And if three magi came later to worship, it is noteworthy that they were wise men, one from each of the great races, an Aryan, a Semite, and a Negro. It is noteworthy, also, that the Hebrews were the first to denounce and then to renounce slavery.

Lastly, if not one of the purposes of the Eranos (union), at least one of the greatest joys of membership, was the right *to participate in fraternal festivals and banquets.* On these occasions the laborer got enough to eat. The disrepute of the Bacchanalia was due to the fact that it was a proletarian festivity (like a May day parade), and for that reason all the upper-class historians and writers took delight in exaggerating its wantonness. (Cicero commented on it with a terrified virulence.) In truth, the taking of meals, of special meals, in common was a general practice among the eranistoi (unionists); and the communal table, with bread broken in sign of fellowship, was among the oldest customs of the Unions.

Labor organizations were particularly strong and widespread in Asia Minor, Pergamos, Cappadocia, Laodicaea, and Canaan; and undoubtedly most of the early disciples belonged to one or another of them. (Under Roman law, all purveyors of food, particularly fishermen, were organized in unions under government supervision. One Pompeian inscription reads, "The members of the fishermen's union nominate Popidius Rufus for member of the board of public works.") An integral part of their tradition was the communal supper I have mentioned. It re-

mained for Jesus to sanctify it, as He sanctified all the simple
works and habits of simple people.

For the same reason that today the Christian converts in India
are largely among the "outcasts," the people "without family"
in the Roman world turned to a religion which recognized
neither rich nor poor, free nor bond, but welcomed all the sons
of God to its bosom. The early Church required no birth certificate, even for its ministers. And, since a priest was legally a
superior and protected person, an optimate by courtesy, as it
were—since by becoming a priest a man automatically changed
caste—the Church was flooded with deacons, not only through
piety but as a means of betterment.

It is not disputed that the foundations of Christianity were
laid among artisans and laborers, but it is rarely conceded that,
by that very fact, the foundations of Christianity were laid in the
labor movement. Yet I cannot see how we can doubt it. Anthro-
pologists, archeologists, ethnologists and sociologists of very
recent years have brought new instances, interpretations and
connections which cannot be ignored. Historians write history
from history, that is, from what previous historians have written.
The tombstone or the shard, the cuneiform tablet or the mine
tunnels still visible at Laurium offer another, a different testimony
—not harking back to other shards or tablets but authentic in
themselves. From such modern researches we know that Christianity was founded on organized labor, on organizations that
were at that very moment seeking cover, on organizations of men
to whom the catacombs were familiar.

Like Christianity, art and politics are inseparable from the
labor movement.

NOTE G   *Tradition versus Heritage*

Herein lies an important distinction. Heritage—an inheritance
—may contain a quantity of rubbish; a tradition must not. As
Dr. Alvin Johnson has pointed out, "by tradition we are associated with Marcus Aurelius and Saint Paul, but also with Nero
and Torquemada. Any quarrel with tradition is with its failure

to keep faith." I think Dr. Johnson has too strongly intermixed tradition and heritage. To my mind, they are not the same thing. Tradition is neither history nor habit nor heritage, but the beneficent residue of the triad. Something has intervened: the discrimination of the artist. And this book has attempted to show that the long line of creators has, in the main, rejected the Neros and Torquemadas, and has kept faith.

Index

311

313